TWO GENTLE MEN

The Lives of
George Herbert
and
Robert Herrick

Marchette Chute has written

BOOKS FOR ADULTS

THE SEARCH FOR GOD

GEOFFREY CHAUCER OF ENGLAND

THE END OF THE SEARCH

SHAKESPEARE OF LONDON

BEN JONSON OF WESTMINSTER

TWO GENTLE MEN:
*The Lives of George Herbert
and Robert Herrick*

BOOKS FOR YOUNG PEOPLE

AN INTRODUCTION TO SHAKESPEARE

THE INNOCENT WAYFARING

THE WONDERFUL WINTER

STORIES FROM SHAKESPEARE

BOOKS FOR SMALL CHILDREN

RHYMES ABOUT OURSELVES

RHYMES ABOUT THE COUNTRY

RHYMES ABOUT THE CITY

AROUND AND ABOUT

TWO
GENTLE
MEN

THE LIVES OF
GEORGE HERBERT
AND
ROBERT HERRICK

by

MARCHETTE CHUTE

E. P. DUTTON & CO., INC.
New York

First Printing, September 1959
Second Printing, November 1959
Third Printing, January, 1966

Library of Congress Catalog Card Number: 59-10780

TO
ELLIOTT MACRAE
*who for eighteen years
has been my publisher
and my friend*

Contents

———

PART ONE
GEORGE HERBERT

CHAPTER ONE

G EORGE HERBERT CAME OF A LONG LINE OF WARRIORS. HIS
great-great-grandfather passed into renown and Hall's
Chronicles by fighting his way through a whole army and back
again. His father was attacked in a churchyard and, with his
skull split through to the brain, routed his adversaries and
walked victoriously home. His own brothers were notable
swordsmen and the ones who took up the trade of soldiering
showed the courage of their ancestors. William, fighting in the
wars in Denmark, overcame his opponent with a broken sword;
Thomas, in the East Indies, took command of his ship when the
captain was killed and forced the Spanish enemy aground; and
Richard, when he died, bore the scars of twenty-four wounds.

Out of this military family came George Herbert, who was a
poet and in the end something of a saint. He fought a different
kind of warfare in his short life, one not less difficult than over-
coming an enemy with a sword. He never conquered a city, but
he became a ruler of words and of his own spirit.

The Herberts were descended from a French family that could
trace its lineage back to the Emperor Charlemagne. The first of
the line in England was a friend of William the Conqueror,
and the lands that were granted to Herbert the Chamberlain
are recorded in the Domesday Book. His descendants became
prominent in both England and Wales, and it was the Welsh
side of the family that produced George Herbert.

The most famous of his ancestors was Sir Richard Herbert of
Colebrook, a magnificent young Welsh giant who fought at the
side of his elder brother, the Earl of Pembroke. It was Sir Richard
who entered the history books by hacking his way single-handed
through an entire army, and he was so beloved that after his

defeat in battle even his enemies tried to save him. "Much lamentation and no less entreaty was made to save the life of Sir Richard Herbert, both for his goodly personage, which excelled all men there, and also for the noble chivalry he had showed in the field." But the tears and entreaties were in vain and young Sir Richard was beheaded, one more victim of that feckless and savage conflict known as the Wars of the Roses.

Sir Richard Herbert died in the service of the House of York, and the civil wars ended when the last of the Yorkist kings was slain at Bosworth Field. If Sir Richard's son had remained in the same service the fortunes of the family would have declined, but by this time the Herberts were fighting under a different banner. Like most Welshmen they were supporting Henry Tudor, a Welsh claimant to the throne. A brother of the dead Sir Richard, Sir Rhys ap Thomas, swung the formidable fighting men of western Wales into the Tudor column, and he became a great man at the court of the new king. Henry Tudor, now Henry the Seventh of England, called him father, and so did his successor, Henry the Eighth.

A nephew of "Father Rhys" naturally found rapid advancement at the English court, and Sir Richard's son became in his turn Sir Richard Herbert. He was also a Gentleman Usher of the Privy Chamber, and ultimately Henry the Eighth gave him the rich grant of Montgomery Castle and its dependencies. Montgomery Castle was one of the string of fortresses that had been built on the Welsh border in an earlier English attempt to keep that wild land in subjection, and it was here, near the river Severn, that Sir Richard Herbert made his home.

The English government faced a special problem in Wales, and one that could not be solved merely by manning the Border castles. Over the centuries Wales had been conquered piecemeal, and some of it had never come under the authority of the Crown. In the wild Welsh Marches, for instance, where Montgomery Castle stood high on its great rock, there were a hundred and forty-three separate kingdoms, each ruled by a Marcher lord.

He had the power of life and death there, for the king's writ did not run in the Welsh Marches and the only real authority was the ancient one of tribal loyalty.

The Tudor kings had won the throne of England through bloodshed, but they kept it by a firm insistence on order. There was to be one authority only in all their domains, and the ancient land of Wales was no longer free to keep to its tribal ways. The Tudors found a simple and radical solution to the problem: by an Act of Union they turned Wales into a part of England. They carved up the Welsh Marches into English counties, they imported the machinery of local English government, and they made English the official language of all the law courts in Wales. They uprooted the ancient culture of the violent, picturesque land but they brought what they intended to bring—order.

Under the Act of Union, the lawless area around Montgomery Castle became the county of Montgomery and was expected to send its elected representatives to the English Parliament as tidily as though its inhabitants were all born Englishmen. It was also expected to police itself by the English system of local magistrates, and the fact that most of the Welsh counties achieved this really difficult feat is a tribute to the kind of Welshmen the Tudor monarchs chose as their local administrators.

Sir Richard Herbert was one of the best of them, and he served his king with the unpaid, selfless zeal that was characteristic of so many Tudor gentlemen. He used his formidable fighting powers only to suppress the thieves and outlaws who roamed the mountains of Montgomeryshire, and under his firm hand the wild land grew tame. He was steward of the lordships of Cedewain, Kerry, Cyneiliog and Arwysthi, and the poets sang Welsh lays in his praise. But he belonged to a different race of rulers, and the old ways never returned.

Sir Richard was a newcomer when he settled down in Montgomery Castle, since his family came from southern Wales. But he took care not to antagonize any of the local gentry and he spread his roots wide and deep. Both his wives came from local families and he had eight sons.

Sir Richard's eldest son by his second wife was named Edward, and he in turn became governor of Montgomery Castle. Like most of the men of his family, Edward Herbert spent his youth in the foreign wars and especially distinguished himself at the battle of St. Quentin, where he fought under his second cousin, the Earl of Pembroke. With such excellent connections he might have made a career for himself at the English court, but instead he went back to Wales like his father before him.

Edward lived to be a magnificent old gentleman of eighty, dying only a few weeks after his grandson, George Herbert, was born. He had reared eleven children and had become the unquestioned patriarch of what was now the most important family in Montgomeryshire. In his old age he built a big, low house just outside the town of Montgomery where he could live the life of a rich country squire and entertain with a lavishness suitable to the Herberts. The Welsh called the place Llys Mawr, the English called it Blackhall; and there old Edward Herbert kept such a splendid table that nearly every wild fowl that flew in the shire ended as an item on the Herbert bill of fare.

George Herbert's grandfather spent a lifetime in public service. Like his father before him, he was "a great suppressor of rebels, thieves and outlaws," arresting local wrongdoers, if necessary, at the point of the sword. He served as Sheriff of the county at a time when the duties of that officer were not yet ornamental, and he served also as a Justice of the Peace, that vital custodian of law and order. His grandson George said truly that "no commonwealth in the world hath a braver institution than that of Justices of the Peace," and Edward Herbert must have been one of the best. For he held the office of *custos rotulorum*, which meant that he kept the records and acted as chairman for his seven fellow Justices in Montgomeryshire.

Edward Herbert asked no return for all this, but he nevertheless expected his authority in the county to go unchallenged. In theory, the two Members of Parliament who went from Montgomeryshire were freely elected, but in practice they had to have Edward's approval. His firm paternalism was not quite so explicit as that of a Welshman to the north, whose tenant signed a written agreement to vote for him and his heirs or for "such person or persons as he and they shall nominate." But the tenants of Edward Herbert understood the right way to cast their votes, either for the master himself or for a suitable man of his choice.

On one occasion, when Edward was seventy-five, a Parliament election was contested in Montgomeryshire and the old man struck back with a vigor that was almost lawless in its intensity. On election day the opposition could find no lodgings in the town of Montgomery for its members, and the Sheriff was strangely flexible in his manner of counting the votes. The Sheriff was Edward Herbert's son-in-law, and the abuse of power was so obvious that the case went to the Star Chamber. The Herberts were law-abiding people but one rule took precedence over all others. They were the chief family in Montgomeryshire and no one could challenge them with impunity.

Edward's eldest son was named Richard, and he resembled his father and grandfather so closely that they might have been cut from the same quarry. Like them he was black-browed and black-bearded, a sternly handsome man with a strong sense of public duty. He acted as Deputy Lieutenant of the shire, and like his father he served in Parliament and was a Justice of the Peace and *custos rotulorum*. Even his enemies turned to him for help, and he fought for law and order at the risk of his life. It was when he was trying to arrest a fugitive from justice that he waged his epic and unequal fight in the churchyard of Llanerfyl. The broad blade of a forest bill cut through his skull to the membrane of the brain and a lesser man would have died of the wound he received.

Like the men of his family, Richard Herbert married well. His bride was the daughter and heiress of Sir Richard Newport, a great landowner in the neighboring county of Shropshire. Shrop-

shire was in England, but the line between the two countries
was so indistinct that half the people there still spoke Welsh.
Magdalen Newport brought with her a great name, for she had
the right to include families like Talbot and Devereux on her
coat of arms. She also brought with her an uncommon amount of
wit and intelligence, and enough efficiency to rule half Wales.

Richard and Magdalen Herbert had ten children. George
Herbert was the fifth of their seven sons, and the others were
Edward, William, Richard, Charles, Henry and Thomas—all
strong conservative names in a strong conservative family.

Magdalen was carrying the last son in her womb when her
husband died in October of 1596. He may have died suddenly,
since he died intestate, and she buried him in the parish church
of St. Nicholas in the town of Montgomery at the foot of the
castle. His ancestors lay there, and his father's body had been
placed in the church only three years earlier. She reared for him
in the south transept a magnificent tomb of alabaster, with his
image lying in full armor as befitted so brave a warrior.

Magdalen Herbert was left to share with her male relatives
the responsibility for bringing up the ten children in the fashion
that the honor of the Herberts demanded. In the case of the
three girls—Elizabeth, Margaret and Frances—her task was to
rear them to be good wives and to make sure they were supplied
with adequate dowries. In the case of the younger boys, her chief
responsibility was to supply them with a good education, of the
kind their father before them had been given. After that they
would probably go abroad to make their fortunes in the wars as
most of the Herberts had done. The alternative was to enter the
Church, for they were the younger sons and did not share in the
inheritance.

It was Edward, as the eldest, who was now the most important
member of the family, for he was heir to all the lands that the
Herberts had accumulated. In the old days, before the Act of
Union, there had been no system of primogeniture in Wales and

the land was divided among many sons. But now the English system prevailed, and for all its injustices it insured a strong hand on the land and a sense of continuing family responsibility in local government. Land was power as well as wealth in the days of the Tudors, and the more land the head of the family held the more power he possessed.

Young Edward Herbert was thirteen years old and a student at Oxford when his father died. If he had been free to choose his own path he would probably have become a doctor, for he was fascinated by human anatomy, which he called "the greatest miracle of nature," and conducted medical experiments all his life. But since he was head of a great house he did not, of course, have the right to choose a profession.

Nor was he free to choose a wife. Mary was selected for him by his guardian, Sir George More, who was proud of his skill in having arranged so suitable a match. It was suitable, that is to say, in the Elizabethan sense, for the bride brought with her a dowry of nearly thirty thousand pounds. In other ways it left something to be desired, for Edward was fifteen when he married and Mary was six years older. She was the daughter of Sir William Herbert of St. Julian's, who had left her all his estates in Monmouthshire and Ireland on condition that she marry someone whose last name was also Herbert. Her suitors included thirteen-year-old Philip Herbert, an English cousin of Edward's who was soon to become the Earl of Montgomery. But Edward was the victor, and he and Mary were married at his mother's home in Shropshire where he had been christened fifteen years earlier.

The young couple went to Oxford, where Edward continued his education and Mary bore his children. Edward was a handsome youth, very dark like his ancestors, with lustrous eyes, an oval face and long narrow fingers. He said later that his marriage helped him at the University. He had more time for his books now that there was "a due remedy for the lasciviousness to which youth is naturally inclined." But when he was presented at Whitehall to the aging Queen Elizabeth she remarked reflectively that it was a pity he had married so young.

Edward's good looks were an open door to the favor of Elizabeth's successor, King James, who delighted in handsome young men. Shortly after he ascended the throne he made Edward a Knight of the Bath, and Edward had a fine time at the ceremony. He was even vainer than the average young gentleman of the Renaissance and was charmed by the magnificence of his appearance in the crimson robes of the Order. He carefully observed the way people were looking at him—"I could tell how much my person was commended by the lords and ladies that came to see the solemnity"—and he had his picture painted in the ceremonial robes so that it could hang in his study.

Edward was expected to be useful as well as ornamental, and although he was only eighteen at the time of Elizabeth's last Parliament he represented Montgomeryshire in the House of Commons. His father had served there before him, and his grandfather before that. In fact, the Parliament that was held at the time of his grandfather's death was the only one for nearly a century in which some member of his family did not represent Montgomeryshire.

Sir Edward Herbert assumed another post that his grandfather had held, and in 1605 he was made Sheriff of the county. The Sheriff was chosen annually from among the leading members of the gentry and by now the position was chiefly honorary, with most of the work being done by the Justices of the Peace. But Edward did not want a post that bound him to Montgomeryshire or even to England. He had set his heart on going abroad and had taught himself French, Italian and Spanish so that he could become what he called a "citizen of the world." His wife was bitterly opposed to his plan, and when he finally got her consent he was probably assisted by the fact that he no longer owned Montgomery Castle. Philip Herbert, his handsome Eng-

lish cousin, was given the newly-created title of Earl of Montgomery the same year that Edward was made Sheriff, and two
years later King James presented the Earl with Montgomery
Castle. It was the following year that Sir Edward Herbert sailed
triumphantly for Europe, with three servants to accompany him.

The twenty-four-year-old Edward had been trained in all the
skills of a gentleman, riding, fighting and hunting, and on the
Continent he found that he possessed a further talent, the art of
making love. He brought to it the intensity that was characteristic of the Herbert family, and by Edward's own account
there was hardly a woman in Europe who could resist him.
Certainly he was incapable of resisting them; and when he
finally sat down to write his memoirs, soberly resolved to report
only what might be "useful" and edifying to his descendants, he
managed to include a highly impressive array of duels and of
ladies.

When Edward was in Paris he sent an amused letter in verse
back to Ben Jonson, one of his London friends, in which he described the stupid English tourists who arrived in France knowing neither the language nor the customs and as helpless as
infants. They did not possess the advantages of Sir Edward
Herbert, who was received with honor by the English ambassador and promptly invited to the country estate of the Grand
Constable of France. As a guest in the magnificent castle of
Merlou, Edward made love with vigor and hunted with equal
energy in the great park. He killed a wild boar single-handed—
a "pretty kind of fight" as he himself remarked in honest admiration—and sent the meat back, well larded, as a gift to his uncle
in Shropshire. At Merlou he also wrote poetry, the civilized,
intelligent verse that was characteristic of him, and the beauty
of the woods near the castle moved him to a sonnet on the loveli-
ness of the light through the leaves,

> . . . a green embroidering through each glade,
> An airy silver and a sunny gold . . .

Edward was as good a poet as he was fighter, for it was not in his nature to permit himself a poor performance in anything.

He was also a philosopher, and another poem he wrote at Merlou concludes that the world is a kind of Noah's Ark—"few men and many beasts." Two years later, when Edward was distinguishing himself at the siege of Juliers, another of his poet friends, John Donne, picked up the same idea of the ark and reached a different conclusion.

> Man is a lump, where all beasts kneaded be.
> Wisdom makes him an ark where all agree . . .

Donne addressed the poem "to Sir Edward Herbert, at Juliers," since in his opinion Edward was a man of wisdom. Ben Jonson agreed with him. And so, for that matter, did Edward himself, for his many virtues did not include modesty.

Edward had every reason to think well of himself, since he was petted by the great wherever he went. The King of France embraced him in the garden of the Tuileries, and the Queen had him next to her chair at the masques and balls. When he served in the Low Countries the Prince of Orange kept him affectionately at his side, and the Duke of Savoy lodged him in a room hung with silk and gold. In England he was held in equal esteem, and many people of high rank ordered copies of his portrait.

In the summer of 1613, Edward's castle was returned to him. The Earl of Montgomery had apparently wearied of it, since Edward got it back for five hundred pounds. He was ill for a while, so ill as to be almost unable to fight duels, and he spent much of his time at Montgomery Castle writing the book that would eventually make him famous as Lord Herbert of Cherbury.

Then King James offered to make him ambassador to France, and Edward accepted with delight. He gathered together "as choice a company of gentlemen for my attendants as I think ever followed an ambassador" and returned to his beloved Paris.

There he lived in the magnificence that was habitual with him and ran up impressive bills for gold and silver lace.

Edward was a fairly good ambassador and he evidently worked hard in Paris. But it is difficult to avoid the conclusion that it was the prestige of the office which attracted that flamboyant personality rather than the opportunity to be of use to his government. He was like his ancestors in many ways—in his dark good looks, his fiery temper and his skill with the sword—but he did not have their sense of dedication.

It was upon George Herbert, the fifth brother, that the family desire to be of service descended with full force. And since he lacked Edward's conceit, his life was not only shaped but nearly destroyed by it.

CHAPTER TWO

G EORGE HERBERT WAS BORN ON THE THIRD OF APRIL, 1593, IN
the Welsh countryside that his ancestors had done so much
to make safe and orderly. The green land that had once bristled
with fortresses had now grown tame, and the comfortable homes
of the Tudor gentry dotted the Vale of Montgomery. Through
it ran the river Severn, and near the east bank of the Severn rose
the hill on whose slope the town of Montgomery had been built.

Overhanging the town on a much higher rock stood Montgomery Castle, still complete with moats and drawbridge. Some
of its east rock had been used to wall the town, but now there
was no need of defenses and the town walls were crumbling
away. Montgomery was like any prosperous little English community, with the inevitable High Street leading past the market
and the town hall, and with Cherry Street turning into Orchard
Street as it rambled towards the open countryside.

There is no record of George Herbert's baptism, and no proof
that he was born in Montgomery Castle. But he was probably
brought up there, since the birth of the next child, Henry, is
recorded in the Montgomery parish records. The castle no longer
exists but in Tudor times it was a "most romancey seat" with a
magnificent view of England and Wales.

The only available information about Herbert's childhood
comes from Izaak Walton, who wrote a series of short *Lives* with
the same affectionate care he lavished on fishing. The biography
of Herbert was written nearly forty years after his death as a
product of Walton's old age, and it is deliberately designed to
be the life of a saint. According to Walton even Herbert's childhood was holy. "The beauties of his pretty behavior and wit
shined and became so eminent and lovely in this his innocent

age, that he seemed to be marked out for piety, and to become the care of heaven."

Walton's biography has a great deal of the sweetness and innocence that he attributes to the subject, and it is difficult to know how much is George Herbert and how much is Izaak Walton. Walton does not mention anywhere in his book, for instance, Herbert's hot Welsh temper. Yet it must have been well known, and Edward Herbert mentions it in a short and otherwise admiring description of his younger brother. "He was not exempt from passion and choler, being infirmities to which all our race is subject."

George Herbert speaks of his own youth in two of his poems. In one he calls it "my fierce youth" and in another he couples "youth and fierceness." This does not indicate a quiet childhood, and Herbert did not live to be a quiet man. He kept his balance by a high degree of tension, and like the hurrying rivers of his native Wales he had a "longing desire to haste ever forward." He combined this with a frail body and an intense desire to achieve perfection, and while he shared this second characteristic with his elder brother Edward, he lacked the self-esteem that gave Edward so calm a conviction of the rightness of his own ways. George Herbert's self-esteem was less durable, and he did not find complete peace until he ceased to trade in that particular commodity.

Such a boy needs an orderly background if he is not to wear himself out, and in this George Herbert was fortunate in his mother. As Walton puts it, he spent most of his childhood "under the eye and care of his prudent mother," who managed to keep an attentive eye on her ten children, run a large household and delight nearly every man she met. It was perhaps just as well that Magdalen Herbert had so many children. With her vigorous intelligence and her vitality, she would have been insupportable if she had been left to concentrate on only one.

As Magdalen was fond of pointing out, she had the same number of children as the patriarch Job. And, like Job, she took their

upbringing with the utmost seriousness, concerning herself with
every detail of their moral and spiritual development. It was an
age in which duty to one's parents was as thoroughly ingrained
as duty to Church and State, and a conservative Elizabethan
writer like Richard Hooker could speak quite casually of the
"supreme power" that was vested in the head of the family. In
Magdalen's case she was father and mother both and had a
special reason to concern herself with her children's welfare.

The average Elizabethan was accustomed to supervision. An
array of school authorities, church authorities and government
authorities kept a close watch on the most minute details of his
behavior, and Magdalen Herbert's ten children had come into
a world where her strict watchfulness would seem normal. The
only one who apparently showed even a flicker of rebellion was
her eldest son, Edward. On one occasion he wanted to learn to
swim and she did not wish him to, offering the rather specious
argument that "she had heard of more drowned than saved by
it." This failed to impress her son's logical mind and so she
directly forbade it. They also differed over money, since Magdalen wished her eldest son to support his nine brothers and
sisters out of his inheritance. Edward felt this to be an injustice,
since his mother was a rich woman in her own right. Nevertheless
she had her way, and it was Edward who gave his brothers their
annual allowance and his sisters their marriage portions.

Yet the young Herberts were fortunate in their mother, for
she was not only a stern and virtuous woman but a thoroughly
charming one also. She had learned the art of graceful living
at the house of her parents in Shropshire, and she brought with
her to Wales a real talent for making people happy. The giving
of alms, for instance, usually degenerated into a routine obligation for the mistress of a large establishment, but Magdalen
brought to it a compassion that made her "eyes to the blind,
and hands and feet to the lame." She loved music and gardens
and the company of lively intelligent minds, and John Donne

remembered her house as "a court, in the conversation of the best."

Her friendship with Donne was a close one, and at one time he was writing her almost daily. It is not surprising that she was attracted to Donne, for he was capable of a "winning behavior, which, when it would entice, had a strange kind of elegant, irresistible art." He needed friends, for he stood in the shadow of a desperate poverty, with no way to support his gently-reared wife and their many children except through the casual kindness of the rich. He wrote flattering letters to more than one woman but his letters to Magdalen Herbert are not quite like the rest, and he gave her a tribute in verse of a kind that few women have ever received.

> No spring, nor summer beauty hath such grace
> As I have seen in one autumnal face . . .
> Here, where still evening is; not noon, nor night;
> Where no voluptuousness is, yet all delight.

John Donne shared with Magdalen Herbert a preoccupation with the things of the spirit, and when he wrote his seven Holy Sonnets he sent them to her as their most suitable recipient. "Harbor these hymns." In his eyes she seemed to have achieved righteousness without torment, and he spoke once of the "greatest virtue in the world, which is you."

This quality that Donne valued so much made a strong bond between Magdalen Herbert and her fifth son. Her mind was alien to Edward's but it was very close to that of George. The family prayers and the daily reading of the Bible that seem to have been more or less routine to most of the family were the outward form of an intense reality to them both, and it was not darkened by the sense of sin that lay so heavily on the Christians of the sixteenth and seventeenth centuries. George Herbert came to his first worship of God with the ease and happiness of a boy in spring. As he himself put it, "There was no month but May."

There came a time, and it was apparently early, when George

Herbert decided to spend his whole life in the service of God.
From the practical point of view it was natural for him to look
for a career in the Church of England, since he did not have the
soldier's temperament of most of his brothers. But it was not the
practical point of view that came first with George Herbert.
This was something that he wanted with his whole heart, and
his mother wanted it also.

Normally young George Herbert would have been sent to
grammar school when he was seven years old. But at about that
time Magdalen moved her household to Oxford, because she
wished to be near Edward and his bride and give him the daily
supervision she felt he needed. There she delighted the men of
Oxford with her wit and her intelligence and made friends with
nearly everyone of "any eminent worth or learning that were
at that time in or near that university." She apparently kept the
younger boys near her at Oxford and had them tutored at home.
The same thing was true when she moved to London, still with
her married son and his family in tow, and took a house at
Charing Cross.

George Herbert grew up in an atmosphere of lively intelligence and serene order. He once wrote a Latin poem in which he
described the way his mother ran her household—the rhythm
of her daily visits to the kitchen and the gardens, the faultless
ease with which she entertained. Her management of the household was as skillful as her embroidery or her beautiful penman-
ship, and she gave her son an environment of civilized harmony.
Later, after he had lost his way, he wrote that "Childhood is
health," and he seems to have looked back on his own as a time
of peace.

When George Herbert was about twelve years old, his mother
enrolled him in Westminster School, which was a short walk
southward from her home in Charing Cross. He was a day
scholar for a time at that famous school and then he won a
scholarship and went to live there.

Forty boys boarded at Westminster School, and since it was a royal foundation they were known as the King's Scholars. They had been selected on the basis of "their teachableness, the goodness of their disposition, their learning, good behavior and poverty," and whatever George Herbert's qualifications may have been in the first four departments he was certainly not eligible in the fifth. But there was a growing tendency among prominent families to enter their sons in Westminster School and the original requirement of poverty was being increasingly ignored.

It was an ideal school from Magdalen Herbert's point of view since it was conducted along the same lines as her own household. Its purpose, as given in the statutes, was to produce boys who were "pious, learned, gentlemanly and industrious," and the headmaster, Dr. Richard Ireland, did his best to produce a string of young graduates well fortified with Latin rhetoric and Anglican piety. There had been liveliness and curiosity in Westminster School back in the days when William Camden was a teacher there; but he left there before the end of the century and the light he had been able to kindle in a youngster like Ben Jonson faded back into the conformity that was the school's real purpose. It did not wish to produce independent members of the commonwealth. It wished to produce sober and amenable ones.

George Herbert had already been trained to obedience.

> Parents first season us: then schoolmasters
> Deliver us to laws . . .

He received his induction kneeling, while the Dean of Westminster recited over him the Latin words that gave him entry in the name of the Father, the Son and the Holy Ghost, and from that time on the routine was almost monastic in its severity. The boys slept two in a bed in a room that had once been the granary of the monks and were wakened at five in the morning to kneel for prayers. At six they knelt again in the great hall south of the dormitory and again recited the Latin prayers that the statutes

prescribed. There were prayers before noon dinner, before play-
time and before supper; and at eight o'clock, when they went to
bed, the King's Scholars knelt once more and prayed.

Not a moment of their day went unsupervised, from the time
they made their beds in the morning and filed out to wash until
they blew their candles out at night. Even on the playing field
it was the business of the authorities to know where each boy
was every moment of the time, and there were eighteen monitors
to assist in keeping a vigilant eye on their behavior. The forty
boys in their sombre russet gowns were of course like normal
boys anywhere, and the explicit tone of the statutes in the matter
of washing alone shows how strictly the King's Scholars had to be
watched lest they revert to the natural grubbiness that was their
birthright.

The course of study was the usual one, and Herbert learned
to talk in Latin, rhyme in Latin and declaim in Latin, with an
unusual amount of Greek as he reached the higher forms. He
studied hard, since it was not in his temperament to take anything lightly, but to judge by his later career his favorite subjects
were music and rhetoric.

Music was an integral part of life in the Renaissance, and even
if the royal statutes had not specified a musical training Westminster School would certainly have given it. Every town in
England had its band of musicians, every great house its music
master, nearly every home its lute, and it was a part of the equipment for a civilized life that every child should know and love
music. George Herbert and his schoolmates spent every Wednesday and Friday afternoon from two to three studying the
"art of music" with the choirmaster, and his skill with the lute
may have been acquired in part at Westminster School.

The school statutes laid a special emphasis on singing, since
"a knowledge of singing is found to be of the greatest use for a
clear and distinct elocution." It was for this same reason, the
necessity of learning to speak well, that the King's Scholars
presented each year at Twelfth Night a Latin play in the school

hall. From the point of view of the boys themselves the performance might mean no more than the buttered beer and com-
fits that came afterwards and a chance to wear the magnificent
costumes that were supplied by the Office of the Revels. But
the authorities viewed it as one more opportunity to build up
the control of the spoken word that was the basis of the whole
school system.

The English method was modeled in part on the Roman, and
the primary purpose of the Roman schools had been to turn out
orators. Rhetoric was almost the whole of a Roman child's education, since he was being trained, in theory at least, to become
a power in the land through his eloquence. Rhetoric was the art
of public persuasion; and the man who possessed that art could
dominate not only the field of law, where Roman education
had its primary concern, but any other area of activity where
eloquence was of use.

Sir Francis Bacon, who was a practical man, had a great respect for oratory. "Eloquence is doubtless inferior to wisdom.
. . . Yet in profit and popular estimation, wisdom yields to
eloquence; for so Solomon says, 'The wise in heart shall be called
prudent, but he that is sweet of speech shall compass greater
things'; plainly signifying that wisdom will help a man to a name
or admiration, but that it is eloquence which prevails most in
action and common life."

Like most schoolroom subjects, the end was lost sight of in a
painstaking pursuit of the means. The boys labored over their
formal Latin declamations, accumulated in their notebooks examples of rhetorical devices and learned all the stock techniques
that were already worn with too much use. But occasionally a
boy like George Herbert valued the subject for its own sake and
really enjoyed the somewhat ceremonious and ornamental exercise it had become.

In general, all this training did not produce a very notable
group of English orators and the best place to find an example of
the art was in the pulpit. The Jacobean sermons were intricately

formed and magnificently delivered, and the preachers who delivered them were experts in the art of rhetoric. It was an age in
which people listened to a vast number of sermons, not only as
a religious duty but also as a form of popular entertainment,
and a churchman like Lancelot Andrewes achieved his high
reputation chiefly because he was "an angel in the pulpit."

George Herbert had a chance to hear many sermons when he
was a King's Scholar, since the school was almost a part of Westminster Abbey. It had been originally the living quarters of the
Abbey monks and lay just to the south near the Abbey garden.
All the King's Scholars attended the great church regularly, and
part of their curriculum was to turn in a detailed report of the
sermon—the smaller boys in English, the older ones in Latin
prose and the most advanced students in Latin verse. The rhythm
of the Abbey became a part of George Herbert's life and it stood
as a symbol of all that was most impressive in the Church of
England, with its soaring arches, its magnificent music and its
great altar rich with blue velvet and cloth of gold.

The ritual of the Church of England surrounded George Herbert all through his school days, and he accepted the religion
of his inheritance not merely with obedience but with wholehearted joy.

> I looked on Thy furniture so fine,
>   And made it fine to me:
> Thy glorious household-stuff did me entwine,
>   And 'tice me unto Thee.
> Such stars I counted mine: both heav'n and earth
> Paid me my wages in a world of mirth.

Such a boy might very well end as a bishop. He had a brain
as good as his brother Edward's, with a high proficiency in both
Greek and Latin, and Westminster School was justified in expecting great things of so brilliant and godly a youngster.

The next step in his career was to go to either Oxford or
Cambridge, since the primary function of both universities was
still the medieval one of turning out churchmen. Six university

scholarships were open to the King's Scholars, three to Christ Church at Oxford and three to Trinity College at Cambridge. Christ Church had the better record for producing graduates who became church dignitaries, but Trinity attributed this to its rival's superior connections, "being also a cathedral church and having canons both richly beneficed and highly dignified, which doth enable them to doctorships, deaneries and bishoprics —a great blessing of God that our college wanteth."

The representatives from the two colleges arrived at Westminster School each year in the spring during the week of Rogation Sunday. Election time was always a festive occasion, with new lute strings provided for the music at the Election Dinner and with the boys earnestly rehearsing their Latin epigrams. A stage was set up behind a railing, and there the electors sat in what was hoped would be grave and unanimous cooperation.

On this particular May morning in 1608 the representative from Cambridge was not in a cooperative mood. His name was Thomas Nevile, and he had grown increasingly irritated by the way King James was behaving over the King's Scholars. In the classic fashion of anxious parents, James had decided that the Westminster boys were being discriminated against at Cambridge and were not getting the fellowships they deserved after they arrived at Trinity College.

Dr. Nevile was master of Trinity College and he wished the College fellowships to be given to the best students rather than to those whose only qualification was that they came from Westminster School. He arrived in an unyielding frame of mind and refused to take the oath that was required of all the examiners. Then he announced that there were no vacancies in Trinity College, having filled them all hurriedly in April. The wrangling continued until dinnertime and long afterwards. In the end Dr. Nevile agreed to accept three boys from Westminster School on the usual scholarships but he flatly refused to guarantee them fellowships after they got there.

By the time the discussion ended it had involved such dignitaries as the Archbishop of Canterbury, the Lord High Treasurer and the Lord Privy Seal. It also involved George Herbert, since he was one of the three boys chosen.

Before he left he was called in by the headmaster, along with another promising boy named John Hacket who had also won a Cambridge scholarship. Dr. Ireland said that the school was sure to be proud of both of them at Trinity College, and he warned them to "study moderately and use exercise." They both had a tendency to push themselves too hard, and the headmaster asked them "not to impair their health with too much study."

George Herbert was in fact ill after he arrived at Cambridge, as he mentioned in a letter to his mother when he apologized for the quality of some verses he had sent her. "I fear the heat of my late ague hath dried up those springs, by which scholars say, the Muses use to take up their habitations."

It was the custom for a good son to send his parents an example of poetic composition as a New Year's gift, and the learned and virtuous Prince Henry had been sending his father Latin verses at holiday time since he was nine years old. George Herbert was also skilled in Latin verse, but the two sonnets he sent his mother as a New Year's gift were in English. They are not especially good poetry, since he had not yet found his own voice, but they concerned a subject on which he had strong convictions.

Many years earlier a distant kinsman of Herbert's, Sir Philip Sidney, had criticized the failure of English poets to write in honor of God. They wrote love songs to women instead, and Sidney thought they overdid it. There had been a movement in French literature to counteract this erotic, somewhat pagan tendency in Renaissance writing, but nothing of the sort had happened in England, except for some vague moralizing about "ungodly songs" and their bad effect on all good Christians. Sidney regretted the fact that no good religious poetry was being written in England, and he was sure that his countrymen would be well employed "in singing the praises of the immortal beauty, the immortal goodness of that God Who giveth us hands to write and wits to conceive."

As his own contribution Sidney translated part of an epic account of the Creation by the Huguenot poet, Guillaume Du Bartas. Sidney's version has not survived, but when Joshua Sylvester made an enormously popular translation of Du Bartas in 1605 he prefaced it with a memorial to Sidney before he began his own account of the Creation as "divinely warbled by Lord Bartas' art."

Whatever the divinity of Du Bartas' original warblings, the English version is painfully earthbound. Its chief interest is that it introduces a new Muse of poetry; Urania, originally the Muse of astronomy, is now the heavenly Muse who wafts Du Bartas up to God. It was to Urania that Milton called for assistance when he began *Paradise Lost*, but by that time her wings had grown considerably stronger.

The one English poet capable of writing sacred poetry was Robert Southwell, the heroic Jesuit who died on the scaffold when George Herbert was two years old. His execution on a charge of treason had no effect on the popularity of his poetry, which was being openly published in London the year he died; and Ben Jonson, who had the highest opinion of his own verse, once remarked that he would be content to destroy much of it if he could have written Southwell's masterpiece, "The Burning Babe." Southwell had started what almost amounted to a campaign to elevate love poetry to the love of God, and although he was a Roman Catholic he was one of the fathers of that great line of Anglican religious poets which includes George Herbert.

At seventeen Herbert agreed wholeheartedly with the great Jesuit, and the two sonnets he sent his mother are a restatement of the position Southwell had taken.

> My God, where is that ancient heat towards Thee,
> Wherewith whole shoals of martyrs once did burn,

Besides their other flames? Doth Poetry
Wear Venus' livery? only serve her turn?
Why are not sonnets made of Thee? and lays
Upon Thine altar burnt?

It is not very good poetry, in spite of the fact that Herbert
had obviously been studying both Sidney and Donne, but it
expresses a conviction that was to become of the highest importance to him. The worship of God was not a service that
should be reserved for a few clearly defined areas. The whole
world belonged to God and was formed for His praise; and a
poet's abilities, just as much as a churchman's, could, as Herbert
told his mother, "be all and ever consecrated to God's glory."

CHAPTER THREE

G EORGE HERBERT FOUND NO CHANGE IN HIS LIFE WHEN HE
went to Cambridge. It continued to be an orderly and disciplined existence, dedicated, in the words of his matriculation oath, to "piety and good letters."

The atmosphere was the matriarchal one he had already known. It was not for nothing that the University was called the fostering mother, the *alma mater*, and Herbert once remarked that he pictured her as "a matron holy, reverend, of antique and august countenance." When John Donne wished to describe the way Magdalen Herbert had installed her sons in the universities, he said that she "recompensed to them the loss of a father in giving them two mothers." The function of this second mother, according to the Privy Council, was to "bring up youth in the knowledge and fear of God, and in all manner of good learning and virtuous education." In return the student was expected to give the same absolute obedience he gave his own parents.

Magdalen introduced her son to Cambridge in the same way she had introduced him to Westminster School, taking him direct to the head of Trinity College. As Izaak Walton put it, "His prudent mother, well knowing that he might easily lose or lessen that virtue and innocence, which her advice and example had planted in his mind, did therefore procure the generous and liberal Dr. Nevile, who was then . . . master of that college, to take him into his particular care, and provide him with a tutor; which he did most gladly undertake; for he knew the excellencies of his mother, and how to value such a friendship." This was the same Dr. Nevile who had been so uncooperative on Election Day, and by this time he had changed his mind about young George Herbert.

35

The name of the tutor that Dr. Nevile chose for him is unknown, but it would have been one of the fellows in the College.
He assumed the responsibility for Herbert's bills, saw that he
met the right people and took up the right kind of sports, supervised his study program, reported his progress home to the
family, and in general acted as a kind of substitute resident
parent. It was the tutor's responsibility to see that the student
behaved himself and spent his time usefully, and some of them
had a profound effect upon their charges.

The statutes of Trinity College were as strict as those of Westminster School, and in fact Queen Elizabeth had signed them
only a year apart. Their purpose was the same, to create learned
and obedient Englishmen, and they provided for the same supervision of the religious life of each student. Every morning and
evening he recited in his chamber the prayer that the statutes
provided. He reported to the chapel each morning at five for an
hour of services, and if he were late for morning prayer, for
evening prayer, or for communion, the exact form of his punishment on the following Friday evening at seven o'clock was also
specified. Twice each day when the students assembled in the
great halls for meals, they listened to a Bible-reading from someone appointed by the deans, and these same deans were responsible for seeing to it that the students fulfilled in the smallest
particular "the pious, religious and becoming performance of the
worship of God."

The life was rigid but the surroundings had an almost cathedral-like magnificence. The revenues of Trinity College made it
the richest foundation in either Oxford or Cambridge, and it was
a beautiful place to live when Herbert arrived there on the
eighteenth of December, 1609. Dr. Nevile had been master for
the past sixteen years and had possessed from the first the ex-
pansive ideas of a minor Renaissance prince. As soon as he took
office he personally advanced three thousand pounds towards re-
building the College, and when Herbert arrived the splendid
Great Court was there to welcome him, with its fountain in the

center and the life of the College going on around it. As Herbert's schoolmate, John Hacket, most truly said, Dr. Thomas Nevile was a "splendid, courteous and bountiful gentleman."

The master of Trinity College worked equally hard to supply the students with recreation, and four years after Herbert's arrival Dr. Nevile finally persuaded the town authorities to let him buy the fields on the other side of the river Cam. The bowling green he had hoped to make there was not achieved until many years later, but at least the young men had space to walk under the willows on the other side of the busy river. Dr. Nevile also opened a tennis court two years after Herbert arrived. It was roofed against the weather and staffed with two court keepers, and some of the undergraduates ran up bills for tennis expenses that topped everything else on their lists.

Like all the colleges of Cambridge, Trinity lived a completely self-contained life behind its beautiful gate. It had its own vegetable garden, slaughterhouse, meat house, hen house, capon house, fish house, brew house and bake house. It had a horse-keeper's house for the man who took care of the students' horses, and even a swan house for the College flock of swans.

The focus of this community life was the great hall, which was used for meals and lectures and hung with greens at Christmastime for the College plays. For relative privacy there was what was then called the parlor, a large room behind the dais which the students used as a general meeting place. No one could achieve the eminence of a room of his own until he became a doctor of divinity, and the students lived by twos and threes in the crowded upper floors. But the window space was good, and each boy had a work cabinet where he kept his books and did his studying. The students ran up bills for buying desks, hiring chairs, putting up shelves and having the walls painted, and most of them acquired the lutes that were as much standard college equipment at the beginning of the seventeenth century as the banjo was at the end of the nineteenth.

Each student was required to own a surplice and to wear it

when he attended services in the College chapel. The chapel was as beautiful as the rest of Trinity College, and by Herbert's time elaborate hangings had been placed in the organ loft. Within this rich, sober and disciplined environment the young men were supposed to lead lives of studious virtue, fitting themselves for "the better service of Church and commonwealth."

Perhaps this somewhat visionary ideal could have been enforced if the sole function of the University had still been the training of churchmen. But by the time George Herbert went to Cambridge every well-to-do Englishman hoped to send his sons to a university, and the nursery for divines was being transformed into a kind of gentlemen's finishing school.

Many of the young worldlings who went to Cambridge had no idea what to do with themselves after they arrived. Henry Peacham, who attended Trinity College at the same time as George Herbert, gives a pathetic picture of a youthful undergraduate in Dr. Nevile's noble structure, his unread books ranged round his chamber and not a thought in his head except how to amuse himself. The statutes permitted a certain amount of dignified recreation and even went so far as to allow playing cards at Christmas, but these concessions were not enough for lively young men with time on their hands. There was a statute forbidding attendance at dancing school, but bills for dancing lessons are among the students' papers. There were laws against heavy drinking, but a sober young man who attended Cambridge at the same time as Herbert was appalled at the "swearing, drinking, rioting" he found there. There was a statute against keeping dogs, but the students kept them nevertheless for hunting small game; and so another statute had to be drafted to threaten with imprisonment any townsman who was willing to house the greyhounds.

This kind of behavior was a constant source of irritation to the authorities. But it was to be expected whenever normal young men were gathered together and it posed no real threat to the foundations of the commonwealth. Of a very different nature was another kind of disobedience which also existed at Cambridge and which the government fought with every weapon at its command. This was a religious radicalism which had made the University its stronghold, and which the authorities believed could destroy both Church and State unless it were rooted out.

A tradition of rebellion against religious authority had existed at Cambridge for nearly a century. When the heretical wind of the Reformation began to blow across the Channel, it brought inflammatory tracts that were smuggled up the river Cam in bales of merchandise from traders in north Germany; and when reformers like Latimer and Tyndale gathered to discuss the strange new doctrines of Martin Luther they met in a Cambridge inn. The men of the University of Cambridge were at the heart of the Reformation in England, and it was in large measure through their ardor that England became a Protestant country.

When Queen Mary ascended the throne, England became Roman Catholic again and the Protestants had their choice of exile, conformity or death. Most of them naturally chose conformity, but many valiant spirits chose the stake and about five hundred chose exile. Most of their leaders came from Cambridge, and after they had regrouped themselves abroad they started a vigorous propaganda campaign against England's devout and well-intentioned Catholic queen.

Many Protestant communities in Europe were open to the exiles; but the most impressive was Geneva, where John Calvin had won his relentless warfare to turn an easygoing Swiss town into the City of God. It had taken him nearly fifteen years to do it, but he succeeded so well that John Knox described Geneva as "the most perfect school of Christ that ever was in the earth since the days of the Apostles." The thin, sickly French lawyer, with his tidy mind and his fierce will, had managed to impose upon its thirteen thousand inhabitants his own ascetic vision of God's will, and those who refused to share his vision had it thrust upon them. There was no longer any wearing of fashionable slashed breeches in Geneva, no dancing at weddings, and

when a man named his son Claude instead of Abraham he was
put on trial by the Council for so irreligious an act.

The nearest approach Europe had seen to Calvin's ideal of
behavior was a well-run monastery, and in a sense Calvin's
discipline was the monastic ideal of behavior transferred by
force to the whole community. But an even closer parallel was
the organization that had been built up long before by the men
who returned to Judah from the Babylonian Exile. There was
the same desire to serve God and the same fierce conviction
that there was only one way to do it, the same high standard
of conduct and the same unrelenting determination to force it
on everyone else.

The English exiles believed that God had permitted a Catholic
queen to come to the throne because the Protestant Reformation
in England had not been thorough enough. Every vestige of the
old religion should have been swept away, and nothing should
have been permitted in the church organization or the church
services unless expressly authorized in the Bible. Anything else,
"seem it never so good, holy or beautiful, yet before our God
. . . it is evil, wicked and abominable."

When a Protestant queen ascended the throne of England in
1558, the exiles trooped back in triumphant excitement. Here
was their opportunity at last to transform the nation into a second Geneva, blessed with the spirit of God and the true Reformed discipline.

Young Queen Elizabeth thought otherwise. She had become
the ruler of a small island ringed with foes and torn by internal
disagreements. She dared not take a rigid stand on the subject
of religion, which was a bitterly divisive force and left a trail
of blood behind it. The emotion she wanted to encourage was
patriotism, both because she felt it so strongly herself and because it was the one thing that could unite the country; and she
succeeded in making patriotism the dominant emotion of the
Elizabethan Age.

As far as religious ceremonies went, Elizabeth knew that there was no way of pleasing all her subjects. So she authorized what she felt to be a reasonable compromise between the elaborate ritual of the Roman Catholic church and the spare observances of Geneva and hoped that the majority of her subjects would be content. In any case, content or not, they were all expected to become members of the Church of England. For there was one church in England as there was one queen.

Elizabeth assumed full control of the church and used it as an integral part of her technique of government. Her bishops operated as a key unit of control in an intricate system that interlocked on all levels and stretched up from the parish church-wardens to the Queen on her throne. Under such circumstances, and faced with the difficult problem of running the country, she had no intention of listening to the returning exiles, who did not wish the ministers to be under the control of the Crown and were convinced that the Bible did not authorize bishops. It authorized only "doctors, pastors, governors and deacons. . . . All else is Antichrist."

This group of Protestant extremists found its first and most eloquent voice at the University of Cambridge. In 1570 a fellow of Trinity College named Thomas Cartwright presented a brilliant series of lectures in which he offered a design for a new and holier English church fashioned after the Genevan model. When he preached at St. Mary's, "grave men ran like boys in the streets to get places in the church" and the clerk had to take down the windows to accommodate the crowd. One Sunday in July, in the chapel of Trinity College, he attacked the custom of wearing the surplice, which was the chief survival of pre-Reformation vestments and therefore to him a wicked popish remnant; and the excited students tore the surplices from their shoulders as an affront to the Lord.

In those days the master of Trinity College was John Whitgift, who was so stern a disciplinarian that he was able to keep the students "in a mannerly and awful obedience." He was convinced that Cartwright was making a direct attack on the government, and in such a case Whitgift did not believe in gentle reasoning. "Insolent audacity . . . is rather to be corrected with due punishment than confuted by argument." This was Queen Elizabeth's view also, and in the end she made Whitgift her Archbishop of Canterbury.

Cartwright was expelled from the University and a new set of statutes instituted to make sure that the matter would not come up again. A heresy board was set up to try any University preacher who attacked the Church of England, and the law against seditious writing was made so strict that anyone who picked up a radical pamphlet could be expelled. In an even more fundamental move to exert the royal authority, the right to govern the University of Cambridge was taken away from the acting body of teachers and vested instead in the heads of the Colleges, whose appointments were under the Queen's control. There were bitter protests against these new statutes, especially from the "younger sort," but there was no shaking Whitgift and the Queen.

Thomas Cartwright was a dedicated man and a determined fighter. Silenced at Cambridge, he and his party tried to work through Parliament, where they had an enormous number of sympathizers. The Queen muzzled the House of Commons and repeatedly refused to let its members discuss anything that related to the Church of England. Patiently, Cartwright's party tried a new device. Boards of young clergymen, mostly Cambridge graduates, were formed in some districts with the idea of quietly taking over the local church organizations and altering them by degrees to the Genevan model. The project was finally uncovered and crushed, and an exasperated Elizabeth wrote to her cousin James in Scotland, "There is risen both in your realm and mine a sect of perilous consequence, such as would have no kings but a presbytery. . . . Look we well unto them."

For some time the radical Protestant reformers had been known as "Puritans." The nickname was given in derision and used indiscriminately, but by the end of the century there were three groups to whom it could be applied. The best organized and the most vocal was the one to which Cartwright belonged, which wished to change the Church of England to a presbyterian organization and remove the bishops. A less radical group did not wish the structure of the Church altered but hoped it might become more Protestant in its ritual. And a very radical fringe, regarded with horror by all other Puritans, denied the value of any state church at all and advocated a series of local self-governing congregations.

All the Puritan factions felt a new hopefulness when Queen Elizabeth died and King James ascended the throne of England. He had been reared in Scotland, where the state church was modeled on the Genevan system, and the English reformers were sure he would sympathize with their aims. A large number of ministers presented what was called the Millenary Petition, requesting certain changes in the Church and assuring the new monarch that they did not desire "a disorderly innovation, but a due and godly reformation." These men belonged to the moderate wing of the Puritan movement, but James was convinced they were all radical Presbyterians and he had had enough of that system in Scotland. "Presbytery . . . agreeth as well with monarchy as God and the devil." James thoroughly approved of the structure of the Church of England, which reinforced the power of the throne while the Puritan system tended to undermine it, and if his measures against Puritanism were less efficient than Elizabeth's it was only because he lacked her intelligence and vigor.

Official Cambridge was much shocked by the Millenary Petition and issued a severe reproof to the ministers who had signed it. The University also passed a formal resolution that anyone who criticized the Church of England would automatically lose his degree. But the spirit of man is not an easy thing to control, and neither statutes nor loyalty oaths could smother the spirit of religious radicalism at Cambridge.

The chief stronghold of the Puritans was Emmanuel College,

established during Elizabeth's reign by a great officer of state
who assured his sovereign that it was not a Puritan foundation.
Nevertheless it was, and its sole purpose was to produce preachers "learned and zealous . . . in the service of the reformed
faith." There were only a dozen young men in Emmanuel College
when it opened, but when George Herbert was at Cambridge
so many students were crowding into Emmanuel that it was
second only to Trinity as the largest college in the University.
Unlike rich Trinity College, Emmanuel could not house all its
ardent young students, and many of them had to disobey the
statutes and live outside the College gates while they pursued
their studies and fitted themselves to spread the Word.

Emmanuel was not an austere college. It had its tennis court,
its bathing pool and its bowling in the orchard, and King James
was sincerely fond of its master. Yet it was the most dangerous
institution in the country from the point of view of anyone who
believed in an absolute monarchy, for education could achieve
what no frontal attack could ever hope to bring about. When
the extent of the damage finally became evident, an outraged
member of the Church of England accused the Puritans of
having worked "like moles under the ground," and in a way he
was quite right.

From the first, Puritanism had appealed to youth, and the reports of the Elizabethan bishops were full of complaints about
the "foolish young men" who were being attracted to it. It was
based on a radical, exacting idealism, and the young intellectuals
of the rising generation fitted themselves like soldiers for a cause
that was worth any sacrifice. Each year the voices of the Cambridge graduates, strong and eloquent and fiercely in earnest,
could be heard in a rising chorus over the land, protected by
the city tradespeople and the country gentry who had supported
them from the first.

Puritanism seemed even more attractive when it was compared
with the remoteness and artificiality of the official curriculum,
which had almost nothing to offer an ardent young modern. It

was based on Aristotle, whose writings were so revered by the educationalists that there were by now nearly twelve thousand books in existence that explained him and commented on him. But none of these books explained what relation his philosophy had to the real world that was changing so furiously outside the college walls.

Back in the days before Dr. Whitgift rose in the world, he had tutored in Trinity College a young man named Francis Bacon. Bacon resented the domination of the old ways of thinking but he did not take the usual route of the restless young and become a Puritan. Unlike most of the men of his age, Bacon had no interest in the unseen. It was the visible world that roused him, and when he dined in the great hall of Trinity College it was not the open Bible that attracted his attention so much as the framed map of the world that was also in the hall.

Young Francis Bacon had a devouring curiosity about the nature of things. There was, for instance, an iron pillar in Trinity College that supported the roof of one of the rooms upstairs. Why did this pillar make a "little flat noise" in the room where it was struck but a loud one in the room beneath? What were the properties of sound? What, in fact, were the laws that governed sound and motion, the color of birds, the action of tides and of all created things?

Bacon found no encouragement at Trinity College, nor would he have found it in any other institution of learning in England. As he said rather bitterly, "The studies of men in these places are . . . imprisoned in the writings of certain authors, from whom if any man dissent he is straightaway arraigned as a turbulent person." He further said that if anyone had "the boldness to use any liberty of judgment" he would find himself almost without company.

It was no wonder. Bacon was attacking the policy not merely of the universities but of all England. It was still a medieval country, still convinced that the ideal commonwealth consisted of authority at the top and obedience at the bottom, and Bacon's plea for "liberty of judgment" was in fact a revolutionary one.

The University of Cambridge, which called itself a "little commonwealth," operated under the same system of all-encompassing rules and tireless supervision that was felt to be necessary for the country as a whole. Individual liberty was as undesirable in subjects as it was in children. Disagreement was dangerous; nonconformity could quickly become treason. Both were enemies of public order whether in the home, the church or the state, and they were especially so at the University of Cambridge. For she was the august mother of many sons, and she was determined to be obeyed.

CHAPTER FOUR

G EORGE HERBERT WAS AN IDEAL STUDENT FROM THE POINT OF
view of the University authorities—an aristocratic young
man who was willing to work and a clever young man who was
willing to be obedient. He was neither a worldling nor a radical,
and the master of Trinity College took him under his wing and
gave him special attention. Dr. Nevile suffered a paralytic stroke
when Herbert was twenty-two and died soon afterwards, but by
that time his protégé was well launched on his university career.

The only area where George Herbert seems to have ignored
the rules was in the matter of dress. The ideal of both universities
was a monastic one, and the students were supposed to wear
their hair short and their gowns reaching to the ankles. The ideal
of dress in the young men themselves was a fantastic glitter of
laces and silks and buttons and bows, and they saw no reason to
leave their curls and their feathers behind them when they went
to college. A Cambridge undergraduate who paid three shillings
for his surplice paid eight shillings for a satin collar and four
times that amount for a pair of garters and roses. Herbert apparently dressed expensively and well. Almost too well, for Izaak
Walton says that his "clothes seemed to prove, that he put too
great a value on his parts and parentage."

Walton was also obliged to admit that Herbert's behavior at
Trinity College was not of the friendliest. "He kept himself too
much retired, and at too great a distance with all his inferiors."
In fairness to Herbert, however, it must be remembered that he
lived in a period when the maintenance of social distinctions was
part of a gentleman's duty. As Henry Peacham put it, "To be
overfree and familiar with inferiors argues a baseness of spirit
and begetteth contempt." It is also fair to remember that the

47

Herberts were an old and distinguished family, and the same
pride of ancestry that pervades Edward's memoirs was equally
strong in his younger brother.

In any case it was a family to be proud of, for all the sons
were distinguishing themselves in various ways. Edward, as
he himself blandly admitted, was held "in great esteem both in
court and city." Richard and William were becoming notable
swordsmen. Thomas had served brilliantly at the siege of Juliers,
"where he showed such forwardness as no man in that great
army before him was more adventurous on all occasion." Charles
had made an excellent beginning at Oxford, becoming a fellow
two years after entering New College, while Henry was already
showing that gift for getting on in the world that made him the
most successful of all the brothers in the end—"dextrous in the
ways of the court."

There was another member of the family by the time George
Herbert went to Cambridge in December of 1609, for Magdalen
Herbert, rather surprisingly, had married again the previous
spring. Even more curious was the fact that she had married a
young man about half her age.

Sir John Danvers was in his early twenties, a pretty youth
with a round face who wore his long hair flowing over his shoulders. He had so beautiful a complexion that when he travelled in
Italy the people gathered on the streets to admire its fairness.
His marriage to Magdalen was a happy one for, as John Donne
put it, "she had a cheerfulness agreeable to his youth and he a
sober staidness conformable to her more years."

Sir John Danvers came from a Wiltshire family, not as old as
the Herberts but almost as prominent. His elder brother was
Baron Danvers of Dauntsey, that "magnificent and munificent"
bachelor who spent three thousand pounds a year on his kitchen
alone and who founded the Botanic Gardens at Oxford. Sir John
Danvers shared his brother's love of gardens, and when he acquired a house for himself and Magdalen he made it one of the
show places of London. It was in the aristocratic suburb of

Chelsea, which was a gardener's paradise because it was not part of the London chalk basin and possessed a very rich soil; and there he created a large and beautiful garden in the Italian manner, with marble statuary and ornamental walks, extending nearly to the Thames. It was a place that "much delighted" Bacon, who was a frequent visitor there and a connoisseur of gardens.

Not all the members of Magdalen's family approved of her new husband. Her eldest son, Edward, who was several years older than his stepfather, apparently did not trust him, although Danvers was the kind of man whom nearly everybody liked. Magdalen wrote imploringly to her first-born: "Mistake him not, but believe me there was never a tenderer heart or a lovinger mind in any man than in him towards you."

Since George Herbert was so close to his mother, he might have been expected to dislike the marriage. On the contrary, he loved his new stepfather dearly, and the letters he wrote him from Cambridge are full of affection and gratitude. He speaks of Danvers' "infinite kindnesses" and "infinite favors" and thanks him over and over again for the loving courtesies he has shown.

George Herbert told his stepfather his troubles and asked his advice in the comfortable knowledge that he could speak freely to an understanding and generous man. "I write to you, sir, because to you I have ever opened my heart." Sir John Danvers sent him expensive and useful presents—the first surviving letter from Herbert is in gratitude for the gift of a horse—but his greatest contribution to his stepson was the active and sympathetic interest he took in his university career.

This career was proceeding in the orderly fashion that anyone would have predicted for young George Herbert, nicely balanced between "piety and good letters." He was writing a certain amount of verse and when he was nineteen had the pleasure of seeing some of it in print. He contributed two Latin poems to a collection of memorial verse issued by Cambridge in 1612 to mourn the death of Prince Henry. Both universities issued suit-

able volumes whenever anything befell the royal family, and
Herbert's poems are the conventional ones of their kind with the
usual classical invocations to Phoebus and Pallas.[1]

George Herbert took his B.A. a few months later, in 1613, and
his name is second on the list that graded the bachelors of art in
the order of their seniority. Two members of Trinity College are
among the first fifteen, and both of them, Hacket and Herbert,
came from Westminster School. It is possible that this list reflected the students' social position as well as their academic
standing, but at any rate it gave Herbert the right to walk in
front of most of his colleagues in the various processions of which
the University was so fond.

In 1616 Herbert became a master of arts and a major fellow of
Trinity College, with the right to a servant of his own and a seat
on the dais at mealtimes. The fellows did all the tutoring in the
College, and Herbert would have spent at least a part of his time
as a teacher. He must have been a good one, for the following
year he was singled out to be one of the College lecturers.

Trinity College was the first to supply this kind of instruction
for the undergraduates, which supplemented the work of the
tutors, and the courses were given in the hall each morning
directly after morning prayer. Four of the lecturers presented
various aspects of Aristotle, while one taught Greek literature,
one Greek grammar, one Latin, and the eighth lecturer did what
he could with arithmetic, geometry, cosmography, astronomy
and music. Herbert gave the course in Greek grammar, a subject
in which Westminster School had given him an unusually thorough foundation, and it was his task to drill the younger students
in grammar and syntax with an emphasis on strict memory work
and many examinations.

---

[1] Prince Henry's untimely death inspired an enormous amount of poetry,
and John Donne and Edward Herbert both wrote elegies on the subject.
Their grief for the prince was wound in with complex meditations on the
nature of things, and Ben Jonson, who was a friend of them both, maintained that Donne deliberately wrote his poem "to match Sir Ed. Herbert
in obscureness."

Again he must have been an excellent teacher, for the following year he was advanced into a higher teaching position and one which was sponsored by the University as a whole. Cambridge did not normally consider itself responsible for teaching and was merely a corporate body to confer degrees, but over the years a few lectureships had been endowed which were open to students from all the Colleges. Most of these were intended for advanced students, but for the instruction of "the younger sort" there were the four Barnaby lectures. These were given in mathematics, logic, philosophy and rhetoric, and in June of 1618 George Herbert was appointed to be the teacher in rhetoric.

The Barnaby lectures had been endowed nearly a century earlier by a public-spirited lord chief justice, and they took their name from the fact that the four teachers for the year were chosen on St. Barnabas' Day. The lectures were presented at nine in the morning at the Common Schools, a unit of buildings south of Trinity College which also housed the University library and the administrative offices.

Herbert must have found his new assignment much more stimulating than the task of drilling Greek grammar into the heads of the young, and his students responded to him. An undergraduate who entered Cambridge that year singled out only two courses which he felt had brought him real profit, "Mr. Downes his public Greek lectures, and Mr. Herbert's public rhetoric lectures." Andrew Downes had been Regius Professor of Greek for more than thirty years and was now a lively old gentleman of seventy, tall, ruddy, bright-eyed and given to sitting with his feet on the table. He was one of the ablest scholars in England, and it was a high compliment to be compared to him.

The rhetoric lectures had originally dealt only with Terence and then had been expanded to include other classical writers. Herbert expanded them still further to include modern masters of oratory and was remembered for the day he analyzed a speech by King James and pointed out how completely it fulfilled all the requirements of approved oratorical technique. A later generation has accused him of trying to curry royal favor, because it has been forgotten how high a reputation James had as an orator in his own day.[2]

All this teaching was of course a side issue with George Herbert. For he was now embarked on the study of divinity, to fit himself to be the churchman his mother had always hoped he would become, and he was studying with the intensity that was characteristic of him. It may have added to his sense of responsibility that he was the only scholar left in the family now. His brother Charles had died in 1617, leaving nothing to show for all his promise except a few lines of Latin verse that he had contributed to a book for a friend.

When Herbert left Westminster School Dr. Ireland had warned him to "study moderately and use exercise," but it was not in him to do anything in moderation. He was possessed by a driving desire for perfection in everything he undertook, and a man like that serves a hard master.

The University of Cambridge was not the ideal place for a young man in frail health who was working too hard. It was plagued by heavy air from the fens, and it was quite customary for the students at Cambridge to fall ill from time to time and be obliged to leave for a change of air. Herbert went occasionally to Newmarket, thirteen miles away, because the heath there was famous for its "good air and pleasure," but the trips did not benefit him much. In the spring of 1618 he had still not recovered

---

[2] Bacon described the King's skill as an orator as "indeed prince-like, flowing as from a fountain, and yet streaming and branching into nature's order, full of facility and felicity." Sir George Carew characterized James' oratory in the Star Chamber as being "more like an angel than a man," and Dr. Montague said of his speeches at Hampton Court, "for learning, piety and prudency I never heard the like." Bulstrode Whitelocke praised his Parliament speeches for their eloquence, wisdom and elegance, and none of these gentlemen would have thought it odd for Herbert to single out the King as an example of rhetorical excellence. James himself, who wrote his speeches out carefully in advance, shared the general admiration and included five of his addresses in his collected works.

from an earlier illness, although he was taking every precaution not to fall what he called "absolutely sick."

Sir Francis Bacon once said bitterly that much time was lost through illness. Yet Herbert was sure that if he kept working steadily, if not quickly, he would master the subject he had set for himself. "It is true (God knows) I am weak, yet not so, but that every day, I may step one step towards my journey's end." He was convinced of the journey's importance, and he had never lost the sense of dedication to God that made him choose the ministry in the first place. He wrote his mother four years later: "I always feared sickness more than death, because sickness hath made me unable to perform those offices for which I came into the world, and must yet be kept in it."

Herbert faced one additional problem. Books on divinity were both numerous and expensive, and he could not make his income stretch far enough to cover all the volumes he needed. His brother Edward gave him an allowance of thirty pounds a year, to which could be added what he received as a fellow and a Barnaby lecturer, with some assorted fees. But his illnesses were expensive, for doctor's bills came high and Herbert was also obliged to pay the costs of a special diet. All this left him very little money for books, which he bought nevertheless. "If a book of four or five shillings come in my way, I buy it, though I fast for it; yea, sometimes of ten shillings. But, alas, sir, what is that to those infinite volumes of divinity, which yet every day swell and grow bigger."

The family did its best to help him. His brother Henry, who was in France in 1618, sent him a package of books which "were not to be got in England," and both his stepfather and one of his sisters offered to pay for them. But Herbert did not like to accept their generosity. "It is high time now that I should be no more a burden to you." He was really ashamed of his "clamorous and greedy bookish requests," and yet, as he said, a workman must have tools.

All this Herbert explained to Sir John Danvers in the letters he wrote him in 1618. He knew that his stepfather was concerned with his problem and he wanted his support for a plan which he felt would solve the whole difficulty. With an extra thirty pounds a year he could manage well. Therefore he wanted his allowance doubled for the time being, with the understanding that he would renounce his claim to it as soon as he was in holy orders and could support himself. Herbert suggested this plan to the family more than once, but he could not persuade them to agree to it.

Then, and it must have seemed almost an answer to prayer, the opportunity to earn thirty pounds a year opened in front of him.

In the autumn of 1619, the Public Orator of Cambridge, Sir Francis Nethersole, was called abroad on government business and decided to give up his University position. George Herbert, whose skill in rhetoric was well known, had been serving as Nethersole's deputy and believed himself fitted to be his successor.[3]

Sir Francis Nethersole was a good friend of Herbert's but he hesitated to recommend him for the post because it might interfere with his studies in divinity. But Herbert himself did not believe that the office of Public Orator was incompatible with the service of God. "This dignity hath no such earthiness in it, but it may very well be joined with Heaven; or, if it had to others yet to me it should not, for aught I yet know."

This statement has been dismissed by a modern editor of Herbert as a "too facile" way of justifying his desire for the post. Yet it was the same point of view he had expressed to his mother nine years earlier when he sent her the New Year's sonnets. He

---

[3] The office of Public Orator carried with it a salary of only forty shillings, which was so far below the salary for the similar office at Oxford that the Cambridge authorities had added to it a whole series of fees. But it was never a fixed amount, and when Herbert says that the revenue from the post is "about £30 *per an.*" he may have been influenced by the fact that this was the sum he had been trying to raise by mortgaging his allowance.

was sure then that his talent for poetry could be "all and ever
consecrated to God's glory" and there was no reason why the
same thing could not be true of his talent for rhetoric.

From the point of view of the twentieth century this may seem
a curious position to take, as inexplicable as the seventeenth-
century admiration for King James as an orator. But the Renaissance placed an extremely high moral value on rhetoric, and one
reason the subject was taught so earnestly in the schools was
that it was considered an indispensable tool to lead men to the
good life. Moreover, it was the duty of the Public Orator to use
his skill to serve Cambridge, that nursery of churchmen, so that
he would indirectly be serving the Church of England itself.
And even if the prospect of thirty pounds a year weighed with
Herbert, as it almost certainly did, it was to buy books of divinity
that he wanted the money.

Once Herbert had decided to try for the post of Public Orator,
he went after it with the single-mindedness that was characteristic of him. Thanks to Elizabeth's sweeping reorganization
of Cambridge, it was only the heads of the Colleges who had to
be convinced of his fitness, and Herbert set out to "work the
heads," as he called it, with the vigor of a born diplomat. There
were influential men like Sir Benjamin Rudyard who could be
approached and Sir John Danvers had many connections. But
George Herbert hoped to win the post without family assistance,
"that you may see . . . I am able to stand on mine own legs."

During this same year of 1619 Sir Edward Herbert went to
France as ambassador, a post which he termed "both noble and
pleasing." His younger brother George uses almost the same
terms when he tries to describe to his stepfather the advantages
of being Public Orator. He feels it is "the finest place in the
University," quite apart from the thirty pounds a year. "For the
Orator writes all the University letters, makes all the orations,
be it to king, prince or whatever comes to the University. . . .
He takes place next to the doctors, is at all their assemblies and

meetings, and sits above the proctors, is regent or non-regent at his pleasure, and such-like gaynesses, which will please a young man well."

There may be a half smile here at his own enthusiasm, but none of the Herberts undervalued pomp and circumstance. Nor did they undervalue themselves, since humility, like calmness of temper, was not a family characteristic. When Henry was in Paris the year before, George wrote him a letter of brotherly advice and his remarks on pride had the full force of a family conviction behind them. "Be proud, not with a foolish vaunting of yourself when there is no cause, but by setting a just price of your qualities. . . . It is the part of a poor spirit to undervalue himself and blush."

George Herbert had no intention of undervaluing himself. He was sure he could acquit himself well in the role of Public Orator, just as he was equally sure, in a deeper part of his being, that the office could be "joined with Heaven." He had spoken the year before of his determination to obey "that spirit which hath guided me hitherto" and which would lead to "holy ends," and apparently he had no difficulty convincing Sir Francis Nethersole that he could conduct a civil post to the glory of God.

On the eighteenth of January, 1620, Nethersole formally resigned as Public Orator, and two days later, on a Thursday, the heads of all the Colleges met to nominate two men for the post. George Herbert was one of them. The day before he had written in confident haste to his stepfather, "All goes well," and on Friday the full Senate met to confirm his confidence. When the senior proctor read out the votes, George Herbert had been elected the new Public Orator of Cambridge.

CHAPTER FIVE

A T CAMBRIDGE IN THE SEVENTEENTH CENTURY, THE PUBLIC
Orator did the work that would now be called public relations. The University depended on the good will of men in high
places, and it was the duty of the Orator to combine a judicious
mixture of flattery and gratitude with an alert eye for future
favors, all couched in the smooth and polished Latin that was
suited to the dignity of the University and the ears of the great.

Above all, the University depended on the good will of the
King, and within four months of his election the new Public
Orator faced a severe test of his ability. King James, that most
determined of literary men, had just had his prose works translated into Latin and he presented copies of the large volume,
handsomely bound in velvet and gold, to both Oxford and Cambridge. There had been a long rivalry between the two universities for the favor of the King, and Oxford bowed before the
book as though it were an honored guest. The Vice-Chancellor
bore it to the library in a reverent procession headed by twenty
doctors clothed in scarlet, and the keeper of the library made "a
very pretty speech" expressing his gratitude for the precious
object. All this was reported back to the King, who had the
natural vulnerability of any author and was "exceeding well
pleased."

The University of Cambridge had unfortunately failed to arrange for similar ceremonies, and it was up to the Public Orator
to compose a letter of thanks effective enough to counteract the
ingenuity of its sister university. George Herbert sharpened his
Latin and his wits and allowed his mind to float in that Renaissance realm where kings are gods. Then he produced a letter so
drunk with exaltation, so quivering with reverence over the great

57

gift, so filled with graceful phrases and even a judicious academic pun, that the twenty doctors clothed in scarlet could hardly have been more effective. As a final touch, and a really clever one, Herbert added an epigram that delicately removed from Oxford its chief triumph over Cambridge, the great library that Sir Thomas Bodley had recently established there. Let our visitors, said George Herbert, talk of the Vatican library or the Bodleian. *Our* library is a single book: the King's.

By birth and breeding Herbert was well fitted to play the courtier in graceful Latin phrases, but behind his rhetorical flourishes lay the sober fact that the University needed all the help it could get from King James. Elizabeth had seen to it that Cambridge was wholly dependent on royal good will, and James was frequently irritated by the way Puritanism was flourishing there. A few years earlier there had been a serious breach with the King when the Puritan element at Cambridge tried to interfere with the election of its Chancellor. "For their error, the whole university was under as black a cloud of displeasure as ever I saw in my time, and floated like a ship in a great storm." The storm was finally stilled when Cambridge sent its most accomplished orator, the Welsh proctor John Williams, to assure the King that the whole difficulty had been caused by the misguided action of a "few headstrong fellows." But the King's displeasure was a serious matter, and it was the business of the Public Orator to help make sure that such a thing would never happen again.

The following month George Herbert wrote a second letter to the King, again in the name of the University and again in gratitude. Cambridge had been fighting a plan to drain the fenland area to the north because the University was convinced it would damage her precious river Cam. She felt that the draining of the fens was a device to bring wicked profits to speculators and deprive her of her river traffic, whereas it was actually an attempt to turn a huge tract of nearly useless land into an economic asset to the whole region. In June of 1620 the plan was temporarily abandoned, and Herbert wrote a letter of thanks to the King. He also wrote letters to other government officials who had been helpful, including two to Sir Robert Naunton. Naunton had once been Public Orator of Cambridge and was now a Secretary of State.

The following winter the University elected Naunton to Parliament, and Herbert sent him a prompt letter of congratulation, taking the occasion to remind him delicately that useful results were expected from him. "Alma Mater most willingly leans her head on thy bosom." Within a period of two months he wrote four other letters of congratulation—to the new Treasurer of England, the new Attorney-General, the new Solicitor-General and the new Chief Justice. There had been a shake-up in the government and Herbert hastened to inform the new officials that Cambridge loved them all and confidently expected their most gracious support of her just claims. Less than a year later there was another Treasurer in office, a London merchant named Cranfield, and the Public Orator transferred the University's affections to him with equal speed. "Thou, my lord, hast triumphed. . . . Since . . . thou art most worthily set over the Treasury, do thou reckon the University also amongst thy treasures."

All these letters to the great were written as a matter of University policy, and the compliments slipped easily from George Herbert's well-trained pen. But there was one public official for whom he really felt the profound admiration that he expressed so skillfully in the letters to them all.

This was Francis Bacon, one-time student of Trinity College and by now one of its most distinguished graduates. After a slow and difficult start in politics he had suddenly shot skyward and become Keeper of the Great Seal and Chancellor of England. He was created Baron Verulam and Viscount St. Albans, and few men were better suited to the coronet he now wore.

For he moved through life with such splendor and so large a
retinue that he was more like a Renaissance princeling than a
Jacobean public official.

Cambridge had kept in close touch with Bacon. It was the
sensible policy of the University to make use of prominent
graduates to aid "their first nursing mother," and however much
Bacon may have disliked the curriculum he was a good and
loyal son. When he was Attorney-General he represented the
University in Parliament and agreed to look out for her legal
interests, and that same year he sent a gift of venison to Trinity
College for the Christmas festivities. When he became a Privy
Councillor he was still acting as legal adviser for Cambridge
and promised not to let his new duties interfere with his services
to Alma Mater. And he kept his word, for now that he was
Chancellor of England he was still her "most loving son."

The first letter George Herbert wrote Bacon as Chancellor was
in gratitude for his services in the controversy over the fens. The
following winter the Public Orator wrote again, to ask Bacon's
help in the battle that Cambridge was waging with the London
book trade. The London publishers were trying to get a monop-
oly, in defiance of the University's charter which gave it the
right to its own press, and if they had succeeded the price of
books would have increased. Herbert wrote Bacon as one scholar
to another, and with almost the same turn of phrase he had used
in a letter to his stepfather. "Thou seest the multitude of books
swelling day by day, especially in theology. . . . If both the
number of writings and the price of them grow greater, what
bottomless pit of a purse will be equal to such expenses?"

But the letter in which Herbert most truly spoke his heart
had been written to Bacon two months earlier, after the Chancellor sent a copy of his latest book to the University. The book was
an extraordinary piece of work, and George Herbert was one of
the few who realized how remarkable it was.

The volume that Bacon presented to Cambridge was only a
section of the great edifice he had been planning. The whole of

it was called *Instauratio Magna,* "The Great Regeneration," and the section he issued in 1620 was called *Novum Organum,* "The New Instrument." The regeneration was to consist of a new way of looking at the universe and the instrument was to be the light of the physical senses and the reasoning ability of man.

Bacon had changed very little since he was an undergraduate at Trinity College, excitedly trying to explore the properties of sound by striking a pillar in an upstairs room. He still experimented endlessly—thrusting a musical instrument first into a damask cushion and then against a woolen carpet to see what happened to the sound, peering into the yolks of eggs, corresponding with experts on the movement of tides, searching for the key that would unlock the secrets of the visible world.

When Bacon tested the weight of a sprouting onion and then called the result "a noble trial and of very great consequence," he was not thinking primarily of the condensed air which was the object of that particular experiment. He had seen a vision, the conquest of nature through man's knowledge, and he worked with a dedication as intent as any priest's. "I am laboring to lay the foundation, not of any sect or doctrine, but of human utility and power." Man could conquer the world if he understood it. And he could understand it, not by studying commentaries on Aristotle, but by conducting intelligently planned and properly integrated physical experiments.

Bacon did not himself have the mind of a great scientist. His attention leaped too quickly from question to question and he was too uncritical about the answers. He could look at the stars and conceive what he called a "strange doubt, viz. whether the face of a clear and starlit night be seen at the instant at which it really exists and not a little later." The next moment he was able to smile at his fancy, which indeed was not suited to the smallness of Bacon's world. Yet he was one of the men who made it larger, not so much by the justness of his experiments as by the greatness of his vision.

When the vision came to him in his youth he put it down im-

mediately on paper. "I composed a juvenile work on this subject, which with great confidence and a magnificent title, I
named 'The Greatest Birth of Time.'" Then, in a strange and
intent counterpoint to his busy public life, he went on rewriting
it for over thirty years, trying to expound his vision of a relationship which would restore the connection "between the mind of
man and the nature of things, which is more precious than anything on earth." Bacon's secretary reported that he saw twelve
drafts of the book, "revised year by year," and there may have
been more. It was the beloved heir of a man who had no children, and when Bacon finally published one section in 1620 it
was not because the book was finished. It was because he was
afraid he might die suddenly and the manuscript be lost.

Bacon dedicated the book to King James, who could make
nothing of it. The King remarked that it was "like the peace of
God which passeth all understanding," and the joke gained cur-
rency since few people liked Bacon and fewer liked his book.
Nor did Cambridge like it, since the University was still dedicated to a worship of the past and Bacon was trying to build a
pathway into the future.

In the opinion of George Herbert, however, Bacon had written
a masterpiece. The graceful letter of thanks which he composed
as Public Orator was the sort of thing due any author who was
also a high government official. But Herbert also wrote three
Latin poems in which he expressed the excitement he felt over
Bacon's call to arms. Herbert did not respond intellectually and
turn himself into a scientist. He responded emotionally, and in
the longest of the three poems he gives Bacon the titles he so
thoroughly deserved: "prince of ideas," "high priest of truth,"
"lord of induction," "steward of light," "driver-away of idols."
It was a much quoted, much copied poem and a worthy tribute
to a very great man.

Bacon had written his book in Latin, partly because he was
addressing an international audience and partly because he was
afraid to trust his work to a young and unstable language like

English. The only philosophical book he had written in English was *The Advancement of Learning,* an introductory work he published in 1605, and he began to worry almost at once about the risk of entrusting even part of his grand structure to so unscholarly a language. He negotiated with a Cambridge professor about a translation, but he produced "such superfine Latinity" that Bacon abandoned the project for the time being. When he took it up again, George Herbert was one of the translators who turned Bacon's vigorous English prose into satisfactory Latin, and Bacon thanked him publicly for help which "I cannot forget."

Herbert was not the only member of the family whom Bacon trusted. He was a frequent visitor at Danvers House, and when he finished his brilliant history of Henry the Seventh he not only sent a manuscript copy to Sir John Danvers for his opinion but was willing to accept the literary criticism that Herbert's stepfather made.

Bacon finished his history of King Henry less than a year after he had sent his earlier book to Cambridge, and in that short space of time he had become a ruined man. Parliament had accused him of taking bribes, stripped him of his high office and sent him to the Tower of London. The King managed to free him almost at once and Bacon held his head so high that one unsympathetic observer said that he had "no manner of feeling of his fall." But Bacon himself once said, "Shame for a great disgrace, and of long continuance, contracts the spirits almost to suffocation." To this was added in his case, not so much a sense of guilt at having taken bribes (since the exact line to be drawn had never been clear in Jacobean officialdom) as a creeping sense of having spent his life on the wrong things. He wrote a prayer the month before he was sentenced in which he asked God to forgive him for having spent his talent on "things for which I was least fit."

Now that his public career was forever ended, Bacon turned back to the first love of his life—books and the dissemination of knowledge. He did not enter into a life of polite leisure. His history of Henry the Seventh was written at high speed in a few months in an attempt to satisfy his creditors. Yet there was no fading of the old brilliance or of that lively, wonderful, restless mind.

Even when Bacon was taken ill, his mind could not stop working; and he gave it occupation by trying his hand at versifying some of the Psalms. Bacon had never been a poet and he did not become one in his old age. The seven Psalms are stiffly and laboriously rhymed, and the most attractive thing about the little book is its dedication.

> To his very good friend, Mr. George Herbert. The pains that it pleased you to take, about some of my writings, I cannot forget; which did put me in mind to dedicate to you this poor exercise of my sickness. Besides, it being my manner for dedications, to choose those that I hold most fit for the argument, I thought that in respect of divinity and poesy met . . . I could not make better choice. So, with signification of my love and acknowledgment, I ever rest,
>
> Your affectionate friend . . .

The little book was published in 1625, when Bacon was sixty-four and an old man by the standards of the seventeenth century. Yet Bacon would not acknowledge old age or death as long as his life work, the *Instauratio Magna*, filled his mind. The whole thing was to be in six parts, of which only two were completed; but he had the next section "already compassed and planned" and he was sure he could finish it. The old man was still in his heart a hopeful, excited boy, and when his death came the following year it had a kind of magnificent suitability about it. The story goes that he had taken advantage of a late snowfall to try the effects of refrigeration on a hen. Bacon called it "an experiment or two, touching the conservation and induration of bodies," and reported triumphantly that it was a great success. But he was also obliged to report that he had caught cold because of it, and he died early in the morning of Easter Sunday, April the ninth, 1626.

The will that Bacon left was characteristic. It established a foundation at Cambridge for a lectureship in the sciences and another at Oxford, for he had said long ago, "I especially disapprove the smallness of the salary assigned to lecturers in arts and professions." He longed to see the two universities take their rightful place in the world of the future and he hoped that his gift would help to shake Aristotle from his dusty eminence. But it was equally characteristic of Bacon that there was no money to pay for the lectureships, since his debts totalled over twenty-two thousand pounds.

When a great man died it was the custom for his university to honor him with a memorial volume. When William Camden had died three years before, Oxford issued a handsome book in his honor with a huge number of contributors, but when Bacon died Cambridge saw no reason to honor one of the greatest of her sons. The small memorial volume in his honor was printed in London, not Cambridge, and Bacon's secretary was the editor. Yet some Cambridge men made contributions, and chief among them was George Herbert. The six lines in Latin that mourn Bacon's death are his final tribute to the man he calls "incomparable."

It is curious that Herbert should have been so attracted to Bacon. There was very little similarity in their temperaments and almost none in their outlook. But it may be that Herbert was assisted by the fact that there was an iconoclast in his own family. The most original and destructive mind in England, next to Bacon's, belonged to George Herbert's elder brother, who was soon to become Lord Herbert of Cherbury.

Behind the glitter and conceit and the worldly success of Edward's outer life there lay a driving purpose as steady and honest as Bacon's own. When he had been a small boy living in his grandmother's house in Shropshire, it took him so long to learn to speak that the family feared he would never begin. But he was unwilling to make the attempt until he was sure he could express himself clearly and intelligently, and when he finally formed a sentence almost the first question he asked was how he "came into this world?" His nurse laughed at him for such talk, but a stubborn desire to find out the truth had driven itself deep in his mind and he persisted.

Just before Edward went to France as ambassador, he experienced the enforced solitude of a long illness and began writing a book he called *De Veritate*, "Concerning Reality." He continued working on it after he arrived in Paris—"all the spare hours which I could get from my visits and negotiations being employed to perfect this work"—and he finished it two years after George Herbert became Public Orator.

De Veritate denied the authority of the church as flatly as Bacon denied the authority of Aristotle. Edward had no doubt of the existence of God, but he was sure that He had created man as a reasoning being who was not to be hamstrung by the pronouncements of organized religion. Man had been set by his Creator in a world where he should be free to ask questions, and the church was not a divinely constituted guide to answer these questions but only a stumbling block to the exercise of man's own reason.

When Edward gazed upon the diversity of religions in the world, he was sure that some spirit of truth must pervade "this shapeless and monstrous chaos of beliefs." But he was equally sure that it was not contained in any of the churches, each one proclaiming itself to be the supreme guardian of revealed truth and each one fiercely denying the claims of all the others. He himself worked out five points of religion which he felt that any reasonable man in Europe or Asia should be able to accept, and he offered this as a substitute for "the inextricable confusion of oral and written tradition to which men have given their allegiance."

Like Bacon when he looked at the stars, Edward could not

quite shake himself free from the mental habits of his own day. He was not sure if he should publish so radical a book as *De Veritate* and so he asked God to give him a sign. He knelt in his room one clear and sunny day with the manuscript in his hand and said a prayer for guidance. "If it be for Thy glory, I beseech Thee to give me some sign from heaven; if not, I shall suppress it." There was a "loud though gentle noise" from the heavens in answer to his prayer, and the rationalist at once prepared for publication.

The book was published in Paris, where the winds of deism had already begun to blow, and was given a favorable reception. Edward dared not publish it yet in England, for that tight little island was always late in receiving any intellectual impulse from Europe, and his friends were sufficiently shocked as it was. Yet it is clear that Edward did not expect his devout younger brother to be shocked, for when he finished the manuscript copy he dedicated it to his secretary (who later became an ambassador also) and to George Herbert.

It would have been more appropriate to dedicate it to Bacon. There is a prayer in Edward's handwriting in which he calls himself "a living, free and reasonable creature . . . capable of seeing and understanding Thy wondrous works." Bacon could have written that prayer in spite of his religious conservatism, for by a different route he, too, had entered that new and headstrong universe where man's reason was to be king.

Such a way of thinking was alien to George Herbert, and yet both these men dedicated a book to him. There must have been a courtesy in his mind that made him welcome a vision he could not share, so that he could sympathize with high purpose even when it led to a conclusion very different from his own.

CHAPTER SIX

G EORGE HERBERT MIGHT BE WILLING TO HONOR HONESTY AND high purpose wherever he found it, but there was one point of view with which he could not sympathize. He was a devout son of the Church of England and he could not bring himself to look with courtesy upon the Puritans.

In 1620, the year Herbert became Public Orator, there appeared in print a set of verses called *Anti-Tami-Cami-Categoria*, written seventeen years before but only just published. It was the work of a learned Scotch Presbyterian named Andrew Melville, and it savagely attacked both the Church of England and the University of Cambridge.

Melville's verses had been inspired by the behavior of the two universities at the time of the Millenary Petition in 1603. Oxford and Cambridge had both attacked as seditious the ministers who signed the petition, and Melville at once attacked the two universities. He used this as a springboard for a general indictment of the ritual in the Church of England, and his verses lost none of their bite in the seventeen years they waited for publication.

In George Herbert's eyes, Melville had committed a double fault. He had attacked Mother Church and Mother Cambridge, and Herbert was the devoted, uncritical son of both. He did not allow himself to be intimidated by Melville's age or his high reputation, and he counterattacked with a vigorous set of Latin verses called *Musae Responsoriae*.

Andrew Melville was a formidable opponent, a scholar in his seventies who was honored all over Europe as a mighty champion of the Protestant cause. When he was young he travelled over half France to get a training in Hebrew and divinity and then walked to Geneva with his Bible at his belt. Calvin had been only five years dead when Melville arrived in Geneva, and militant Protestant refugees were still thronging the holy city. Thomas Cartwright was there, renewing his strength for his long battle with the Church of England, and Melville was made of the same fighting spirit. For thirty years he strove for the cause of Presbyterianism in Scotland, and he never retreated from the basic Puritan position that the Church of England had a ritual that compromised with popery. He once seized a startled English prelate by his wide lawn sleeves and informed him that they were "Romish rags and a part of the Beast's mark," and he had been an open enemy all his life of the episcopal system that George Herbert considered holy.

Once, in what was probably a later poem, Herbert recommended a gentle tone in controversy.

> Be calm in arguing: for fierceness makes
> Error a fault, and truth discourtesy.

But Herbert did not worry about calmness when he wrote *Musae Responsoriae*. He jeered at Melville's complicated title, criticized his choice of meter, and suggested that the cold climate of Scotland might have encouraged the immoderate heat of his zeal. In the end his heart misgave him a little for his rudeness and he expressed regret that a man like Melville, whose learning was "such as words are weak to praise too much," should have allied himself with a misguided group like the Puritans. Moreover he pointed out, and it was quite true, that he had used less violent language than Melville himself, who had likened the Anglican baptismal ceremony to screech owls, the church anthems to bellowing, and who had assured the University of Cambridge that it would go straight to hell for supporting the wrong side.

The argument on church ritual had been raging now for generations, and neither side had anything new to say on the subject. Back in 1572, Cartwright's party had drawn up a list

of "Popish abuses yet remaining in the English church," and
it contained practically the same items that Melville attacked
and Herbert defended in the following century. The Puritans
said that these ceremonies were "stinking abominations," the
defenders of the Church of England said that they were "meet
and convenient"; and since neither side had the slightest intention of listening to the other, they were both reduced to hurling
insults. The obvious and humane solution would have been to
establish two churches, but this was inconceivable. There was
one church, as there was one state, and the only point that could
be argued was the kind of church it should be.

From the first the bishops had been a main target of Puritan
abuse, since they were the officers responsible for maintaining
church ritual and church discipline. By 1620 the very word
"bishop" had become in the Puritan mind a stereotype for
wickedness, and Andrew Melville was echoing a host of previous writers when he described the "pomp-fed prelates," vicious
and insolent, gorging their bellies and strutting in display while
the vengeance of a Puritan God drew nigh.

It is true that some of the bishops were very wealthy. The
Bishop of Winchester, for instance, entertained King James so
lavishly during this same year of 1620 at his country place in
Farnham that he spent nearly three thousand pounds in three
days. Yet the Bishop of Winchester was no fat and strutting
prelate. He was a holy and gentle scholar, so unconcerned with
practical details that he never knew what was planned for dinner
until he arrived at the table, and so generous that he gave away
a great deal of his wealth to the London poor.

His name was Lancelot Andrewes and he was one of George
Herbert's close friends. It is possible they had met at Westminster School, when Andrewes was Dean of Westminster and
encouraging the "young fry" around him to discover that Greek
could be as delightful as any game. But Andrewes left at about
the time Herbert entered, and they probably met when Herbert
was at Cambridge. Andrewes had given standing orders to his

chaplains and his friends to be on the lookout for promising young men, and few young men were as promising as George Herbert.

The reverence that Herbert felt for Bishop Andrewes is shown in the long Latin letter he wrote after a visit. He returned to the University "grown greater and fuller for joy" because of Andrewes' company. Since this was the year in which he was serving both as rhetoric professor and Public Orator he was obliged to spend nearly all his time at Cambridge, but he wanted Andrewes to know that he did not overvalue either office. "I would not take six hundred little properties of this kind in exchange for thy favor. . . . No concerns (certainly not those which claim the head rather than the heart) are able to lessen the power of thy dominion over me." The letter is signed "thy most obedient son" and certainly he could not have chosen a better father than the learned, loving, holy Bishop of Winchester.

In the course of his letter Herbert spoke of the "whiteness" of the Bishop's mind, and it was an accurate word. The sixty-four-year-old Andrewes had spent most of his career in the silly, conniving atmosphere of the Jacobean court and had still managed to remain gentle, serene and incorruptible. He was saved in part, perhaps, by the fact that he was a scholar rather than a courtier. He tried earnestly to keep his mornings free for study, and once made the rather touching remark that "they were no true scholars, that came to speak with him before noon."

Lancelot Andrewes had a sense of order as fundamental as Herbert's own. It shows in the complex, patterned prose of his sermons and especially in the seventeen Christmas sermons that he preached at Whitehall. Many ambitious young divines set themselves to imitate Bishop Andrewes' way of preaching but they could not imitate the man himself, with his mind in full control of the intricate oratorical structure he was building and his heart full of love for God and His creation. His favorite exercise was walking because it gave him an opportunity to meditate on the beauty of the world—"corn, trees, cattle, earth, waters, heavens"—and his chief desire was to make the Church of England into a holy, single-hearted and ceremonial hierarchy of praise.

Andrewes thoroughly disliked religious controversy—"this cockpit," as he called it—but since his beloved church was threatened by Puritans and Roman Catholics he was inevitably drawn into attacking them both. He labored conscientiously on his heavily written arguments against the Church of Rome, and he was a tower of strength against the Puritans.[1]

When George Herbert finished his own attack on Puritanism, the *Musae Responsoriae*, he dedicated it to Lancelot Andrewes. He protested that his pen could "produce nothing worthy of thy perfection," but he gave the Bishop credit for whatever merit it might have had.

Herbert included two other dedications, one to Prince Charles and the other to King James himself. Dedications to James were so numerous that the King would have been a busy man if he had paid attention to them all, but there were two reasons why he may have felt a special interest in Herbert's manuscript.

In the first place, any attack on Andrew Melville would be welcome to the King. That determined Puritan had arrived back in Scotland from Geneva with the firm conviction that the Kirk was under the authority of God and the King therefore under the authority of the Kirk, and James had imprisoned him for it. He imprisoned him again after he became King of England, when Melville wrote some insulting verses on the services in the royal chapel. It was men like Melville who made James take so dark a view of the more moderate English Puritans. He felt they

---

[1] Bishop Andrewes' most famous achievement, his vast contribution to the King James Version of the Bible, would probably not have come into existence without the Puritan controversy. When James came to the throne, most of the English churches were using the Genevan Bible, a translation made by the English Protestant exiles in the days of Queen Mary. Some of their annotations had political overtones, such as the one in *Exodus* that justified disobedience to monarchs. James announced that such annotations were "untrue, seditious and savoring of traitorous conceits" and one of the first acts of his reign was to order a new translation.

were all "plotting and contriving . . . to bring in a form of presbytery, to the utter dissolution of all monarchies."

In the second place, the King would be likely to welcome any piece of writing that was sponsored by his old and dear friend, Lancelot Andrewes. The Bishop had taken part in James' coronation as Dean of Westminster, and ever since then the King had been listening to his sermons and delighting in his company. In Andrewes' presence the King avoided the oaths and the horseplay that usually characterized his behavior, and he once slept with the notes of Andrewes' sermon under the royal pillow. The Bishop returned his affection, and during twenty-two years of close association with that odd monarch he never lost his love and respect for him.

This side of King James is almost forgotten now, and many people find it hard to understand why a wise and gentle man like Lancelot Andrewes should have valued him so highly. James is usually remembered for his shambling gait and his slobbering tongue, his unseemly devotion to his favorites, his lack of political realism, his childish dislike of tobacco, his pedantry and his conceit; and therefore the modern reader is inclined to feel that the praise he received from his contemporaries must have been the flattery of sycophants.

Perhaps the chief reason why it is difficult to admire King James is that he admired himself so warmly. He believed himself to be a wise and experienced monarch, as he knew he was a well-intentioned one, and he moved through his corrupt, predatory court like a placid Scotch dominie. When anything especially outrageous occurred he blamed it on the "ill government of those whom I have trusted" and saw no reason to connect himself with the results. As he grew older and increasingly bored with government, he permitted a rank growth of faction and intrigue and then blandly refused to admit its existence. "I am the shepherd and this is my flock," he proclaimed when he ascended the throne that Elizabeth had made great, and he clung to this picture of himself as an all-wise, benevolent mon-

arch, slipping into old age without the slightest doubt that he
was running the country supremely well.

James was equally pleased with his achievements as Defender
of the Faith, for he was a valiant if muddle-headed supporter of
the Church of England and did his best to steer between the
twin rocks of Puritanism and the Papacy. He took his responsibilities seriously and once remarked in perfect good faith that
"the state of religion through all Christendom . . . almost
wholly, under God, rests now upon my shoulders." He pursued
his paper wars with energy, dragging his reluctant bishops after
him, and bombarded all Christendom with his pamphlets. He
also wrote on religious topics for the edification of his own subjects, supplying them with educational thoughts on the *Book of
Chronicles,* the *Apocalypse* and the Lord's Prayer, for he never
doubted his competence in the field of theology. Few of his
subjects did either, and a churchman remarked with real respect
that he "deserved to be a bishop."

Not only did King James feel himself to be a latter-day incarnation of King Solomon for wisdom but he also inclined to
the opinion that he resembled King David, since he was a royal
singer of songs in praise of the Lord. In his youth he had been
deeply impressed by the Huguenot poet, Du Bartas, and when
he translated some of the popular Frenchman's work he invoked,
quite naturally, the assistance of the Lord:

> O Thou that mightily does tune
> My warbling holy harp . . .

Du Bartas returned the compliment by translating some of
James' verses into French, presenting him to an international
audience as "the Apollo of our time," and the King became a kind
of patron saint of Christian poets. He encouraged their efforts
at sacred poetry and continued with his own, and when he died
he was still puttering about with a cherished project of turning
all the Psalms into English verse.

James was also a patron of scholars, and here again there was a misdirected ardor that could not altogether hide a certain dignity of intention. He pursued knowledge with an almost reverent devotion when he had time for it and honored it in others. When he was in Denmark he paid a special visit to Tycho Brahe, the great astronomer, and wrote some excited verses in his praise. He himself had been stuffed with book learning in his youth and went on adding to it throughout his life. "The reading of some books before him was very frequent while he was at his repast. Otherwise he collected knowledge by variety of questions."

Most of the knowledge he collected is now as out-of-date as the speeches for which he was once so admired. The pamphlets and the poems he labored over go unread, and the latter-day Solomon has been reduced by time and history to a rather stupid and ineffectual old Scot. Yet if King James is given credit for nothing else, the twentieth century might well honor him for a single conviction which he held, and held almost alone.

The King hated war. In an age when the average monarch threw away his subjects' lives with no more thought than he might give to a game of tennis, James believed that war was an act of murder to be resorted to only as a final extremity. Almost his first act when he came to the throne was to put an end to the war with Spain; and all his foreign policy from that time forward, pitifully unrealistic though it might be, had the single end of keeping England at peace.

James had been King of England for fifteen years when a religious war began in Europe that became the most horrible conflict of that tormented century. It was called the Thirty Years' War and, since it involved the interests of James' Protestant son-in-law in Bohemia, most Englishmen felt that their country should take part in it also. But James refused, over and over again and against great pressure. In 1619 he wrote an anonymous pamphlet called *The Peacemaker* in which he pic-

tured his realm as a blessed haven, safe from the "perpetual
deluge of blood and enmity" in which the rest of the world was
drowned.

Lancelot Andrewes helped James to write *The Peacemaker*
and he believed the King's efforts were truly holy—"a prince of
God, a man that hath prevailed with God to plant His peace
with us." Everything that the King valued the Bishop valued
also, peace and scholarship and the welfare of the Church of
England, and they moved in a world of hopeful innocence that
had very little connection with the violent realities of power
politics.

Few Englishmen shared this love of peace, but one of the
few was George Herbert. His hatred of war is curious in a man
who came from a long line of soldiers. Yet he went so far as to
write a Latin poem called "The Triumph of Death" in which
he bitterly traced the growing savagery of "red slaughter"
through the ages until it culminated in the invention of gun-
powder. His imagination was haunted by the capacity of the
new weapon to destroy whole cities, and he was one of the few
men of his time who shared the King's loathing of war.

At the end of *Musae Responsoriae* Herbert wrote an address
in praise of King James. He spoke of his protection of the Church
of England and the care with which he had shepherded his flock
along the middle way that yielded neither to Papist nor to
Puritan. He spoke of James' knowledge of the Bible and all the
other qualities that made him truly the Defender of the Faith.
He was the monarch who loved books, the scholar who loved
God, and George Herbert felt nothing but reverent admiration
for such a paragon.

Musae Responsoriae contains a promise that Herbert will de-
vote all his future poetry to glorifying King James, and then
he adds that his poetry belongs to God. He saw no inconsistency
here. For the King was God's deputy on earth and worthy to be
so, and any man who served the King served God also.

CHAPTER SEVEN

WHEN GEORGE HERBERT TOOK HIS OATH AS A FELLOW OF Trinity College, he agreed to take holy orders within seven years or give up the fellowship. At the time he had expected to get a degree as Bachelor of Divinity and then enter the Church. But by the time the seven years were ended Herbert had altered his course and decided to go into government work instead.

On the basis of the available evidence, there does not seem to have been any shift in Herbert's fundamental point of view. He still intended to serve God. But he now believed that this could be done not only in the Church but also in the world outside.

The line of demarcation between the things of the world and the things of God was not as strong in the Renaissance as it later became, and in Herbert's eyes it had never been so. When he was seventeen he had declared that the art of writing sonnets— that pride of secular poets—could be turned to the glory of God. When he was twenty-six he had decided with equal conviction that the office of Public Orator could be "joined with heaven." And now he apparently felt that the same thing could be true of a government office, as long as the government was that of so Christian a ruler and so dedicated a man of peace as King James.

It must be remembered that it was not possible for Herbert to look upon the King with the well-informed hindsight of an historian. He saw him through the affectionate and idealistic eyes of his friend, Lancelot Andrewes, and to both men James was a scholar-king who was using his great office to save England from war and England's church from dissolution. To serve such a monarch was to serve the purposes of God Himself.

Sir Edward Herbert once described King James as "that in-

nocent and single heart," and the phrase was equally suited to
his own younger brother. George Herbert knew nothing of the
realities of seventeenth-century politics. He had lived a sheltered
life at Cambridge where, as he said, there was "peace with all
but bookworms," and his close friendship with Bishop Andrewes
would have done nothing to open his eyes to the fact that
James' efforts to defend the Church of England were inadequate
and his dream of peace impractical. The King and the Bishop
believed that certain good things were possible, and George
Herbert believed it with them.

Magdalen Herbert must have shared this idealism, for Herbert would never have taken so decisive a step against her
wishes. Several years later, when Herbert was thirty-three,
mother and son had a slight difference of opinion and Herbert
suggested that she might for once permit him to be "an undutiful
son." Since he had never been so before, he must have had his
mother's blessing when he decided to enter government service.
She must have felt that he was still "obeying that spirit" which
had always guided him.

The office Herbert wanted was that of Secretary of State. It
was one in which he could work for international peace and in
which his skill in composing letters could be put to good use.
Earlier in the century the office of Secretary of State had been
the pivot on which the whole government turned, and Herbert
could never have aspired to so exalted a position. But there were
now two Secretaries of State who divided the work between
them and who took orders rather than dictating policy, and it
was an office legitimately within Herbert's reach. One of the
current Secretaries was Sir Robert Naunton, who had once been
the Public Orator of Cambridge, and there was no reason why
Herbert should not follow in Naunton's path.

Herbert's chief disadvantage was his lack of any firsthand
knowledge of Europe. "His mother would by no means allow him
to leave the university or to travel . . . though he inclined very
much to both." It was normal for young men of birth and breed-

ing to finish their education abroad, and when Henry Herbert went to France in 1618 George wrote him a rather wistful letter. "You live in a brave nation. . . . Be covetous, then, of all good which you see in Frenchmen, whether it be in knowledge, or in fashion, or in words." George Herbert had never had the opportunity to do this for himself, and it imposed a handicap on a man who hoped to become a Secretary of State. "Those infinite volumes of divinity" which he had labored over so faithfully were no use to him now. What he needed was a working knowledge of the modern languages of Europe—French, Spanish and Italian—and he learned them all "very perfectly" with the same intensity he gave to everything else he attempted.

When Herbert had tried for the post of Public Orator, he knew that his chief problem was to "work the heads." For a government post the technique was the same on a larger scale, and the successful office-seeker had to know how to please the right people at the right time. Normally the correct procedure in Jacobean circles was a large and open bribe. Sir Robert Naunton, for instance, achieved his Secretaryship by a financial arrangement with the King's favorite, the Marquis of Buckingham, in which he endowed Buckingham's younger brother with an estate. Herbert had no connections with Buckingham, as far as is known, and no money to buy his way into public office even if he had been willing to stoop to such a thing. But he had the good will of two highly influential courtiers in the Duke of Lennox and the Marquis of Hamilton.

These two men, like Lancelot Andrewes, belonged to that small segment of the Jacobean court which was neither predatory nor corrupt. Both of them were kinsmen of the King but neither one had any personal ambitions, and they had a natural courtesy that made them really popular in the English court. The Duke of Lennox had been the King's boyhood companion in Scotland and remained one of the closest of his personal friends. For a time he held the only dukedom in England, and when Buckingham was made a duke in 1623, Lennox was hur-

riedly presented with a second title, that of Duke of Richmond,
a day earlier. The Marquis of Hamilton was another Scottish
nobleman who had succeeded in "avoiding intrigues and designs
at court," and to do him additional honor the King had revived
the ancient title of Earl of Cambridge.

Izaak Walton describes these two noblemen as George Herbert's "most obliging and powerful friends," and to them could
be added William Herbert, the third Earl of Pembroke. This
amiable and literary gentleman had always maintained excellent
relations with the rest of the Herberts and had been especially
helpful to George's younger brother, Henry. Like the two Scottish
noblemen, he was "exceeding beloved in the court, because he
never desired to get that for himself which others labored for,
but was still ready to promote . . . worthy men." George
Herbert was unquestionably worthy, and with the support of
three powerful and honorable men there was no reason why he
should not eventually achieve his quite reasonable goal.

When Izaak Walton, half a century later, wrote his life of
George Herbert he did relatively little research on this period
of the early 1620's, and he came to the conclusion that Herbert
wanted the office of Secretary of State only to satisfy his personal ambition. As the subject developed in Walton's hands it
became the study of a saint seduced by the "outward glory of
the world," and such an interpretation became a foil against
which the last, holy years of Herbert's life could be made to
shine with a special brightness. But there is no evidence for the
correctness of this interpretation outside of Walton's own pages,
and Walton has been proven in other instances to be less than
reliable.[1]

Yet if it would probably be untrue to say that Herbert was
seduced by the pleasures of the world, it is still reasonable to
suppose that he enjoyed himself in a court atmosphere, for he
was not fitted by temperament for the secluded life of a scholar.

---

[1] See the appendix for a fuller discussion of Walton as a biographer.

As long as he believed that the best way to serve God was to study divinity, he worked faithfully at his books and endured the marshy air of Cambridge with what patience he had. But a new path had opened before him, one which was not a repudiation of his goal but an enlargement of it. He had a wider horizon now for his dream of serving God, and it must have been with a real lift of the heart that the scholar set out to turn himself into a statesman.

Even in his sober undergraduate days, Herbert had been fond of fine clothes and conscious of his birth and breeding. His instinct was for bright silks instead of the long dark gown of the academic life. He delighted in "mirth and music," in lively manners and intelligent conversation, in the "quick returns of courtesy and wit." The men he knew best at court were people of intelligence and breeding, and he found himself once more in the easy, aristocratic, civilized atmosphere in which Magdalen Herbert had reared her sons.

Since George Herbert was still active as Public Orator, he would not have seen much of the court if it had remained at Whitehall. But the court followed the King, and the King was spending more and more of his time at his three hunting seats, where he could indulge his passion for the chase and relax in the fresh air. One of these, Newmarket, was thirteen miles east of Cambridge, and another, Royston, was about the same distance to the southwest. Both little towns were so crowded with courtiers that some of them had to look for lodgings in the surrounding villages, and since the University stood between them it made an excellent headquarters for anyone who wished to be near the King.

Moreover, the Public Orator could sometimes be of direct service to the Crown. Late in the winter of 1623, for instance, the ambassadors from Spain and Brussels lodged at Trinity College to be near the King at Newmarket, and it was part of Herbert's official duty to make them welcome. It was vital that the Spanish ambassador should be pleased with his reception, since a marriage was currently being negotiated between the King's son Charles and the Spanish Infanta.

The Public Orator addressed the two ambassadors on the twenty-seventh of February when they were given honorary degrees, and the speech had to be delicately worded since both men were Roman Catholics. Herbert managed the assignment with his usual skill, weaving in "the Catholic king" and "the most renowned Princess Isabel" with that "protecting saint" of England, King James. The speech was of course given in Latin, but it was translated and printed with the rest of the oratory inspired by the occasion. The government needed any good will that might be gleaned from what was a very unpopular visit in Protestant England.

Ten days earlier Prince Charles had secretly left England to woo his Spanish bride in person, and he arrived in Madrid on the first of March. The University of Cambridge rang its bells and lit its bonfires in rejoicing, and the University of Oxford, a little less alert than usual on this occasion, "took the alarm and did the like," with the addition of some hastily written verses in praise of the match.

King James had a streak of incurable romanticism and he was much excited by the whole affair. He himself had gone overseas for his bride, as had his father and grandfather before him, and for lack of a more suitable chronicler he composed some verses of his own on his son's quest. When he arrived at the University of Cambridge twelve days later, to eat dinner and see a play, he did little but talk steadily about the two "boy adventurers," as he called them, Prince Charles and his companion Buckingham.

George Herbert composed a Latin epigram for the occasion which so impressed the King that he bore it back to Newmarket with him. Into four lines Herbert ingeniously packed the idea that the King had shown greater love in coming to Cambridge than the Prince had shown in going to Spain, since the University was farther from the King in intelligence than Spain was from

England in miles. Herbert also delivered the farewell speech in the late afternoon, while the royal coach and the royal trumpeters waited at the door, and on the whole it was a most successful day for a Public Orator who hoped to become a Secretary of State.

King James was convinced that a marriage alliance between Protestant England and Catholic Spain would bring peace to all the warring nations, and throughout the summer of 1623 he clung with hopeful hands and shut eyes to his "darling design." But the marriage negotiations wavered and stalled, and early in October the Prince returned without his bride. All England abandoned itself to a wave of hysterical rejoicing that the heir to the throne was not going to marry a Spanish papist, while the Infanta herself, a grave, self-contained girl, was equally pleased not to be the bride of an English heretic. A new anthem was sung in the special services at St. Paul's Cathedral: "When Israel came out of Egypt and the house of Jacob from among barbarous people."

The University of Cambridge celebrated also, and the bells of St. Mary's rang for three days in rejoicing. The church was used by the University for all special occasions, and on the afternoon of the third day the student body assembled there to hear an address by the Public Orator. Since it was a joyful occasion, George Herbert inserted a little academic teasing into his august Latin sentences. "Our prince has come back. . . . Throw away your books. . . . There is no room for seriousness, not even amongst you. Alma Mater will dance, though advanced in years; even an old woman jumping up and down may raise a good deal of dust."

Most of the speech was a routine celebration of the wonders and wisdoms of Prince Charles, delivered by a public official who knew what was expected of him. But there is one section of the speech that is not routine, and it is extraordinary that George Herbert should have included it.

The middle part of the speech—nearly one-fifth of the whole

oration—is taken up with a picture of war even more bitter than
the one in his "Triumph of Death." Herbert speaks of the
scholars who died under the heels of soldiers and of the learning
destroyed by militarism. "I know that the name of war is
splendid and glorious. . . . Know you not, I pray, the miseries
of war? . . . Slaughterings of every kind, mangled bodies, the
mutilated image of God, a little span of life long enough for
weeping, the burning of cities, crashings, plunderings, violated
virgins, women with child twice killed, little infants shedding
more milk than blood; images, nay shadows of men, with hunger,
cold, filth, vext, crushed, disabled. How cruel is glory which is
reared upon the necks of men; when it is doubtful whether he
who achieves it, or he who suffers, is the more miserable."

If George Herbert had been thinking of his own future welfare he would never have written this into his oration. It was
common knowledge that Prince Charles had come back from
Spain furiously determined to declare war on his former hosts,
and if Herbert had possessed the tact of any normally ambitious
politician he would not have uttered so ardent a plea for peace.
But Herbert was not ambitious for himself. He was ambitious
to be of service. Only the year before he had written his mother
and spoken of "those offices for which I came into the world,
and must yet be kept in it"; and a man so sure of his destiny and
his responsibility does not think first of expediency. He thinks
first of his relationship to God, and for Herbert He was not a
God of battles.

CHAPTER EIGHT

NOW THAT GEORGE HERBERT HAD EMBARKED UPON A POLITICAL career, it was natural for him to follow in the footsteps of other members of his family and serve in Parliament. His grandfather, his father and his elder brother had all represented Montgomeryshire in the House of Commons, and interlocking members of the clan had served from other parts of Wales.

In theory, a member of the gentry was sent from each Welsh county and a local burgess from the chief county town, but in practice the gentry had been moving into both positions. It was common for the head of a prominent local family to represent the shire while one of his sons represented the town; and it would have caused little surprise in Montgomery on a winter's day early in 1624 when the votes were counted and it was found that George Herbert had been elected to represent the town in the next Parliament.

There was intense competition for seats in this election of 1624, since King James had attempted to interfere with the voting on an earlier occasion and the gentlemen of the shires were determined to have no more of such practices. They were taking their political responsibilities with increasing seriousness, and it was a sober and conscientious group of men—no age "afforded a better pack"—who met in Westminster early in February.

George Herbert was a newcomer in Parliament but he could not have felt himself a stranger. His grandfather had served there before Queen Elizabeth came to the throne and the members of his family ever since. Moreover, he had many friends there, and some of them had been serving in the House of Commons for a long time. It was the fourth Parliament for his stepfather,

Sir John Danvers, and the eleventh for Sir George More, a well-loved friend of the family who had once served as guardian for Edward.

George Herbert drew his two shillings a day as a borough representative and met each morning with his fellow Members in St. Stephen's Chapel. The long, high-ceilinged room stood at right angles to Westminster Hall and a flight of thirty-two steps led from the Hall to the lobby of the House of Commons. Before the Reformation St. Stephen's had been a royal chapel, glorious with paint and gilding, and even in its present more sober form it was still a handsome room. The Members sat within it, ranged in tier-like seats, wearing their cloaks against the winter weather and finding the single room increasingly cramped for so vigorous a body as the House of Commons.[1]

The first week was given over to the forming of committees, which were growing steadily more powerful and being chosen with increasing care. There was no room for them to meet in St. Stephen's Chapel or in the lobby at the head of the stairs, and so the committees met all over town, giving first preference to a room that had a square table rather than a long one. In order to leave the afternoons free for the work of the committees, the House met at eight in the morning, and George Herbert seems to have been very interested in the whole procedure. He said later that every English landowner ought to serve in Parliament, "and when he is there, he must not only be a morning man, but at committees also." Herbert of course had a special reason to pay close attention to what was going on, since a Secretary of State would be in regular attendance on Parliament.

On opening day Bishop Carew gave a speech in Westminster Abbey in which he pointed out the blessed peace enjoyed by

---

[1] When Geoffrey Chaucer served as a Member of Parliament the accommodations were even more unsatisfactory. The House of Commons met in the Chapter House of the Abbey monks, where the acoustics were poor; and since it was located in the east cloister of Westminster Abbey, the Members were an inconvenient distance from the House of Lords.

England in a world otherwise torn by war. Herbert had written
a brief Latin poem on the same subject, *"In Pacem Britannicam,"*
and he would have listened with a sympathy that was unshared
by most of his fellow Members. It was shared, however, by King
James, who in his opening address to the assembled Parliament
made the same point. "You have found the fruits of my government if you consider the peace which my kingdoms enjoy." The
speech was an effective one, and a listener was reminded of the
day, five years earlier, when George Herbert as professor of
rhetoric had praised the royal skill in oratory. "The speech
which was had at the opening of the Parliament doth commend
Mr. Herbert for his censure. . . . The whole contexture was a
right purple robe that became majesty."

Another listener praised the speech also, calling it "very gracious and plausible," but from the King's point of view it hid
disaster. James' Spanish policy, on which he had labored so
long, was in ruins, and instead of the union with Spain that he
had hoped for, his son Charles had come back clamoring for
war. During the past autumn King James had drooped at Newmarket as though it were an "infirmary," with no heart even for
his beloved hunting, and now he faced a Parliament as hostile
as his son to his own dream of peace. More than half the Members had served in the last Parliament and petitioned him then
to take up the sword "speedily and effectually." He had told
them not to meddle, but he could not say so again. However
hopefully he might now refer to "the general peace of Christendom, wherein I have always constantly labored," the real point
of his speech was that he was now ready to ask Parliament for
advice.

The advice which Parliament was prepared to give was ac-
celerated by a theatrical gesture engineered by Prince Charles.
The following Tuesday he gathered both Lords and Commons
in the great hall of the palace, where the acoustics were especially good, to hear a report on his trip to Spain. The chief
speaker was the Duke of Buckingham, and Buckingham made it

clear that the Prince had taken an heroic Protestant stand in
Spain with himself as a faithful follower. Parliament was much
impressed. "The general suffrage was that the Prince had
marched valiantly like a captain of holy truth, and that the
Duke deserved a great name as a lieutenant, that maintained
the cause of God under him."

George Villiers, Duke of Buckingham, was by now the most
powerful man in the kingdom. Seven years earlier he had been
a pretty youngster pushed forward by a court faction to dislodge
the current favorite, and James' susceptible heart had melted at
the sight of him. He became the golden, rising sun to which
every courtier turned, and for a time Prince Charles had hated
his father's new favorite. But if Buckingham knew nothing else
he knew how to be charming, and by the time of the Spanish
trip the Prince was completely under the spell of the most headstrong man in England. Buckingham was convinced that the
Spaniards had insulted him, and he would be content with
nothing less than war. When he spoke to Parliament in the
palace hall he was "mortally anti-Spanish, and his anger was
headed with steel."

Parliament had never liked Buckingham, but if he opposed
the perfidious Spaniards it was willing to forgive him anything.
The hatred of Catholic Spain that existed in England was almost
pathological in its intensity, and James' determination to bring
about a union between the two countries had only made matters
worse. His marriage plans had unfortunately coincided with the
opening of the Thirty Years' War, and the average Englishman
had watched in terror while the Protestant armies met defeat,
the King's Protestant son-in-law was driven from Bohemia, and
an apparently irresistible wave engulfed lands that had once,
in their eyes, been free. They saw Roman Catholicism as a giant
international conspiracy with Spain at its head, and every year
their fear and hatred increased.

Queen Elizabeth had succeeded in substituting patriotic zeal
for the religious emotionalism that had threatened to tear her

kingdom apart; but under the well-intentioned bungling of her successor the two emotions joined together and a new force arose in England. It saw itself doing the will of God in politics, and the wise and gentle Hooker had foreseen where that would end. "The mind once imagining itself to seek the execution of God's will, laboreth forthwith to remove both things and persons which any way hinder it." Buckingham knew that this force existed and he thought he could manipulate it for his own purposes. Actually he was merely moving for the moment in the wind's direction, "the darling of the multitude, for bringing home the Prince to safety, and discovering the Spanish designs against our religion and country."

The excited young Prince of Wales was so zealous in his attendance that he never missed a day in Parliament. He and Buckingham had worked vigorously before Parliament opened to shape the peace party to their will, and even the government officials who were most reluctant to enter a war with Spain were equally reluctant to antagonize the heir to the throne and the King's powerful favorite.

The only real support the unhappy King possessed was his Lord Keeper, a shrewd politician whose name was John Williams. Like George Herbert, Williams was a Welshman who had made a name for himself at the University of Cambridge, but unlike Herbert he was a man of driving ambition and had become a bishop chiefly to further his own ends. When he was a small boy he had tried to fly from the town walls of Conway, and ever since then he had been attempting what seemed to be impossible. He became the best orator at Cambridge in spite of a Welsh accent so thick that his fellow students laughed at him when he first arrived. He became Lord Keeper when he was less than forty, although that lofty post required legal training and Bishop Williams' only knowledge of the law came from a brief term of service as a Justice of the Peace. But he had once been the attentive chaplain of a Lord Keeper, and he made up for whatever else he lacked by the incredibly long hours he was

willing to work. A trim man, with a small mouth and elegant
mustaches, Bishop Williams had managed to please both King
James and Buckingham, and he owed his present eminence to
their joint efforts. But now he found himself in a position where
he could only protect the King's policy by risking his own future,
and while Williams "saw no expediency in war" he saw even
less in openly opposing the Duke of Buckingham.

The pressure on James increased and he piteously tried another speech. "It is an unchristian thing to seek that by blood
which may be had by peace." He hopefully asked Parliament's
help in preventing "the effusion of Christian blood, of which too
much hath been shed, and so much against my heart." He also
pointed out that wars cost money, and since his former Parliament had seldom been in a hurry to vote supplies perhaps he
hoped the matter would end there. But his loyal subjects at once
voted a substantial sum for so worthy a cause as war with Spain.

The King had retreated step by step, and now there was nowhere for him to go. His son and his favorite were against him
and so were most of the people of England. On the twenty-third
of March he dissolved the treaty with Spain and the streets of
London were filled with happy citizens, lighting bonfires of
rejoicing and throwing stones at the Spanish embassy. "And in
this order and method the war was hastily entered into against
Spain."

It was a dark season for anyone who loved peace. Even the
weather was vicious, a bitterly cold winter with a savage wind
from the northeast as late as April. On the nineteenth of April,
funeral services were held for the Duke of Richmond and Lennox, who had been Herbert's good friend and patron. He had
died suddenly in February on the day Parliament was scheduled
to open, and the servant who came to dress him in his robes of
state found him lifeless on the bed. Because King James loved
him, his funeral was a magnificent one with a hearse higher
than Queen Anne's and with Lord Keeper Williams to preach the
funeral oration. There was a huge throng of mourners in West-

minster Abbey, and George Herbert must certainly have been among them.

Parliament adjourned the end of May, expecting to meet again in November, and thirteen days later Herbert made a formal application to the University of Cambridge for six months' leave of absence. He said he needed it "on account of many businesses away" and it may be that he was doing government work in connection with the next meeting of Parliament, which was supposed to be held in six months' time. In that case, he would probably have been working with Lord Keeper Williams, who was still the King's trusted lieutenant.

Parliament was not held in November after all; but early in December Herbert received a gift that could have been in return for services rendered. The gift was the right to draw part of the revenue of the parish church at Llandinam, a sinecure that could be held by a layman since it carried no religious obligation. The church was in Herbert's own Montgomeryshire, southwest of his birthplace, and it was in the hills of Llandinam that his grandfather had narrowly escaped injury when an outlaw's arrow drove into the pommel of his saddle. But in this particular case the living was not in the gift of the Herbert family. It belonged to the executor of one Eleanor Panton, and this executor was Lord Keeper Williams.

The year of 1624 drew to its close with Parliament still waiting to be called back into session and with King James still trying to work out a policy that would involve him in as little fighting as possible. The death of his kinsman, the Duke of Richmond and Lennox, had hit him hard, and he received a further shock at the beginning of March when a second kinsman and Herbert's second patron, the Marquis of Hamilton, also died. When James gave the directions for Hamilton's funeral he was so depressed that he told his attendants he did not expect to live much longer.

On the fifth of March, the lonely and confused King became seriously ill. He seemed for a time to be improving and then took a turn for the worse. He called for Lancelot Andrewes to come to him, but his friend was himself ill and could not come. It was Lord Keeper Williams who came to the bedside of the dying man and who stayed with him to the end. He was kneeling by the King's side when James died on Sunday morning, the twenty-seventh of March, 1625.

The body was brought back to London in a rain so heavy that little could be seen except the coaches and the torchlight. It was placed in state in a room hung with black velvet and surrounded by the six silver candlesticks that the new King Charles had brought back with him from Spain. The burial was in Westminster Abbey, after a costly funeral for which there was no money, and Lord Keeper Williams preached a funeral oration that lasted until seven in the evening. He modeled it on a famous one a French cardinal had delivered for Henry of Navarre, and he tried to prove in a series of complicated parallels that James had been a modern Solomon.

The King was no Solomon. He had never been wise. He had lived a rather foolish, fumbling life, and nature had never intended him for a ruler. But he had clung throughout his life to one ideal, his dream of peace, and it was his tragedy to live long enough to see it destroyed. Some people thought it may have helped to kill him, "that he was forced to rush into a war, now in his declining age, having lived in a continual uninterrupted peace his whole life."

His was not the only defeat. George Herbert also had dreamed a dream of peace, and it was apparently because he had hoped to make it a reality that he had changed the course of his life. But the King he had thought to serve was dead now, and Herbert's own dream with him.

CHAPTER NINE

KING JAMES DIED IN A MONTH OF EVIL WEATHER—SNOW AND rain and hail and high winds—and if the new king had been a superstitious man he might have taken it as a portent. But Charles ascended the throne placidly and told John Williams, his reluctant Lord Keeper, to summon a new Parliament. He needed money for his army and navy, and since Parliament had voted for war they would surely vote the money too.

Again there was a battle for seats. Sir Henry Wotton, who was a friend of Herbert's, tried to get elected for Canterbury and "spent almost fifty pound in good drink upon his followers," only to be defeated by one Captain Fisher. But he successfully ran for Sandwich, and in general it was the same men who served in James' last Parliament who returned to serve in the first of Charles'. Among them was George Herbert, who again represented the town of Montgomery.

George Herbert's second Parliament, like his first, had a delayed opening, this time caused by the coming of the plague. Parliament was scheduled to meet in the middle of May, 1625, but there was so much sickness in London that it was a question whether it was safe to meet there at all. But Charles could not wait indefinitely, and on the eighteenth of June he told his assembled Lords and Commons that he needed money to carry on the war they had recommended. Unlike his father, Charles was no orator and left most of the speechmaking to Williams, but his intent was clear enough.

The intention of the House of Commons was equally clear: no reforms, no money. They had grown to power under a tactful Elizabeth and a lazy James, and the lawyers and country gentlemen who made up the bulk of the House had a potential strength

of which Charles had no conception. He considered himself an
absolute monarch—he who had no standing army and not even
the right to levy taxes—and he looked upon Parliament as a gov-
ernmental convenience anxious only to obey his gracious will.
Queen Elizabeth had always known exactly how far she could
go without public approval, but her rigid and inexperienced
young kinsman had no knowledge whatever of the delicate art
of government.

Things began well, for the Commons was full of respectful
loyalty to the twenty-five-year-old monarch who had behaved so
winningly at the last session. But King and Parliament no longer
wanted the same thing, and the session which had begun so
"hopefully and cheerfully proceeded turbulently and suspi-
ciously."

It was no assistance that the air was thick with plague. Each
week the mortality bills rose higher, until by July the rate in
London was equal to that of the Black Death. God's evident displeasure might still be averted by fasting and prayer, and on the
second of July Parliament spent the whole day in church. The
Lords met in Westminster Abbey, the Commons next door in the
parish church of St. Margaret's. George Herbert and his fellow
Members of Parliament spent nine hours without food listening
to a series of sermons, "during all which time it was observed
that not any one man of their company fainted." But nine days
later Parliament had to be suspended, for men were dying in the
streets and London had become a city of ghosts.

A wiser monarch would have given up for the time being, but
Charles decided that Parliament could meet in Oxford instead.
An embittered Commons gathered in the Divinity School at the
University and began to harp once more on that ancient string:
religious grievances. The Members also set about trying to get
rid of the Duke of Buckingham, whom they regarded as the root
of all their difficulties, and Charles dissolved his unruly Parliament on the twelfth of August.

By now Bishop Williams had broken with the Duke of Buck-

ingham, and he knew that his days in public office were num-
bered. In October he ceased to be Lord Keeper, the second of
Herbert's friends to lose that office, but he was no Bacon to
struggle in a sea of debt. Williams had kept a tenacious grip
on all his ecclesiastical offices and he was still both Dean of
Westminster and Bishop of Lincoln. His episcopal residence
was at Buckden, and he arrived there in the midst of a muddy
and desolate winter to transform it into a show place worthy of
his vigorous presence. He ransacked the nurseries near London
for rare fruits and flowers, he sang tenor in his own excellent
choir, his servants presented plays in the evening in the great
hall, and his friends flocked from nearby Cambridge to his
famous dinners. From the safety of his huge diocese he commented freely and unfavorably on Buckingham's behavior, and
in general behaved like a true son of the ancient Welsh houses
of Penrhyn and Cochwilliam.

Like Herbert, Williams had lost his career; but, unlike Herbert, the disaster made remarkably little difference to him and
he was described by a friend as "merry and heart-whole." He
had always been an opportunist who served Williams first, and
in spite of his succession of church offices he had never been
under any illusion that he was serving God. When he fell he fell
skillfully, biding his time until he could rise again, and there
was never any real loss of direction. But George Herbert apparently lost direction completely. The whole of his sheltered, orderly life and his intent, driving spirit had been focussed on one
thing only, his desire to serve God. One move had led to another
with such apparent logic that there had never been any reason
to turn back, and now he suddenly stood at the end of the road.

In December of this plague year of 1625, George Herbert was
staying with his mother in Chelsea at Danvers House. She had
made the beautiful place a haven for those who wished to escape from stricken London, and John Donne had spent the
summer revising his sermons at her house. Magdalen had always
been a steady light to her fifth son, and, as Walton says, he "did

always submit to her wisdom." But she had been losing her
normal serenity, and in the last years of her life she was prey
to the intense melancholy that visited so many people in that
troubled and self-conscious century. John Donne spoke of this
depression of hers when he delivered her funeral sermon two
years later—"not that she ever lay under that water, but yet had
sometimes some high tides of it."

Donne knew those tides well, for he had spent a long time
trying to find mental peace. He could find no pattern for his
life and no place for himself in the world. "I would fain do something. . . . To be no part of any body is to be nothing." Yet he
could find nothing to support himself, his family or his restless
heart until he finally took holy orders in the Church of England.
The suggestion had come from King James, and Donne never
ceased to be grateful. "When I sit still and reckon all my old
master's royal favors to me, I return evermore to that—that he
first inclined me to be a minister."

When George Herbert saw Donne during that Christmas season at Danvers House, his mother's friend had risen to be Dean
of St. Paul's and was now one of the most admired preachers in
England. The sermons on which he lavished so much care had
a wit and strength greater than Lancelot Andrewes', for Donne
had a more profound knowledge of the heart of man.

It may have been Donne, or Donne's example, that prompted
George Herbert to become a deacon. It may have been his
mother's suggestion. Or he may have been moved by the example of a man who became the dearest friend he possessed,
a Londoner named Nicholas Ferrar.

The Ferrars were a merchant family with an ancestry dating
back to William the Conqueror. Drake and Raleigh were familiar
figures at their table, and the five sons were brought up to love
music and the arts. Their mother, Mary Ferrar, was a handsome,
strong-willed woman who seems to have made Nicholas her
favorite. He was born six weeks before George Herbert, a sensitive dreamy boy and a clever one. Like Herbert he fell ill in the

marshy air of Cambridge, but unlike Herbert his mother let him go abroad. Nicholas hurled himself into his travels with the same intensity that George Herbert had recommended to his brother Henry. He took voluminous shorthand notes on everything from Dutch architecture to nautical terminology and then returned home hoping to become a doctor. But his father died, his mother needed him, and his older brother John was struggling helplessly with the complicated family finances.

The most intricate of these financial operations was the Virginia Company, a great speculative venture at colonizing-with-profit in which Sir John Danvers was also heavily involved. He and the two brothers worked long hours in the big Ferrar house in London which was used as company headquarters, and if hard work could have kept the company afloat it would have prospered. But the venture was badly planned, in spite of an impressive list of subscribers, and there always seemed to be more colonists than grain. Sir John Danvers and Nicholas Ferrar fought hard to save the Virginia Company when they both served in James' last Parliament. But there was too much evidence against the well-intentioned management and the Company was dissolved.

The failure of the Virginia Company did not affect Nicholas Ferrar's reputation. He was rightly considered one of the most brilliant young businessmen in London, and it came as a real shock to his large circle of friends when he announced that he was going into holy orders.

The decision had a long root. When Nicholas Ferrar was six years old, he was already tormented by religious questions and once left his bed on a night of frost to lie weeping in the garden because he did not know how to serve God. The sober little boy who refused to wear lace on his clothes changed outwardly into a cosmopolitan young traveller who returned from Europe with plays and novels and love poems in his luggage. But Ferrar still met with God in "the closest walks of his mind" and still longed to serve Him.

The Parliament of 1624 was almost as painful for Ferrar as it must have been for George Herbert, if for a different reason. His efforts to save the Virginia Company brought him into direct opposition with King James, a situation which did not trouble his friend Sir John Danvers but which seemed almost unendurable to Ferrar's sensitive conscience. He said later that he would be willing to lose his right hand if he could be "assured of pardon for that sin," and his experience in Parliament evidently brought to a climax his growing conviction that it was impossible to serve God in the world.

The only solution that Nicholas Ferrar could find for himself was a complete retirement into meditation and prayer. He consulted with his mother, a devout woman who once estimated that she had attended twelve thousand sermons, and Mary Ferrar agreed that neither the town house nor her country estate would make a fit place for retirement. Nicholas Ferrar found a property off in Huntingdonshire, with the manor house falling to ruins and the brick church piled with hay, and there he moved his willing family to set up the famous secular retreat of Little Gidding. It was about ten miles from the gaily flowered episcopal seat of his friend Bishop Williams, and Williams gave him permission to have services conducted once more in the deserted church.

In the spring that followed the plague year, Nicholas Ferrar was in London to say goodbye to his friends and to be ordained a deacon in the Church of England. The ceremony took place in Westminster Abbey on Trinity Sunday, 1626, and after that June day Nicholas Ferrar ceased all concern with the ways of the world. Nor did he make any effort to rise further in the Church. He was able as a deacon to conduct the services at Little Gidding, and he refused every offer of advancement.

Less than a month after Ferrar became a deacon, George Herbert is identified as being a deacon also. It is not known when or where the ceremony occurred or what bishop officiated. According to the usual formula, Herbert promised "to serve God, for the promoting of His glory and the edifying of His people," and the bishop gave him authority to read Scripture, assist in communion, instruct the young in the catechism and perform the various offices that the Church of England permitted.

It is not possible to know why George Herbert became a deacon. If it had occurred back in the days when he was studying divinity, it would have been the normal preliminary to becoming a minister. But this was clearly not the reason now. It was not until several years later that Herbert decided to enter the ministry, and by that time the circumstances of his life had radically altered.

Perhaps, like Ferrar, Herbert felt that he was not worthy of a benefice with its heavy spiritual responsibility for the cure of souls and "durst not presume to step one inch higher" than the office of deacon. Perhaps he thought that a single step across the threshold would bring him peace. But peace does not always come with the laying on of a bishop's hands, and Herbert did not lose his sense of drifting and of uselessness to God.

When Nicholas Ferrar became a deacon he wrote out a formal statement on a piece of vellum, vowing to dedicate his whole life to the service of God. George Herbert needed no words on parchment to reaffirm his goal. What he needed was a chart to tell him how to reach it, and neither Donne's success in the church nor Ferrar's retirement from the world gave the key that could bring peace to his own disordered life. Nor could he relax and bide his time as his third friend, the Bishop of Lincoln, was able to do.

John Williams, Bishop of Lincoln, was no longer a power at court. But he still had enormous resources as an ecclesiastical patron and was able to indulge his generosity towards men he admired.[1] Williams had already given George Herbert one gift,

---

[1] One of the recipients was Herbert's school friend, John Hacket, who had become Williams' chaplain. The Bishop gave him two livings in a single year, one in Holborn so that he could winter in London and another at Cheam so that he could have his summers in the country.

the sinecure at Llandinam, and eighteen months later he gave him another, making him a prebendary of Lincoln Cathedral.

The acceptance of the money carried with it almost no religious obligation. In the old days a prebendary at Lincoln had been an active member of the Cathedral chapter, helping in the management of the great building and the maintenance of the services. But over the intervening centuries the work had come to be done by deputies and the position was largely honorary. Herbert's only obligation was to preach in the Cathedral once a year, and even this could be done by a deputy. Nor did he appear in person when he was instituted in the Cathedral on the fifth of July, 1626, and his place was taken by Peter Walter, clerk, who acted as his proxy and took the necessary oaths.

Herbert had only one real obligation as a prebendary. Lincoln was a cathedral of the Old Foundation, moving to a rhythm that had been set in motion six hundred years earlier, and it was the duty of the Cathedral chapter to recite the whole of the Book of Psalms daily. This was achieved by parcelling it out among the prebendaries, and over the magnificently carved choir stall that belonged to Herbert as prebendary of Leighton Ecclesia were the Latin titles of the two Psalms he was expected to recite daily, "In Thee, O Lord, do I put my trust," and "Blessed is he whose transgression is forgiven." When John Donne became a prebendary of St. Paul's Cathedral he found a comforting sense of spiritual fellowship in the fact that he and his fellows united to offer "howsoever we be divided from one another in place, the sacrifice of praise." But Donne was already at peace when he received his prebend, and Herbert was not.

The one thing that Herbert did derive from Williams' gift was a strong sense that it was undeserved, and he did a most abnormal thing for that covetous age. He tried to give it away. The revenue that supported it came from the parish church at Leighton Bromswold, which was only a few miles from Ferrar's community at Little Gidding. Herbert decided that the prebend should go to Ferrar instead and wrote him "with much earnestness" asking him to accept it.

Ferrar had good use for the money, for the expenses of establishing a new community in a ruined manor were heavy. In this particular year of 1626 he was planning to start an orchard and stock the fishponds. There were bills from the glazier for repairing the church, and within the building itself everything had to be of the finest materials. The service book was adorned with a velvet cover, the candlesticks were silver, the pulpit was hung with silver lace, and the benches were cushioned with tapestry and blue silk. In the serene and well-ordered atmosphere of Little Gidding, "Mr. Ferrar and his happy family" united to serve God, and it was perhaps a desire to contribute to something he could not otherwise share that made Herbert attempt to give Ferrar his prebend.

Nicholas Ferrar refused the offer with as much vigor as Herbert made it. But he was apparently wise enough to see what lay behind it, for he suggested an alternative. The church at Leighton Bromswold, like too many others in England, was standing roofless and the vicar was holding services in the hall of the local manor house. There had been talk of repairs, but the estimates ran to about two thousand pounds, which was a large sum in those days. Ferrar suggested to Herbert that he might help repair the church, and Herbert threw himself into the task as though it were a life line to God.

Lady Danvers heard what her son was planning to do and sent for him to come and see her in Chelsea. It was not fitting, Magdalen said, for a man with his "weak body, and empty purse, to undertake to build churches." Herbert listened carefully and then returned the next day with the patient request "that she would, at the age of thirty-three years, allow him to become an undutiful son." Nor was Magdalen, in her turn, an unreasonable mother, since she ended by subscribing to the building fund herself. She also persuaded the family kinsman, the Earl of

Pembroke, to donate fifty pounds, and Herbert, "by a witty and
persuasive letter," got him to double it.

The weak body of which his mother spoke was still a burden
to George Herbert, a dragging chain that must have seemed even
heavier now that his spirit was burdened also. He was especially
ill in this year of 1626 and to get a change of air he went to stay
with his brother Henry. Henry was living about nine miles north
of London in the village of Woodford in Epping Forest.

Henry was two years younger than George and unlike him in
every way. Henry was the practical member of the family and
for the last decade he had been industriously turning himself into
a rich man. His marriage brought him a considerable fortune,
and in 1623 he was given a knighthood and became a Gentleman of the Privy Chamber. In that same year he bought the
right to manage the Office of the Revels, although the Master
of the Revels was still living.

Sir Henry Herbert paid a hundred and fifty pounds a year for
the privilege but he got his money's worth. The Master of the
Revels not only supervised the court entertainments but also
controlled the London theatres, and Henry raised the subtle art
of collecting fees to a new height. The actors of the company
that had once been Shakespeare's suddenly discovered they must
pay him an annual fee for the right to have music in their own
theatre, and by 1626 they were staging two benefit performances
a year for his sole profit. In time Sir Henry decided that the play
scripts in London must all be licensed over again, with the payment of a new fee, "since they may be full of offensive things
against church and state." In this case Henry's gift for making
money coincided with his natural temperament, since he had a
tidy, conservative mind and disliked even mild profanity.

The year in which George Herbert came to stay with him at
Woodford was a busy one for Henry. He served as a Member of
the House of Commons in Charles' second Parliament, repre-
senting the town of Montgomery as George had done the year
before. In this year also his first and only son was born, baptized

on the first of May by Mr. Isaacson, the Woodford parson. Lady
Danvers arrived for the christening to be the baby's godmother,
and its godfathers were those "most noble and incomparable pair
of brethren," the Earls of Pembroke and Montgomery to whom
Shakespeare's First Folio had recently been dedicated. The Earl
of Pembroke had been especially kind to Henry, keeping a helpful hand under his elbow during his rise, and it was at the Earl's
estate at Wilton that Henry had been knighted.

By now Sir Henry Herbert's career was in sharp contrast to
that of his brothers. William and Richard were dead, leaving
nothing behind except a reputation for valor in Flanders and
Holland. Thomas, the sailor brother, had distinguished himself
in the East Indies and had captained the ship that brought
Prince Charles back from Spain. But his naval career became
blocked and he "retired to a private and melancholy life," giving
free rein to a family tendency to oversensitivity.

Even Sir Edward Herbert, the eldest and most famous of the
seven brothers, had not been doing well for himself lately. He
had been dismissed in 1624, rather unfairly, from his post as
ambassador to France, and since his salary was in arrears he
could not pay the many debts he had incurred. But Edward was
not the man to endure injustice patiently, and the week after his
small nephew was christened at Woodford he addressed a petition to King Charles. He announced that he had been publicly
insulted because he had not been rewarded with a "place of
honor and preferment," and he suggested a seat in the House
of Lords, membership in the Privy Council and some sort of
financial restitution.

For once the government moved with relative speed, possibly
assisted by the fact that Edward's creditors in France presented
a petition of their own for two thousand pounds. In July of 1627,
four months after this second petition, Edward and his brother
George and a first cousin named Thomas Lawley were given the
joint grant of the manor of Ribbesford.

The manor was a heavily wooded property in Worcestershire,

with "an ancient moated house," and Sir Henry Herbert had
already been thinking of buying it. He hesitated only because
the house was in poor condition and might not be "healthful in
the winter." But later in this same year he finally purchased it
from his relatives, paying them three thousand pounds; and however the money may have been divided, it seems clear that
George Herbert no longer had the empty purse of which his
mother had spoken.

While he was still at Woodford he heard of the death of two
of his close friends. Sir Francis Bacon died in April of 1626 and
was buried next to his mother in St. Alban's. In September
Lancelot Andrewes, his friend and Herbert's, slipped into death
after a long time of waiting. One of his brothers had died in the
plague year and another soon after, and the tired old man had
lost his will to live.

Early in June of the following year, George Herbert's mother
died quietly at her house in Chelsea. Two hours before her death
Magdalen was able to join the people gathered at her bedside
in a final prayer, and then she lay motionless "without any struggle, any disorder." Disciplined to the last, her final words revealed the source of the discipline: "I submit my will to the will
of God."

She was buried on the eighth of June in the parish church of
St. Luke's, which stood east of Danvers House on the other side
of the lane, but her funeral sermon was delayed until the first of
July so that John Donne could deliver it. He had known and
loved her for a quarter of a century, and Izaak Walton, who was
in the church that day, saw him openly weeping. Walton saw
George Herbert also, tall, "very straight" and very thin.

Herbert had been writing a series of poems for his dead
mother, and when Donne's funeral eulogy was licensed for publication on the seventh of July Herbert's own memorial was ready
to go with it. He called it *Memoriae Matris Sacrum* and it is a
curious piece of work, as odd as those ornate funeral monuments
that the seventeenth century sometimes reared, in all love and

honor, to the memory of the departed. It consists of nineteen poems, five in Greek and the rest in Latin, written in the strained and ornamental style which Herbert evidently felt was suited to a public occasion. He speaks of his grief being mixed with Thames water to produce ink; he invokes mythological characters like Astrea, daughter of Themis; he brings in complicated Latin puns, and he even manages to introduce current events by mentioning the English fleet that was being equipped to sail to the Isle of Rhé. Occasionally there is a natural, human touch, such as the mention of his mother's love of gardens, but in general the memorial is stiff with rhetoric and as heavy as marble. Herbert says in the last stanza that he wrote it because "my mother's honor claims it" and that he would write no more thereafter. Perhaps he meant that he would write no more for an audience, and if so he kept his word.

Six months later, on the twenty-eighth of January, 1628, Herbert gave up his post as Public Orator. Walton says that he had kept it so long only because his mother had wished him to. He had not been at Cambridge and the work was being done by his deputy, a brilliant young Orientalist named Herbert Thorndike who delivered the Orator's address when King James died. Herbert's successor in the post was Robert Creighton, who had been educated at Westminster School and Trinity College and was an equally brilliant scholar. He had served as Andrew Downes' assistant and succeeded him as Regius Professor of Greek when the old man died.

There is in existence a letter which George Herbert wrote his friend Creighton on the subject of the Oratorship. It is an easy, charming letter in which he offers some advice on the style to be employed in the official University speeches and letters. Then he adds that Creighton knows this already and that he has been chattering needlessly, but that "love is generally talkative."

This was apparently Herbert's usual manner in public, the pleasant half-teasing courtesy that showed very little of what he was really thinking. Izaak Walton noticed somewhat the same thing during the brief time he saw him. "His aspect was cheerful, and his speech and motion did both declare him a gentleman. . . . They purchased love and respect from all that knew him."

A gentleman keeps his emotions to himself, and there was evidently very little in Herbert's outward manner to show his loneliness, his rootlessness, the anguish of a man who has lost his way. He kept this for the poems he wrote in English, the poems that were not published during his lifetime and in which he showed his heart.

CHAPTER TEN

G EORGE HERBERT WROTE FIVE POEMS THAT HE NAMED "AFFLIC-
tion" and the first of them is an account of the servant who
has lost his way. It describes the joyful beginning of Herbert's
service to God, "no place for grief or fear." It describes his loss of
health, his loss of friends, and his sense that his gifts were not
put to their best use.

> Whereas my birth and spirit rather took
> The way that takes the town;
> Thou didst betray me to a ling'ring book
> And wrap me in a gown.

The poem ends with the conviction that he cannot "change the
service" and seek some other master, even though his own "ways"
have been taken from him. But in one wistful stanza that is
almost childlike in its wording, Herbert expresses his longing for
some sort of uncomplicated usefulness.

> Now I am here, what Thou wilt do with me
> None of my books will show:
> I read, and sigh, and wish I were a tree;
> For sure then I should grow
> To fruit or shade: at least some bird would trust
> Her household to me, and I should be just.

He again uses the image of the contented tree in a poem called
"Employment," when he thinks with envy of the orange tree,
"that busy plant." Like the image of working bees, which he uses
in four different poems, the usefulness of ordinary things haunts
him. For he can find no place for himself in the hierarchy of
natural order that ascends to God.

> I am no link of Thy great chain,
> But all my company is a weed.

To feel nothing but disorder in a world of natural order, nothing but uselessness in a universe of use, made Herbert long for some kind of a simple, innocent solution that would bring his life into a clear pattern again. But he knew quite well that this sort of remedy was not available to him. He was a tense, complex, highly educated man who had dedicated his life to the service of a difficult God and who now knew the agony of being more distant than ever from his goal.

> To have my aim, and yet to be
> Further from it than when I bent my bow . . .

Herbert could not cease trying to take aim. He could not leave God's service and "seek some other master out." And yet he could not shape his life into the clear direction it had once had. He could not even control his thoughts, which tempted him to abandon what had apparently become a useless struggle.

> As good go any where, they say,
>   As to benumb
> Both knees and heart, in crying night and day,
>   *Come, come, my God, O come,*
>   But no hearing.

The sense of hopelessness continued, a mental torment so violent that Herbert calls his thoughts "a case of knives," the thrust that he could not withstand which nevertheless did not show him where he should go. It was a state of uncontrollable inner warfare endured by a man who was not fitted for that kind of pain.

To a degree, the problem that tormented Herbert was one that troubled many men in the first half of the seventeenth century. It was a period when the sense of separation from God weighed with special heaviness upon Western man and the yearning to be at peace with Him had a greater intensity. Christians might war against each other, but each of them fought an even more strenuous battle against the common enemy of them all. The burden of the Fall, the agonized sense of estrangement from

God, and the hourly impassioned effort to return to Him were shared equally by Roman Catholic, Anglican and Puritan. They shared also an acute realization of the shortness of the time available—what Herbert calls "my hour, my inch of life"—and the knowledge that failure was irrevocable.

As long as Herbert was sheltered by an orderly career and the conviction that he was spending it in God's service, these winds of the mind had less force. He wrote a letter to his mother once to console her in an illness and he listed as one of her chief sources of comfort the fact she had lived a useful life. He himself had thought he was useful once and had known shelter. Nothing was left to him now except the discord of his own thinking and the unending pressure of the "curse in Adam's fall."

George Herbert had one refuge only, one area in his disordered life where he could impose order. He was a poet, and it is a poet's business to reduce formlessness to an exact control. Even if he records chaos he cannot be chaotic. His whole business is with order, the perfect shape of the cup that will contain the otherwise uncontrollable wine.

As long as Herbert lived a tidy and limited existence his verse was relatively commonplace. There was nothing to restrain, and therefore no necessity to exert the kind of strength that is indispensable to a poet. It was not until his life was formless that form became a vital necessity, and it was in writing poetry that he found the sense of order without which it was almost impossible for him to exist.

Herbert's poetry cannot be dated, but it seems reasonable to assume that his success as a poet was a gradual achievement. It is known from the available manuscripts that he rewrote constantly, and since skill grows with use it is probable that his finest work is the result of a long inward training. He learned how to report a mood until it became no longer a report but a work of art.

He experienced many times, for instance, a furious sense of having been trapped into giving his life to a service in which he

could not succeed and from which he could not escape. All the
worlds of love and courtliness and learning were open to him as
an aristocrat, and it sometimes infuriated him to be bound by so
tight a tether.

> Full of rebellion, I would die,
> Or fight, or travel, or deny
> That Thou hast aught to do with me.

This is the truth of fact but it is not yet the truth of poetry.
It is hardly more than a rhymed statement. Yet the idea it expresses is a reality—one of the foes that Herbert encountered
in the house of his mind—and therefore it remained with him
until he brought it to complete expression in that most beautiful
of poems, "The Collar."

> I struck the board, and cried, No more.
> I will abroad.
> What? shall I ever sigh and pine?
> My lines and life are free; free as the road,
> Loose as the wind, as large as store.
> Shall I be still in suit?
> Have I no harvest but a thorn
> To let me blood, and not restore
> What I have lost with cordial fruit?
> Sure there was wine
> Before my sighs did dry it: there was corn
> Before my tears did drown it.
> Is the year only lost to me?
> Have I no bays to crown it?
> No flowers, no garlands gay? all blasted?
> All wasted?
> Not so, my heart: but there is fruit,
> And thou hast hands.
> Recover all thy sigh-blown age
> On double pleasures: leave thy cold dispute
> Of what is fit, and not. Forsake thy cage,
> Thy rope of sands,
> Which petty thoughts have made, and made to thee
> Good cable, to enforce and draw,
> And be thy law,

> While thou didst wink and wouldst not see.
> Away; take heed:
> I will abroad.
> Call in thy death's head there: tie up thy fears.
> He that forbears
> To suit and serve his need,
> Deserves his load.
> But as I rav'd and grew more fierce and wild
> At every word,
> Me thoughts I heard one calling, *Child!*
> And I replied, *My Lord.*

"The Collar" mirrors disorder in a frame of perfect control. The apparently broken construction of the lines, the brilliant audacity of the rhyme scheme, the jerk and pull and effect of increasing frenzy—all these are held safely in a hand that knows exactly what it is doing. In the last lines the hand closes gently and the poem moves from resistance to peace, with the rhyme scheme following the emotion and quieting into order.

To an extraordinary extent Herbert was able to convey an emotion through the actual physical movement of his lines. He experimented endlessly with the shape of his poetry, choosing or inventing a rhyme scheme that would precisely match the meaning of the poem as a whole, and more than half his poems are cast in stanza forms he did not use again. He will end a conventionally shaped poem like "Grief" with a sudden break in the pattern that is like a cry, or he will withhold the rhyming word the reader is expecting in a poem like "Home" in order to force attention on what he is saying. He will even use the seventeenth-century trick of spreading his words into a visual pattern on the page, so that they take the shape of an altar or a pair of wings, and there is almost no technical device that he does not try somewhere.

Herbert did not play games as a writer, using experimentation for its own sake. Every poem he wrote was an orderly attempt to speak the exact truth at a given moment and to provide the best vessel he could for the contents. Donne once remarked, only half joking, of his own poetry, "I did best when I had least truth for my subject." George Herbert could never have said that. He was dealing in his writing with the most important thing in his life, his relationship to God, and what he said he meant. It was because of this quality that even the Puritans admired his poems. As Richard Baxter said, "Herbert speaks to God like one that really believeth a God, and whose business in the world is most with God."

Yet Herbert brought no special reverence of tone to his discussions with God, in the sense that the eighteenth and nineteenth centuries understood reverence. He brought the whole of himself and left nothing behind on the threshold. He brought his wit, the easy wit of an aristocrat and a good conversationalist. He brought his passion and turned many of his lines into outright love poetry. He brought his delight in puns and proverbs and his interest in everyday things, and he did not object to writing religious poetry that used images like playing cards and watering pots and clocks.

When a later day had succeeded in turning religion into a formal, Sunday part of life, George Herbert's colloquial approach seemed wrong. Equally wrong to a later generation was the sensitive violence with which he used the symbols of the Christian religion, the blood, the cross, the banners, the tears. A later age called this emotionalism, which it was not. It was the context in which the mind of the average Christian moved in the early seventeenth century, as truthful as the equally visual emotion of the men who wrote the Psalms.

In a sense, Herbert was talking to himself in his poetry, and he did it against a background of experience that he shared with nearly all the Englishmen of his day. The images in his mind were chiefly formed by the Bible and by the liturgy of the Church of England, and he used them as unconsciously as a painter depends on his colors. He was almost as dependent on the images that came from music, for he was a highly skilled instrumentalist and could not resist the technical terms that gave him an almost mathematically precise image for what he wanted to convey. It is accuracy rather than vagueness that makes his work sometimes obscure, for the reader needs as exact a knowledge as Herbert's own to understand the precision of his use of words.

Moreover, he had Donne's way of seeing a likeness in unlike things, the intellectual quickness that will charge a line with a double meaning and then turn it back upon itself. He shared with his period a liking for verbal shorthand and packed his phrases tight: "the shells of fledge souls," "noise of thoughts." Coleridge was displeased with him for writing a line like "anguish of all sizes" but Emily Dickinson would have approved of it; she might have used it herself. She shares with Herbert that curious, tense combination of subtlety and directness with which he turned even the Day of Judgment into something casual and familiar.

> Summon all the dust to rise,
> Till it stir, and rub the eyes . . .

New England dust or seventeenth-century English dust, it is all one. The images are used with deceptive simplicity, but the minds that use them are not simple.

George Herbert had never succeeded in bringing the whole of himself to any career he could find in the world, but he did bring the whole of himself to his poetry. Lover, courtier, musician, craftsman, he could turn all his skills into servants when he picked up his pen, and he did not need to suppress any part of himself when he talked to God. The one thing he did suppress, and the fact is worth noting, is his learning. The classical jargon and the obscure allusions that the Renaissance loved and that Herbert had used in the Greek and Latin verses on the death of his mother are wholly absent in the English poems in which he turns to God.

His older brother Edward admired George Herbert's Latin poems more than the ones he wrote in English. Edward says that the English poems, "though they be rare in their kind, yet are far short of expressing those perfections he had in the Greek and Latin tongue."

Edward Herbert had a vigorous and even brilliant mind, but his notions of order and his set of values were less subtle than those of his brother. Both men, for instance, wrote a poem on the same subject—the tendency of the repentant sinner to relapse into sin—and the difference in their approach is evident from the first line. This is Edward Herbert's opening:

> Lord, thus I sin, repent and sin again . . .

This is George Herbert's:

> Sorry I am, my God, sorry I am . . .

Edward casts his poem in the shape of a sonnet and ends it on a note of smoothly conventional self-reproof.

> . . . but oh! my sins renew,
> Whilst I do talk with my Creator thus.

George Herbert uses a pattern, apparently of his own invention, in which each stanza is linked to the next by a repetition of the last line. They move in a kind of weary circle and in the end they have been nowhere, for the last line of the poem is the same as the first:

> Sorry I am, my God, sorry I am.

He calls it "Sin's Round" and that is exactly what it is, both on the page and in the reader's mind. Its much greater effectiveness is partly due to the fact that George Herbert is the better poet and partly because he knew so thoroughly what he was talking about.

Herbert wrote all his poetry out of his own experience. None is the result of hearsay, none is born of secondhand emotion, and when peace comes at the end of a poem it has been hard won. In some cases it was almost certainly the act of writing the poem itself that brought him a sense of at least temporary victory. He could focus the whole of himself, however briefly, on the attain-

ment of a single object and forget his own existence in the
process. He might have echoed his distant kinsman, Sir Philip
Sidney, who once wrote a friend, "I am never less a prey to
melancholy than when I am earnestly applying the feeble powers
of my mind to some high and difficult object." The writing of a
good poem falls into this category, and it brought Herbert some
of the peace that Sidney describes.

Like Sidney, he also found peace in music. Herbert was not
unlike a lute himself, delicate and difficult to keep in tune, and
he found in music almost the only other medium that could be
trusted to take him out of himself. Walton says that he was "a
great master" of the lute and viol and that he made musical settings for many of his poems. They are lost now, and perhaps he
never wrote them down. But a quarter of his poems reflect his
love of music, and the image of the untuned instrument is the
one he most often applies to himself.

Herbert knew how to tune a lute or a viol. He knew how to
exact obedience from his pen. But he did not know how to re-
shape his life and it remained formless and broken. He was useless, and one of his poems gives to uselessness almost the shudder
of death.

> . . . We freeze on,
> Until the grave increase our cold.

He called the poem "Employment," and employment was the one
thing he could not find.

So he went on existing, moving from place to place. He was
now thirty-four years old.

CHAPTER ELEVEN

I ZAAK WALTON SAW GEORGE HERBERT ONLY ONCE AND REPORTED
that he was "lean to an extremity." This must have been when
Donne preached the funeral sermon for Magdalen, since Walton
attended the service and Herbert certainly was there. He had
spent the past year at his brother's house in Woodford, but
instead of being benefited by the change of air he had acquired
what the seventeenth century called a consumption. Looking
for a better climate, he went to a manor house in Wiltshire which
was owned by his stepfather's elder brother Henry, Lord
Danvers.

The house was a "noble" one, set in a park of magnificent oaks.
The meadows of that peaceful, airy place were famous for their
pasture, and the fattest cattle that went to the London market
came from the manor of Dauntsey. The house stood on a terrace
set back from the river Avon, with the broad sweep of the meadows beyond; and tucked in next to it was the parish church of
St. James, with the Dauntsey shield in front of the altar and the
family coat of arms on the benches.

The Danvers family had come to Dauntsey in the fifteenth
century, when the first Sir John Danvers became the third husband of the "lady of Dauntsey." The father of George Herbert's
host had been named John also, a handsome man of gentle
temper who distinguished himself in the preparations against
the Armada. He became a great landowner through his marriage
with Elizabeth Nevile, Lord Latimer's daughter, a brilliant and
beautiful woman who read Chaucer and managed her huge
estates with equal vigor.

Old Sir John was no longer living, but his picture hung in the
parish church and George Herbert wrote the little rhymed epi-

116

taph that was fastened to it. Sir John's virtue and good looks were shared by the whole family in Herbert's opinion.

> What makes a Danvers
> Would you find?
> In a fair body
> A fair mind.

There were ten children in the Danvers family and three of them were sons. The youngest, John, who was named after his father, was George Herbert's stepfather; the second son, Henry, was Herbert's present host, and the eldest, Charles, had lived a violent life and come to a tragic death. When Charles was twenty-three he murdered a man, in one of those county feuds that were so common in Elizabethan England, and was forced to flee to the Continent. The Earl of Southampton, to whom Shakespeare was currently addressing his poems, helped him to escape, and Charles always felt that he owed his life to the young nobleman. Therefore, when Southampton entered the Essex conspiracy, Sir Charles Danvers was drawn into it also through gratitude and friendship, and when that harebrained enterprise failed he was beheaded on Tower Hill.

Henry Danvers had been involved with his older brother in the murder and escaped with him to the Continent. He nevertheless grew up into a "sedate and solid" man and by the time he was twenty-five had been called the best sea captain in England. King James made him Baron Danvers of Dauntsey as soon as he ascended the throne and a way was found to release the estate, which on Charles' execution had been forfeit to the crown. In the next reign Lord Danvers became an earl, and when he was installed as a Knight of the Garter it was done with such splendor that it was remembered as "the greatest solemnity ever known in the memory of man."

It was a year or so later that George Herbert came to live with Lord Danvers at Dauntsey, and the tall, gentle, slightly balding bachelor was very good to him. Walton reports that he "loved Mr. Herbert so much, that he allowed him such an apartment in it as might best suit with his accommodation and liking."

A gentleman who was living in the village remembered Herbert as having "a very good hand on the lute," and that he spent some of his time at Dauntsey setting his own poems to music. There was much harmony in that pleasant place, with its "choice air" and loving, relaxed atmosphere, and Herbert's health improved so much that he was able to achieve "a good degree of strength and cheerfulness."

About a dozen miles from Lord Danvers' estate and at the foot of Salisbury Plain lay the parish of Edington. A branch of the family had settled here, and a cousin named Charles Danvers had inherited a manor. Baynton House was a handsome resi dence of brick and stone, with gardens and terraces, and here Charles Danvers and his wife Maria brought up their fourteen children.

The third daughter was named Jane, and it was said that her father loved her the best. She must at any rate have been very close to him, since it was to Jane rather than to any of her brothers that Charles Danvers willed his College Cup.

Jane's father died at about the time that Herbert came to Dauntsey, but he had spoken to her about his cousin's guest. Jane Danvers met George Herbert early in the year of 1629, if Walton's story is correct, and the two of them fell instantly and completely in love.

Herbert married Jane Danvers on the fifth of March, 1629. The ceremony took place in the bride's parish church of Edington, that beautiful stone structure that reared its almost cathedral-like height about a mile from Baynton House. Twenty years ago on another spring day his mother had married Sir John Danvers, and now Herbert was marrying into the same family. Jane was the great-great-great granddaughter of the first Sir John Danvers of Dauntsey, and George Herbert went to live at her mother's house of Baynton.

It was a very happy marriage, "indeed so happy that there was never any opposition betwixt them, unless it were a contest which should most incline to a complaisance with the other's wishes." There were many men in the seventeenth century who believed it was the husband's right to "govern like a master," but George Herbert was not one of them. His successful marriage to Jane Danvers was a combination of love and courtesy, and their "daily obligingness to each other" increased the joy they had together.

During this same spring of 1629 George Herbert delivered the first sermon that is recorded of him. Up to this time he had evidently been presenting his annual sermon in Lincoln Cathedral through a deputy, but on the seventh Sunday after Easter, not long after his marriage, he preached in the Cathedral itself.

Herbert's body was stronger now, thanks to the good air of Dauntsey and the affectionate care he had been given there. His personal life was much happier, thanks to Jane Danvers and the love she brought him. All this must have helped him in his search for peace, but the final answer had to come otherwise and in its own fashion.

George Herbert had been brought up a Calvinist in matters of doctrine, as most English Protestants were in his day. The dispute with the Puritans was over ritual, not doctrine, and when Herbert attacked Andrew Melville on the subject of church services he assured his Puritan opponent that they nevertheless agreed wholly as to the nature of God.

To the average Protestant, whether Anglican or Puritan, God was infinite, omnipotent Will, separating the saved from the damned by an absolute fiat from which there was no hope of appeal. A few members of the Church of England, such as Lancelot Andrewes, disliked this iron doctrine of predestination and he and Herbert once had a "debate" on the subject, after which Herbert wrote him a long letter in Greek explaining his point of view. He had apparently not changed it since, for the God he describes in one of his poems is the God of the Calvinists,

Who gives to man, as He sees fit, } Salvation.
                                   } Damnation.

Yet in spite of his conservative upbringing and his long training in divinity, this was a view of God that Herbert could keep
in his mind but not in his heart. With the exception of this single
line there is nothing in his poetry to support the orthodox Calvinist position. The God with Whom he struggled was sometimes
a friend and sometimes an enemy, but He bore little resemblance
to the stern deity whose laws Calvin had codified so brilliantly.

Herbert wrote a poem called "Discipline" in which he might
have been expected to abase himself before the unyielding Judge
of the Protestant nations. Instead he took what was almost a
contrary point of view.

> Throw away Thy rod,
> Throw away Thy wrath:
> O my God,
> Take the gentle path.

It is not wrath that brings man to salvation, but love.

> Love is swift of foot;
> Love's a man of war . . .

It is a beautiful poem, written with the sureness of technique
that Herbert achieved when he knew what he was talking about,
but it is not the normal approach of early seventeenth-century
theology.

The power of love and the power of God came in the end
to mean the same thing to George Herbert. When he wrote a
morning song called "Matins" he closed it with the prayer,
"Teach me Thy love to know," and the prayer was well answered.

Since Herbert was a poet, the answer is recorded in his poetry.
He wrote four poems that he entitled "Love." One of these he
discarded, and two of the remainder are reasonably conventional
sonnets. But the fourth poem is not in the least conventional; it
is the living voice of a man who speaks from the height of an
experience that is wholly his own.

> Love bade me welcome: yet my soul drew back,
> Guilty of dust and sin.

But quick-ey'd Love, observing me grow slack
    From my first entrance in,
Drew nearer to me, sweetly questioning,
    If I lacked any thing.

A guest, I answer'd, worthy to be here:
    Love said, You shall be he.
I the unkind, ungrateful? Ah my dear,
    I cannot look on thee.
Love took my hand, and smiling did reply,
    Who made the eyes but I?

Truth, Lord, but I have marred them: let my shame
    Go where it doth deserve.
And know you not, says Love, who bore the blame?
    My dear, then I will serve.
You must sit down, says Love, and taste my meat:
    So I did sit and eat.

The conversational tone, the everyday images and the easy familiarity of the dialogue are all based on an extraordinary control
of the material. It is the control that Herbert always seems to
possess when he reaches the final statement of what has become
a fundamental conviction, and this was one he had been ap-
proaching for a long time.

It was not to the Calvinist God of wrath that George Herbert
surrendered. It was to the God of love. And he surrendered so
completely that he gave up everything to Him.

He gave up the idea, which he had held so tenaciously, that
he might serve God in a fashion worthy of the Herberts. He gave
up the hope that

                . . . not only I,
    But all my wealth and family might combine
    To set Thy honour up, as our design.

He gave up the right to say, "My will doth study Thy renown,"
because he gave up the possession of a will of his own. In so
doing he left behind him the torment described in "The Cross,"
from which the foregoing lines are taken, and entered instead

into that holy country which is filled with the glory of God and
where no man casts the shadow of his own willfulness. "The
man who once against Thee fought" relaxed into the peace of
God by discovering that he could not build a private peace of his
own making; for God was the sole maker and possessor of all
things.

> . . . Even to trust in Him, was also His:
> We must confess that nothing is our own.

All this did not come in a day. But it gave George Herbert a
clear path where there had been nothing but confusion before,
and it was one he followed with increasing steadiness for the rest
of his short life.

CHAPTER TWELVE

A YEAR AFTER HE PREACHED THE PENTECOST SERMON IN LINCOLN
Cathedral, George Herbert was offered a benefice in the
Church of England.

A rectory in southern Wiltshire had become vacant when its
nonresident rector, the Bishop of Rochester, was promoted to
another see. The King had promoted Dr. Curll and had the right
to name his successor; but the rectory was normally in the gift
of the Earls of Pembroke, and the new Earl, Philip Herbert,
suggested that it be given to his kinsman George.

The benefice consisted of two churches on the highway that
linked the Earl's seat at Wilton with the cathedral city of Salisbury. There was the parish church of St. Peter's near the entrance
to Wilton House and about a mile away the little chapel of St.
Andrew's at Bemerton, built to take care of the extra needs of
what had once been a flourishing community. The rector's house
was at Bemerton, so neglected that it was almost uninhabitable,
and all three buildings were in need of repair.

Herbert hesitated over the offer for more than a month, not
because he thought it unworthy of him but because he believed
himself unworthy of it. When he was a young man studying
divinity at Cambridge, he had worried about his books and his
finances but he had apparently never questioned his worthiness
to be a minister in the Church of England. Now, twelve years
later, he questioned it profoundly. The minister was the deputy
of Christ, the accredited instrument to bring men to salvation,
and Herbert believed he was not fit for so high an office.

The answer, when it finally came, was the same as before. It
was not his private capacities that mattered. He had none. Every-

thing he possessed belonged to God, and he could rest in that fact.

When this became a conviction in Herbert's mind he cast it into poetry. He named the poem "Aaron" after the first high priest in the Bible, and he shaped it into five stanzas of five lines each to correspond to the five letters of Aaron's name. The same rhyming words are repeated in all the stanzas, and the lines swing back and forth with an extraordinary effect like the sound of bells.

Herbert opens the poem by describing the perfect priest.

> Holiness on the head,
> Light and perfections on the breast,
> Harmonious bells below, raising the dead
> To lead them unto life and rest:
> Thus are true Aarons dressed.

He himself possesses no such brightness and can produce no such harmony; "defects and darkness" are all he owns. But in Christ he is newborn and newly dressed, possessing a holiness that is not his. As such he is fit for the priesthood, and the poem curves to its sudden, delighted conclusion in the last line.

> Come, people; Aaron's dressed.

According to Walton, Herbert did not make up his own mind on the subject. Walton's theory is that he went to Wilton House, still undecided, to thank the Earl of Pembroke for his offer and that Bishop Laud was there with the King. "The Earl acquainted Dr. Laud, then Bishop of London and after Archbishop of Canterbury, with his kinsman's irresolution. And the Bishop did the next day so convince Mr. Herbert, that the refusal of it was a sin, that a tailor was sent for to come speedily from Salisbury to Wilton, to take measure, and make him canonical clothes against next day; which the tailor did: and Mr. Herbert being so habited, went with his presentation to the learned Dr. Davenant, who was then Bishop of Salisbury, and he gave him institution immediately."

There are several difficulties with Walton's picturesque story. King Charles was almost certainly not visiting Wilton at this date. Nor would Laud have been there without him, since the Bishop and the Earl were on bad terms over a position at Oxford they both wanted. Nor is it true that Herbert was instituted immediately. The deed of presentation that made him a rector is dated from Westminster on April 16, 1630, and it was ten days later that he appeared before Dr. Davenant to be instituted.

Herbert's bishop, John Davenant, was a fellow graduate of Cambridge and had been preferred for his present post by Herbert's friend, John Williams. He was a gentle, scholarly man, and abnormally scrupulous even for that era of intent consciences. He once was late for an appointment with King James because he considered it a sin to travel on Sunday, and when he lay dying "he thanked God for this His fatherly correction, because in all his lifetime he never had one heavy affliction, which made him often much suspect with himself, whether he was a true child of God or no, until this his last sickness."

George Herbert appeared before this most scrupulous of bishops in Salisbury Cathedral on the twenty-sixth of April, 1630. He could not legally be ordained a priest until the next Ember week, and Bishop Davenant did not perform this ceremony until the nineteenth of September. But since Herbert was already a deacon he could function in most of the church offices, and on the same April day he was instituted at Salisbury he was inducted as rector in his own church of Bemerton about a mile away. Herbert was rector of three parishes—Fugglestone, Quidhampton and Bemerton—and of two churches. But the larger church of Fugglestone St. Peter was to be served by a curate while Herbert conducted services in the little church of Bemerton St. Andrew next door to the rectory.

When a new minister was inducted, it was the parish custom to lay his hand on the key of his church or the ring of his church door. Then the bell rope was put into his possession, and when he tolled the bell the congregation knew that he had come into his own. The bell at Bemerton was an old one—one of those called Alphabet bells—and Herbert's friends waited outside a long time to hear it ring. Finally one of their number, a man named Arthur Woodnoth, went to the window to see what was causing the delay and saw Herbert lying at full length before the altar.

He later told Woodnoth that he had been making "rules to himself for the future manage of his life." He did not need to rededicate himself to the service of God, for he had never left it. But as rector of Bemerton he was embarking on a wholly new way of life, exchanging his silks and his sword for the sober black of a country parson, and George Herbert, aristocrat, could exist no longer.

For some time Herbert had been doubtful of the value of birth and breeding. He had come a long way from the young man at Cambridge who put "too great value on his parts and parentage," and poem after poem reflects his gathering conviction that place and prestige have no relation to Christianity. But it is one thing to hold a conviction in theory and quite another to make it a reality. Herbert was able to achieve this by throwing his intensity into an entirely new channel, where his pride of family, his self-will and his love of the world ceased to have any control over him.

When Herbert preached his first sermon at Bemerton, he did it in the fashion in which he had been trained. He had devoted many years to the study of rhetoric, and all his skill went into a sermon that was filled "with great learning and eloquence." He never did it again. From that time forward he spoke to his congregation in a way they could understand, and the man of learning ceased to exist as far as Bemerton was concerned.

Herbert wrote a little book in which he described the behavior of the ideal country parson, chiefly because his orderly mind wanted to set down on paper a "mark to aim at." He called it *A Priest to the Temple, or, the Country Parson* (it was later published and sold for twelvepence) and the title reflects the combination of spiritual intensity and practical good sense with which Herbert approached the problems of his new life.

George Herbert had always been attracted to common things, and the man who used watering pots and puns in his religious poetry was not likely to show any condescension in dealing with country matters. On the contrary, he was convinced that the more a parson knew about farming the better, since a good teacher could make "great use" of such images when he was speaking to the people about God.[1]

Herbert was a realist, and he knew that his congregation was likely to be more interested in weather and crops than in its relationship to God. As John Earle, later Bishop of Salisbury, remarked of the English farmer, "He is capable only of two prayers, for rain and fair weather . . . and thinks Noah's flood the greatest plague that ever was, not because it drowned the world, but spoiled the grass." Herbert knew that country people led a hard life and he did not expect too much from them. He felt that the rule of no farm work on Sunday should have exceptions "in the cases of extreme poverty, and in the seasons of seedtime and harvest." He believed that the best time to visit the members of his congregation was on weekdays, when they had doffed their Sunday clothes and their careful Sunday deportment, and although he hated the stench in the cottages he let it make no difference to him; for "God is there also." He knew that if he invited a cottager to dinner he would have to make sure that everyone else in the congregation got an invitation later, "because country people are very observant of such things." He knew the difficulty faced by the churchwardens, who were

---

[1] Herbert's pleasure in common things is especially evident in a collection of folk sayings that he gathered together and called *Outlandish Proverbs*. He used the adjective in its older meaning of "foreign," and while most of his proverbs come from abroad they are the kind that any Wiltshire farmer would have grinned over. "Love and a cough cannot be hid." "Every path hath a puddle." "He that lies with the dogs, riseth with fleas." "The eye is bigger than the belly." "Better a snotty child, than his nose wiped off." A man who enjoyed and collected such proverbs as these would have had no difficulty in dealing with a rural congregation.

responsible for parish discipline, if some important gentleman
arrived late to services. In such cases, if "the poor churchwardens
be affrighted" and unable to do their duty, the parson must do
it himself.

What shows most clearly throughout the book is Herbert's
courtesy of mind. As he himself said, "He that will be respected,
must respect." Herbert respected everyone in his congregation,
and he did not share the common notion that religion must be
cheapened in order to be understood by country folk. He took
a vital interest in the catechism, which was usually a gabbled
question-and-answer, and would vary the wording of the questions with all the excitement of a good teacher, "helping and
cherishing the answerer, by making the question very plain."
Like Socrates, he believed "that the seeds of all truths lay in
everybody," and he worked devotedly to encourage the people
of his parish to think for themselves. He had the wisdom to bring
in analogies from ditch digging or plowing, and to use "stories
and sayings," and he knew how to make things easier by the
gift of laughter.

There was a gentleness in Herbert now that could not be
shaken. He mentions the possibility that there may be Puritans in
the congregation, but there is none of the fury that he once di-
rected at Andrew Melville. Instead, he recommends "a very loving and sweet usage of them, both in going to and sending for
them often, and in finding out courtesies to place on them." He
did not cease to hope for the conversion of both Roman Catholics
and Puritans but he would not try to gain it by contentiousness.
Nor was he capable of frightening his congregation with threats
of damnation, although he admitted that country people are
"thick and heavy . . . and need a mountain of fire to kindle
them." He gives one brief line in his handbook to God's judgment but he gives twenty to the certainty of God's love for His
creation. The reasons he gives are born of Herbert's own conviction and are those of a poet both in their logic and their eloquence: "for no perfect Artist ever yet hated His own work."

Since he had come to a small rural congregation at a time when the ritual of the Church of England was still comparatively unfamiliar, Herbert did not try to impose a meaningless ritual upon his people. He wanted them to "pray with understanding," and he explained each step so that the dullest could comprehend. He taught them the reasons for feast days and fast days, for Twelfth Day and Good Friday and Whitsunday. He explained the reason for the prayers of the congregation, for the repetition of the Creed, for the hymns to be sung after the first and second lessons. These were all second nature to Herbert himself, bred in the bone and almost a part of his breathing, but he would not impose a mindless obedience upon his congregation. Like a good teacher, he always gave the reason why.

He had for his assistance the beautiful rhythms of the Book of Common Prayer, and he might have taken for his text the collect for the first Sunday in Advent. "Almighty God, give us grace that we may cast away the works of darkness, and put upon us the armour of light." It was grace and light that Herbert sought for his congregation, and he went about it with a saint's devotion and a poet's skill.

He had also for his assistance the fact that his people were countrymen and had their own yearly rhythm of seedtime and harvest. He could by analogy swing them into the greater rhythm of the Christian year, "because people by what they understand, are best led to what they understand not." His little church mirrored the passing of the seasons and the recurrence of the religious festivals; and although neither the canons nor the Prayer Book recommended it, Herbert held to the old fashion that each church should be "at great festivals strewed, and stuck with boughs"—holly and ivy at Christmastime, palm and box on Palm Sunday, roses on Ascension Day, the herb named woodruff on Corpus Christi day, and birch boughs at midsummer.

Herbert's profound sense of the meaning of the holy days is reflected above all in his poetry. Poems like "Christmas" and "Easter," "Good Friday" and "Trinity Sunday," are not conven-

tional repetitions of someone else's meditations but a deeply felt
and personal reliving of the meaning of such days. His "Whitsunday," written for the festival that celebrates the descent of
the Holy Spirit at Pentecost, is an expression of longing for the
light that once shone on the Apostles and a prayer that it will
shine again.

> Lord, though we change, Thou art the same;
> The same sweet God of love and light:
> Restore this day, for Thy great name,
> Unto his ancient and miraculous right.

At Pentecost the Apostles were given the gift of tongues and each
listener heard them "in his own language." In his own small way,
Herbert achieved the same thing; and the Cambridge scholar,
through love, was able to speak to the people of Bemerton in a
way they could hear and understand.

After George Herbert died, his brother Edward reported that
he was remembered in the countryside around Bemerton as
"little less than sainted," and it seems to be true that he was able
to bring the people of his congregation, by the light of his own
example, to a sense of service to God. He himself, and all his
household, prayed twice each day in the little church, and the
people working in the fields "did so love and reverence Mr. Herbert, that they would let their plough rest when Mr. Herbert's
saint's bell rung to prayers, that they might also offer their devo-
tions to God with him; and would then return back to their
plough."

Some of Herbert's contemporaries felt that he had not used his
talents and training wisely when he accepted an offer like Bemerton and devoted the rest of his short life to an attempt to bring
a few cottagers to God. As Barnabas Oley said, "I have heard
sober men censure him as a man that did not manage his brave
parts to his best advantage and preferment, but lost himself in
an humble way. That was the phrase, I well remember it." A
parson's life was no trade for a learned and cultivated man. It
was poorly paid work in a very limited sphere, and burdened

by the contempt which most men feel for anything that carries with it neither social authority nor money. As Sir Benjamin Rudyard put it during a speech in the House of Commons, "Though the calling of ministers be never so glorious within, yet outward poverty will bring contempt upon them, especially among those who measure men by the acre and weigh them by the pound."

Few Englishmen were as wise as Sir Thomas Fairfax, father of one of Herbert's closest friends at Trinity College. When he learned that his son Henry wanted to become a country parson he gave that promising and well-educated young man his complete approval and called it "the happiest profession that can be. All other services be bondage, but this is perfect freedom."

George Herbert echoed the wording of his friend's father when he himself, many years later, followed the footsteps of Henry Fairfax into the service of God—"in Whose service I have now found perfect freedom." For Herbert had not lost himself when he became a minister. He had found himself, and since he possessed an acute and highly self-analytical mind he knew it very well. It was in the previous years that he had been lost, wandering in the labyrinth of his own mind and struggling in the confusion of his own ways—

> My crooked, winding ways, wherein I live,
> Wherein I die, not live: for life is straight,
> Straight as a line, and ever tends to Thee . . .

John Donne made the same point in one of his sermons. "Upon this earth a man cannot possibly make one step in a straight and direct line. The earth itself being round, every step we make upon it must necessarily be a segment, an arch of a circle. . . . To God Himself we may always go in a direct line, a straight, a perpendicular line." It was this straight line that Herbert finally found, and when he found it he was at peace.

No doubt he could have spared himself a great deal if he had entered the church direct from Cambridge. With his birth, his

talents and his court connections, he would have been a bishop
at least, and perhaps a bishop as rich, as gentle and as kind as
Lancelot Andrewes. He would never have known the long years
of mental struggle and recurrent defeat. On the other hand,
neither would he have acquired the strength that came with
them. As he himself said, "Fractures well cured make us more
strong." In the end the pattern of his life achieved a perfect
shape, one that would not necessarily have been right for any
other man in England but that was precisely right for George
Herbert.

Again he was able to record it in his poetry. He had once
described, in the poem he called "Employment," the winter chill
of uselessness. Now he had found employment at last, and in a
poem called "The Flower" he records the coming of warmth.

> Grief melts away
> Like snow in May,
> As if there were no such cold thing.

The poem continues with a meditation on the flower that grows
in Paradise and Herbert admits that there is no assurance against
frost on earth. Nevertheless the poem as a whole gives an impression of the most moving delight.

> Who would have thought my shrivell'd heart
> Could have recovered greenness? It was gone
> Quite underground; as flowers depart
> To see their mother-root, when they have blown;
> Where they together
> All the hard weather
> Dead to the world, keep house unknown.

> These are Thy wonders, Lord of power,
> Killing and quick'ning, bringing down to hell
> And up to heaven in an hour;
> Making a chiming of a passing-bell.
> We say amiss,
> This or that is:
> Thy word is all, if we could spell . . .

And now in age I bud again,
After so many deaths I live and write;
I once more smell the dew and rain,
And relish versing: O my only light,
It cannot be
That I am he
On whom Thy tempests fell all night.

CHAPTER THIRTEEN

THE NEW MINISTER AT BEMERTON WAS FORTUNATE IN HAVING A wife as loving and as concerned with the welfare of the congregation as he was himself. Jane Herbert could not leave Baynton House for her new home until the rectory had been repaired, but her husband brought her accounts of the parishioners he had met. The first of these was an old woman, stricken with poverty and burdened with many troubles, and Jane at once made the trip to Salisbury, about twenty miles away, to buy her a pair of blankets. She sent them to the old woman with a message that they were "a token of her love" and that the two of them would become acquainted as soon as she could move into the rectory at Bemerton.

Not many women could have endured with grace the change from the easy living of Baynton House to the rigid requirements of a small country parish. George Herbert had warned his wife that his new profession was held in "general ignominy," but Jane Herbert seems to have been one of those delightful women, rare in the seventeenth century, who had very little sense of social degrees. She could love an old woman who needed blankets just as easily as she could love any of her illustrious Danvers cousins. She was loved, naturally enough, in return by her husband's congregation, and "this love followed her in all places as inseparably as shadows follow substances in sunshine."

With such a nature, Jane Herbert would have had no difficulty in learning one of the basic skills of her new life—the art of healing. Any woman of the period with a household of her own had to have some knowledge of it, but a minister's wife served the needs of the whole community. Twice in his handbook on the duties of a parson, Herbert emphasizes the fact that a parson's

134

wife must have skill in the "curing and healing of all wounds and sores." He made his wife a "good garden" at Bemerton, sloping down to the little river that ran through his grounds, and in that or in the surrounding fields would grow the herbs she needed—valerian and yarrow and St. John's wort for salve, camomile and mallow for poultices. If Jane lacked recipes she borrowed them from the Ferrar household in Little Gidding, and in the autumn of 1631 she made a special request for their famous balsam recipe since she had the oil of elder already.

Another service that Jane Herbert performed for her husband was in the distribution of alms. His congregation paid him a tenth of their earnings as tithes, and Herbert put aside the same percentage of what he received. Every tenth measure of corn in his barn and every tenth penny was handed over to his wife to distribute as she thought best. Most of it went into blankets and shoes, and Jane's chief regret was that she did not have more to spend in that fashion.

Herbert's finances were not in a prosperous state, since he had been obliged to put two hundred pounds into repairs for the two churches and the rectory, but he and his wife both had a clear idea of the proper use of their money. On one occasion he was reproved by a friend for giving so much to the poor instead of saving his money for possible heirs. But he had made sure that his wife was financially protected if he died, and he refused to believe he could harm his family by generosity. As he says of his ideal parson: "He resolves with himself never to omit any present good deed of charity, in consideration of providing a stock for his children; but assures himself, that money thus lent to God, is placed surer for his children's advantage, than if it were given to the Chamber of London." He also said that it was better "to be charitable than wise," and he was fortunate in having a wife who agreed with him.

Herbert's endearing combination of generosity and common sense can be illustrated in the case of his three orphaned nieces. They were the daughters of his younger sister Margaret, who

had married into the Vaughan family, and their names were
Dorothy, Magdalen and Catharine. When their widowed mother
died and was buried among her ancestors in Montgomery, the
estate passed to the nearest male relative and the three girls
were left to the rather haphazard care of their uncle Edward.
Edward Herbert was not a domestic man, although his daughter
Beatrice apparently did what she could for them, and as soon as
his brother George had a home of his own Edward offered him
one of the girls.

George Herbert did not take the view that his three nieces
were inconvenient pieces of furniture, to be passed around to
anyone who had a place for them. They were young and lonely
human beings, and if one of them came to his house to live she
would have no one of her own age for company. So he offered
to take two of the girls, although he could not really afford it,
and Margaret's two older daughters came to live with him at
Bemerton.

The problem of the third and youngest niece remained. The
obvious person to take her into his home was her uncle Henry,
who had a handsome manor house, plenty of money and two
small daughters of his own. Sir Henry Herbert apparently wished
to be obliging; but he was a man of sound business instincts
and he wrote his brother George that in his opinion one could
expect nothing but "unthankfulness" from young relatives who
were taken into the household. So George Herbert, whose funds
were infinitesimal in comparison with either Edward's or Henry's,
took all three of Margaret's girls into the rectory at Bemerton
and managed to stretch his income to cover them all.

He showed the same sort of loving consideration to his servants and wrote an unusually sharp criticism of the people who
feel free to treat a servant like a piece of wood as long as they
pay his wages. There were six servants at Bemerton in the end:
Elizabeth, who was evidently the oldest and most valued, Margaret, Ann, Sara, William and John. The women helped run
what had become a fairly large household while the men did

the work outdoors. The Bemerton parson had his own orchard, yard and barn, and he farmed his double strip of the common land like any member of his congregation. Herbert's attitude towards pigs and chickens was one of respectful admiration that the Lord had arranged to have them eat what was "unuseful to man"; but he had no real knowledge of farming, and John and William must have been a necessity.

For help in running his little church he probably had the usual services of a clerk and a sexton, the clerk to ring the bell and lead the congregation and help with the sacraments, the sexton to light the fires and keep the church clean. Herbert himself was in the church so constantly that it was almost a second home, and even its furniture was holy to him and full of meaning. The outward form was the visible shaping of an inward spirit, and everything within the building spoke to him of the presence of God. In the same way that he wrote poems about Easter and Trinity Sunday, he wrote poems about the church key, the church floor and the church windows, and now that he had a church of his own he cared for its outer fabric reverently.

He also wrote a poem on church music, which had always been one of his greatest joys. The little church at Bemerton was apparently too small for a choir and too poor for an organ, but Herbert was not accustomed to living without church music, which he called his "heaven upon earth." A mile away across the meadows from his garden he could see the beautiful spire of Salisbury Cathedral; and twice a week he would leave the church services in the care of Nathaniel Bostock, his curate, and walk over to the city to hear music.

Salisbury Cathedral had always had high musical standards, and in the Middle Ages the chief function of its vicars had been to sing the services. When the supply of vicars was reduced by the Reformation, a system of lay vicars was introduced to supplement the voices of the blue-robed choristers, and they constituted a magnificent balance of tenors, basses and counter-tenors to match the architectural glory of the Cathedral itself.

The lay vicars were men of high musical standing. There were seven of them, including the organist and the teacher of the choristers, and they were known as the singing men of Sarum.[1]

After George Herbert had attended services in the Cathedral, it was his custom to go to a "music-meeting" in the city. He and some of his friends gathered together with their viols and lutes to perform in one of those contented and dedicated amateur ensembles that were filling all England with their music. Once he arrived at a meeting in a very dishevelled state because of an encounter he had had, and Walton tells the story with his usual gentle eloquence.

> He saw a poor man with a poorer horse, that was fallen under his load; they were both in distress, and needed present help, which Mr. Herbert perceiving, put off his canonical coat, and helped the poor man to unload, and after, to load his horse. The poor man blessed him for it, and he blessed the poor man; and was so like the good Samaritan, that he gave him money to refresh both himself and his horse; and told him, "That if he loved himself, he should be merciful to his beast." Thus he left the poor man, and at his coming to his musical friends in Salisbury, they began to wonder that Mr. George Herbert, who used to be so trim and clean, came into that company so soiled and discomposed; but he told them the occasion: and when one of the company told him, "He had disparaged himself by so dirty an employment," his answer was, "That the thought of what he had done would prove music to him at midnight; and that the omission of it would have upbraided and made discord in his conscience whensoever he should pass by that place; for if I am bound to pray for all that be in distress, I am sure that I am bound, so far as it is in my power, to practice what I pray for. . . . And now let us tune our instruments."

---

[1] Sarum was the name of the city in which the cathedral had once stood. A spirited bishop of the thirteenth century disliked the location and built a new cathedral in a meadow a mile and a half away, working with such speed that the building was consecrated only five years after the foundations were laid. A new city, whose name was Salisbury, grew up around the beautiful structure, and the old name of Sarum survived only for the Cathedral itself.

At an equal distance from Bemerton, but west instead of east, lay the great estate of the Earls of Pembroke. Wilton House had acquired a new owner just before Herbert came to Bemerton, for the easygoing and literary William Herbert died suddenly on the tenth of April and was buried in the family vault in Salisbury Cathedral. The new Earl of Pembroke was his younger brother Philip, who was chiefly noted for his interest in sports and his savage temper.

John Aubrey, that most engaging and unreliable of gossips, says that Philip made George Herbert his chaplain. It is true that he was entitled to several chaplains in his household (a duke was allowed six, an earl five and so on) but it is not likely that so conscientious a man as George Herbert would take on additional duties which he had neither the time nor the strength to perform. If he served as chaplain at Wilton House, it was probably only in the informal sense of a friend and adviser in holy orders. John Donne, for instance, was never officially in Sir Edward Herbert's service, but the day he took holy orders he signed his letter to Edward "your very humble chaplain."

George Herbert had a close relationship with Wilton House, but it was not so much with the Earl as with his devout and lonely new wife. Anne Clifford, the new Countess of Pembroke, was forty years old when Herbert knew her and had taken Philip for her second husband a month and a half after Herbert came to Bemerton. The talent she later showed as a builder and administrator was still dammed up within her and she spent her second marriage as she had spent her first, mostly in restless retirement on her husbands' great estates while they amused themselves betting in London. The Earl of Pembroke was no real improvement on the Earl of Dorset, and Anne was as unhappy at Wilton House as she had been at Knole. "I gave myself wholly to retiredness, as much as I could in both these great families, and made good books and virtuous thoughts my companions."

When Herbert knew her she was a short, dark, bright-eyed,

middle-aged woman whose wide reading had carried her from
Turkish history to Montaigne. She had reared the first monument
to Edmund Spenser, Samuel Daniel had been her tutor, and
her alert and civilized mind found a special comfort in the Bible.
Since she was an ardent member of the Church of England, she
was fortunate in having so devoted a minister as George Herbert close at hand. She was at court during the Christmas season
of 1631, and he sent her a note that had a special kindness in it.
For it mentioned her mother, the Dowager Countess of Cumber-
land, who had died fifteen years earlier to her daughter's "un-
speakable grief" and who still remained "my dear and blessed
mother" in her prayers. Herbert said that his letter was not
written in the court style, which may have been true; but it had
something better in its real, imaginative thoughtfulness.

About fifteen miles north of Wilton House was the country
estate of Herbert's stepfather, Sir John Danvers. After Magdalen's death he had married Elizabeth Dauntsey, daughter of
Ambrose Dauntsey of West Lavington, and he laid out in the
estate she inherited an Italian garden even more elaborate than
the one he had in Chelsea. It lay about five miles east of Baynton House, where Jane Herbert's mother and her unmarried
sisters were living, and to the north was his elder brother's
estate at Dauntsey. George Herbert had friends and relatives
all over Wiltshire, to say nothing of the "many gentlemen in the
neighborhood" who visited the little church at Bemerton because
Mr. Herbert was there.

The man he loved the best he never saw. This was Nicholas
Ferrar, who would not leave his retreat at Little Gidding. At one
time Herbert was thinking seriously of exchanging his benefice
at Bemerton for one "nearer to his dear brother," even though
it would have meant a smaller income, but he died before the
plan could be carried out. The two men did not see each other,
but they tried to make up for the separation by exchanging "loving and endearing letters."

Ferrar was a brilliant executive and he had succeeded in

transforming Little Gidding into so efficient a unit of praise that it was drawing throngs of respectful visitors. Everything that Herbert tried to do at Bemerton was achieved brilliantly at Little Gidding. Ferrar had divided the work among the various members of the household so that the teaching of the young, the curing of the sick, the making of music and all the other tasks of a Christian community were shared among those most skilled to perform them.

Ferrar even worked out a system by which God could be praised continually. In Lincoln Cathedral it was the duty of the cathedral chapter to recite the whole Book of Psalms every twenty-four hours, and Ferrar achieved the same thing at Little Gidding by a system of night watches that the members of the household observed in rotation. He did not put the plan into effect until he had first made sure that no one's health would be endangered by lack of sleep, and one of the men whose advice he asked on the project was that of "Mr. George Herbert, his most entire friend and brother."

Herbert himself was still a member of the cathedral chapter at Lincoln and reciting his own share of the Book of Psalms daily. Nor had he forgotten his plan of restoring the church at Leighton Bromswold. It had evidently not been easy to raise the money, but by the spring of 1632 enough had been gathered so that building operations could begin.[2]

Herbert was not in a position to come north and supervise the work on the church, but Nicholas Ferrar lived only a few miles from Leighton Bromswold and was prepared to plan the design and oversee the workmen. He went at the task with his usual efficiency. By July he had eighteen masons at work, with ten carpenters due to follow, and by October it was completed,

---

[2] Sir Henry Herbert was a great help to his brother in this. He approached both the Earl of Bolingbroke and the Earl of Manchester, and he persuaded the Duchess of Lennox to contribute a hundred pounds. Her son was lord of the manor at Leighton Bromswold, and later on he added a steeple to the church as his memorial to George Herbert.

a trim church, newly roofed, with the furnishings very like those at Little Gidding.

Nicholas had an adoring older brother, John, who took over the responsibility for supplying the materials and making a day-to-day supervision of the workmen; and their equally devoted first cousin, Arthur Woodnoth, kept track of expenditures. It was Woodnoth who accompanied George Herbert to Bemerton the day he was inducted, and he made another trip to Wiltshire the following year.

Arthur Woodnoth seems to have been an amicable, rather self-centered individual who leaned heavily on both his saintly friends. He was vaguely considering the idea of leaving his goldsmith business in London and entering the service of Sir John Danvers, apparently as some kind of an informal chaplain. But he could not make up his mind on the subject and he hoped that either Ferrar or Herbert would do it for him. When he visited Herbert in the autumn of 1631 he spent a long time explaining his problem, and Herbert took the trouble to sit up that night and write out a paper to give him in the morning. It was neatly entitled "Reasons for Arthur Woodnoth's living with Sir John Danvers," and Herbert in his orderly way had divided it into seven sections.

On the same day the two of them went over to Wilton House, and while Herbert spent an hour with the Countess of Pembroke, Woodnoth used his solitude to brood further over his problem. He also asked Herbert's advice about getting married, but when he finally proposed to Ferrar's niece, Nan Collett, she would not have him. Herbert was evidently fond of Woodnoth, both for his own sake and as a link with Little Gidding, and there was always a room ready for him when he came to Bemerton.

When Herbert wrote letters to Ferrar he addressed him as "my exceeding dear brother," and even in minor matters their interests were very close. Both of them, for instance, were firm believers in the importance of diet and they were jointly responsible for a little book on hygiene that was translated from the Latin. Herbert's contribution was his translation of a treatise on temperance written by a lively Italian of the preceding century. Luigi Cornaro had ceased to eat such things as sausages and pie crust and cake, and therefore at eighty-three he was climbing hills, composing a comedy and singing in a clearer voice than ever he had in his youth. His little treatise is a rather exuberant study of "the power of order and disorder" in the physical realm, and since Herbert was so firmly on the side of order Cornaro's book seemed worth translating.

Nicholas Ferrar started a translation of his own early in 1632 and as soon as he had finished it he sent it to Herbert, his "most precious friend," for an opinion. It had been written by the Roman Catholic humanist, Juan de Valdes, and Herbert marvelled that anyone "in the midst of popery should . . . understand and express so clearly and excellently the intent of the Gospel." Herbert was ill when the manuscript arrived; but he read it with great care and made long notes wherever he disagreed, his most frequent objection being the Protestant one that the author had "too slight a regard for the Scripture."

Herbert wrote these annotations at the end of September in 1632, less than six months before his own death and at about the time that his eldest niece, Dorothy Vaughan, died at Bemerton. Yet he took the same care with Ferrar's manuscript that he did with everything else, from Woodnoth's personal dilemmas to the services of his church.

He was only thirty-nine but his hair was beginning to turn white. He wrote a poem on the subject, a singularly beautiful one, which he called "The Forerunners." He begins with the image of the harbingers, the royal servants who requisition lodgings and chalk the doors behind them as a sign they have passed that way.

> The harbingers are come. See, see their mark;
> White is their colour, and behold my head.

They may take everything from him—his brain and his cleverness

—but they will nevertheless leave him his "best room," his heart. In this poem Herbert bids farewell to his skill in words, the skill he had once wished to turn to God's service.

> Farewell sweet phrases, lovely metaphors . . .
> Lovely enchanting language, sugar-cane . . .

Nothing is left in his possession except the bare statement, "Thou art still my God." But he is content to let the embellishments go, even that "honey of roses" which the English language is to him, and the poem closes with a perfect willingness to leave all such things behind.

> Go birds of spring: let winter have his fee;
> Let a bleak paleness chalk the door,
> So all within be livelier than before.

The poem in which Herbert claims to have left metaphors behind is in itself a most beautiful and sustained metaphor, but that is only to say that the more Herbert gave up the more he received. He left nothing of value behind when he came to Bemerton, and the straitened existence there was a glorious one for him.

Herbert's favorite term for himself was an adaptation of a phrase that Jacob had used, with perhaps only momentary conviction, on the bank of the river Jordan: "I am not worthy of the least of all the mercies . . . which Thou hast shewed unto Thy servant." Nicholas Ferrar says that Herbert adapted this for "his own motto, with which he used to conclude all things that might seem to tend any way to his own honour: *Less than the least of God's mercies.*" It was the custom in the seventeenth century to use little personal slogans called "posies" which were engraved in rings or on fruit trenchers or even on window panes, and Herbert wrote almost a lover's verse to announce his own choice.

> Let wits contest,
> And with their words and posies windows fill:
> *Less than the least*
> *Of all Thy mercies,* is my posy still.

John Donne once preached a sermon on this statement of Jacob's and remarked that "a disclaiming of merit" is the basis of all true prayer. Donne's sermons and Herbert's poems often parallel each other, since they both draw on the stock of ideas that was the normal equipment of a seventeenth-century Christian. The last sermon that Donne preached is an exact echo of one of Herbert's poems, in which life is described as a series of deaths from the time the baby is wrapped in its clout like a little winding sheet. The chief difference is that Donne goes even further back for his analogy, back to the womb itself, and the sermon has a dark, terrifying magnificence that is no part of Herbert's poem.

When Donne preached this sermon he was openly dying, and the fashionable Whitehall audience that looked at his ravaged face knew that he had preached his own funeral sermon. Two months earlier he made his will, leaving one of the paintings in his large house to his "honorable friend Sir John Danvers." He also gave memorial seals to some of his closest friends, made of bloodstone and engraved with the design of Christ crucified on an anchor. He sent one to George Herbert, and Herbert kept it wrapped in the paper on which he had written some verses on the gift.

Donne died on the last day of March, 1631, with the same almost theatrical tension with which he had lived. He posed for his portrait in his winding sheet, naked except for the sheet tied in knots at his head and feet and with his skull-like head turned towards the East as the painter worked. He kept the picture beside him for the fifteen days until he died and left instructions that it was to be carved in white marble as his memorial. For Donne met death with the same intensity he had met life and wasted no part of the experience.

Two years later Herbert's own time of dying came, and he accepted it without Donne's bravura magnificence but with the quiet lack of fear that shows in his poetry. He tried to conduct the church services as he grew weaker, until his wife persuaded

him to let his curate do the work, and then he was finally obliged
to have a second curate also. Herbert had known much pain in
his short life, and as a good Christian he had never rebelled
against it. As he said in one of the five poems he named "Affliction,"

> We are the trees, whom shaking fastens more . . .

and in his last illness he remained unshaken.

A friend of Nicholas Ferrar's came to see him, to get firsthand
news for Little Gidding, and Edmund Duncon could still remember, forty years later, how deeply the dying man had impressed him. Jane Herbert gave the visitor supper and a room,
and when he came back five days later Herbert had a "little
book" to give him. It was the manuscript of his poems and he
sent it to Ferrar with a message—to read it, to publish it if it
would be helpful to anyone, and otherwise to burn it.

On the last Sunday of his life he got up from his bed and
asked for one of his musical instruments. Herbert had always
loved Sunday, because of "the joy of the day," and he could not
do better than to spend some of it in song. He had once written
a poem called "Sunday" and set it to music, and he sang it then:
"Thou art a day of mirth."

When Herbert's distant kinsman, Sir Philip Sidney, lay dying
nearly half a century before, he also had turned to song. The
two men were alike in many ways, in their gentleness, their high
aspirations, their easy, aristocratic grace and the intensity with
which they lived, and each of them turned to music when "the
glory of mortal flesh was shaken."

The following day Herbert wrote his will, which was witnessed by his curate, Nathaniel Bostock, and his servant Elizabeth. He wrote it carefully on two sheets of paper and left
nearly everything, including his books, "unto my dear wife." He
remembered his curates and his servants and left twenty pounds
to the poor of the parish "to be divided according to my dear
wife's discretion." He made Sir John Danvers the overseer of

the will and he made Arthur Woodnoth, who was hovering devotedly around the house, its executor.

On Friday his wife and his two nieces were by his bedside, weeping so bitterly that Herbert asked them to go into the next room if they loved him. Like Sidney, who asked his brother to leave the room, he could not endure their grief. When he was left with Woodnoth and Bostock, he gave Woodnoth his will and asked him to take care of the three women, and Woodnoth, who hated responsibility, agreed. Herbert said, "I am now ready to die." Like his mother he went quietly, "without any apparent disturbance," and the two men beside him closed his eyes.

He died on the first of March, 1633, only one month short of his fortieth birthday, and was buried the following Sunday. It was Shrove Sunday, the first before the holy season of Lent and the funeral took place in his little church at Bemerton. George Herbert was laid in the chancel under the altar, and the services for the dead were performed, as he had requested, by the singing men of Sarum.

CHAPTER FOURTEEN

THE MANUSCRIPT THAT GEORGE HERBERT SENT TO FERRAR AS HE lay dying was not a miscellaneous collection of verses. It was a book, shaped with the same care as the individual poems within it, and when Herbert gave permission to have it burned he was giving up the last and most legitimate of all his prides— the pride of a good workman. He had made the book as perfect as he could; but now he possessed nothing, not even his own poetry.

The book had one value in Herbert's eyes. It was a record of what he had gone through before he found peace, "a picture of the many spiritual conflicts that had passed betwixt God and my soul, before I could subject mine to the will of Jesus my Master, in whose service I have now found perfect peace." If such a record could help anyone else in his own struggle, Herbert was willing to have the book published. But for the rest, he had ceased to care about anything "that might seem to tend any way to his own honour," and he was quite content to leave it to its fate.

This had not always been his intention. He had obviously planned the book for publication and even worked out its basic pattern before he entered the ministry. There is in existence a small manuscript, with corrections in Herbert's own hand, which contains sixty-nine of the poems and the skeleton structure of the final version; and since none of the poems mentions the ministry it seems safe to assume that this manuscript was in existence before he went to Bemerton.

In this earlier version Herbert had already planned the shape his book would take, opening with a rather witty study of Christian behavior called "The Church Porch" and closing with a view of Christian history called "The Church Militant." Also included were the dedication, the rhymed connecting links and the envoi. There were several poems both in Latin and English that he later decided to omit, but the structure was there and a clear pattern of intention.

In the final version this pattern has not been altered. But there are ninety-five more poems, some of them obviously written after he came to Bemerton, and the earlier ones have been revised and rearranged with that passionate concern for order that was so fundamental a part of Herbert's nature. The earlier version had no title, but the final book is called *The Temple* and it is well named.

Herbert possessed almost an architect's sense of structure. It was an expression in poetry of the same quality that made him take the liturgy so seriously—the form shaped by the contents and really a part of it. He reworked *The Temple* as a sculptor will rework clay, shaping and reshaping both the individual poems and the book as a whole until it more nearly satisfied his fastidious ear and his alert heart. The famous opening stanza of "Easter" was good enough in its earlier version to satisfy anyone but Herbert.

> I had prepared many a flower
> To strew Thy way and victory,
> But Thou wast up before mine hour,
> Bringing Thy sweets along with Thee.

But Herbert was not content, and he reworked the lines until they reached their present form.

> I got me flowers to strew Thy way;
> I got me boughs off many a tree:
> But Thou wast up by break of day,
> And brought'st Thy sweets along with Thee.

If Herbert had been given a longer life, he would probably have worked further on his book. Not everything in it could have satisfied him. But he had to leave it now that he lay dying, and he turned it over to Edmund Duncon with no further thought for its welfare.

Duncon brought the manuscript back to Little Gidding, and Nicholas Ferrar read it with profound excitement. His brother says that it was "many and many a time read over, and embraced and kissed again and again." The next step was to get it published, and Ferrar set about this with his usual efficient vigor. The copy which was prepared for the licensers was almost a work of art in itself, done in expensive paper in folio size, the lines set within a frame ruled in red.

The Temple was to be published at Cambridge, and that meant it had to be licensed by a University board consisting of the Vice-Chancellor and three of the masters. The Vice-Chancellor was Benjamin Lany and he objected strongly to two of Herbert's lines in "The Church Militant."

> Religion stands on tip-toe in our land,
> Ready to pass to the American strand.

Lany felt that the line might give support to the Puritans, who were leaving for New England in large numbers to escape the increasingly rigorous pressure of the bishops, and there was some point to his objection. Two years later a Puritan minister of Ipswich was imprisoned for stating, among other things, that "the Gospel stood on tip-toe, as ready to be gone."

But Nicholas Ferrar was the kind of editor for whom every author longs. He was convinced the book should be published as Herbert wrote it, "without the diminution or addition of a syllable," and he would have no part of it censored. He won his point and the text was licensed, unaltered.

Since the printing was done by the University press it came under the direct and benevolent supervision of Thomas Buck. Buck was a Cambridge graduate who became a fellow the same year as Herbert, and when he was appointed University printer in 1625 there was an immediate improvement in both the quality and the quantity of the Cambridge books. His business partner was inclined to feel that Mr. Buck was "inexperienced, having led a student's life." But he had a student's respect for the written word, and he was determined to produce as accurate and as handsome a printed text as his press could achieve.

Buck and Ferrar saw eye to eye on *The Temple* and the work was done with the most loving care. If there were any errors in the first edition they were corrected in the next, and when the fifth edition was being prepared for the press it was checked against the manuscript copy to make sure that it was as perfect as possible. Buck was almost as scrupulous and orderly as Herbert himself, and even Ferrar's high standards were satisfied.

The two men worked with such speed that there were two editions of *The Temple* in print the year of Herbert's death. Most of the books went into the London market as edition followed edition, and Walton reports that at the time of his writing there were twenty thousand copies in print.

The success of the book was almost inevitable. It concerned a subject—man's relationship to God—about which Englishmen cared deeply, and it was written with an honesty that spoke to the heart. Most of its readers were probably not interested in poetry. Some of them by that time were in direct conflict with the Church that Herbert loved. But a Presbyterian like Thomas Hall, with only five books of poetry in his large library, counted *The Temple* among them, for Herbert spoke from a level of experience on which Christians knew no division.

If this had not been so, Herbert's book would have been ill-suited to the harsh temper of the day. The agony that Hooker had foretold was increasing, the religious controversy was being pursued with heightened bitterness on both sides, and within less than a decade after Herbert's death it culminated in the final agony of civil war. Yet Herbert's little book went on being read by both sides, and King Charles studied the "divine poems" the year before his execution.

Herbert had never ceased to long for peace, with the desire he had expressed so eloquently when he was Public Orator at

Cambridge. When he designed *The Temple* he closed the central section with his final and most beautiful poem on love, and he placed after it the angels' song from the Gospel of Luke.

> Glory be to God on high
> And on earth peace
> Good will towards men.

And then the envoi that closes the whole book repeats the same theme.

> King of glory, king of peace,
> With the one make war to cease;
> With the other bless Thy sheep . . .

A preoccupation with peace had shaped the whole of Herbert's career, first a desire for peace in the world and then a desire for peace within himself. He failed in the first. He never became Secretary of State, he contributed nothing to the peace of England, and no wars ceased on his account.

In the second he was victorious, and by making a record of the battle he won a double victory. For the grave beauty of *The Temple* is triumphant proof that he was able to shape his poetry as perfectly as, in the end, he was able to shape his life.

PART TWO

ROBERT HERRICK

CHAPTER FIFTEEN

G EORGE HERBERT AND ROBERT HERRICK WERE BORN LESS THAN
two years apart and they had several things in common.
Both of them graduated from the University of Cambridge, both
of them became country clergymen in the same year of 1630, and
both of them produced a single book of poems. But the Church
of England needed a wide roof to accommodate two men as unlike as the saintly rector of Bemerton and the somewhat pagan
vicar of Dean Prior.

Like George Herbert, Robert Herrick was born into a large
and closely-knit family, but in his case it was not an aristocratic
one. Herrick came from a middle-class background and his
ancestors were prominent in the business life of Leicester.

Leicester could not claim the dignity of being called a city
since it did not have a cathedral. But it was the richest town in
a large district, supplying goods and services to an area heavily
populated by sheep and cattle raisers. The old part of town stood
behind a circular wall that still followed the Roman pattern,
with room for the gardens and orchards of well-to-do people like
the Herricks. The poorer families huddled in the crowded
suburbs outside the east gate, for even a wealthy market community like Leicester knew something of the poverty that
plagued the inland towns of sixteenth-century England. Yet in
general it was a prosperous place, with two weekly markets and
four annual fairs, and generations of Herricks flourished within
its walls.

Most English communities knew how to enjoy themselves, and
Leicester was especially skilled in the art. Its company of waits,
with the seal of the borough on their badges, might have been
matched in almost any town in England, but very few had the

distinction of owning a public library. It was housed in St. Martin's, the most important parish church in town and the one that the Herricks attended, and in time it acquired rooms of its own in the town hall. Leicester was also devoted to the theatre, and the chamberlains' accounts are full of payments, year after year, to the acting companies that came down from London. Leicester became an increasingly Puritan town but its love of the stage remained undiminished. When Stratford-on-Avon was fining any official who permitted actors in town, the Leicester officials were still expected to make personal donations to all the major companies of visiting actors, of which Shakespeare's was one.

The town was even livelier in the days before the Reformation, when St. George rode in glorious annual pageantry through the streets. And it was also in those days of Henry the Eighth, in the springtime, that the town records delightfully report that the mayor received his gift of "hawthorn budded forth, bean-flowers and a columbine."

It was during the days of Henry the Eighth that Robert Herrick's great-grandfather came to Leicester from the village of Houghton on the Hill about six miles away. He spelled his name Eyrick and came of a substantial family, for he bore a coat of arms. Thomas Eyrick settled down in Leicester, where the spelling of the name gradually changed, and there he established a family whose vigor and industry made them a real power in the community.

His second son, John Herrick, was Robert Herrick's grandfather. John served the town twice as mayor, and he started the family business of ironmongery which flourished in the hands of the Herricks for a hundred years. He married a vigorous, bright-eyed woman named Mary Bond and they had a long and happy life together. When John died in 1589 and was buried in the Herrick chapel of St. Martin's church, it was the first death in the household during their fifty-two years of married life. Mary Herrick herself lived to be ninety-seven, and she "did see

before her departure of her children and children's children and
their children to the number of 142."

The eldest son of John and Mary was named Robert. His
nephew the poet was named after him and became his godson,
so that the relationship between them was probably close. This
Robert Herrick was an even more distinguished citizen of Leicester than his father had been, for he represented the town in
Parliament and served three times as its mayor. His second term
of service fell during the bitter plague year of 1593, and he drove
himself into debt trying to help the tragic poor of Leicester.

The family business of ironmongery prospered under Robert's
skillful guidance, partly because he enjoyed it so thoroughly. A
charming letter he wrote near the end of his happy life describes
a business trip he had just taken. It was "a pleasant journey . . .
for him that hath got most of his wealth for this fifty years . . .
that way; and now find as good iron as was there this forty year,
as good weight, as good workmen, as honest fellows, as good
entertainment." He had heard "in the pleasant woods of Cank
. . . the sweet birds sing, the hammers go," and all of it made
music to him.

Herrick's uncle Robert enjoyed work days and feast days with
equal enthusiasm. For forty-seven years he celebrated St.
Stephen's Day with feasting and music and "as many guests as
my house would hold," and although the official portrait of
Alderman Robert Herrick looks sober enough, with his long
beard and his black cap, he could be gay in private. The will
of that successful businessman lists his playing-tables and pic-
tures, his virginals and cittern, his silk stockings and wrought
velvet breeches, as well as that characteristic object of a class-
conscious age, the gilt bowl with his grandfather's arms upon it.

The second son of John and Mary Herrick was named Nicholas, and he was the poet's father. Nicholas also was interested
in metals but he wished to become a goldsmith, a luxury trade
for which there was no market in Leicester. So Nicholas Herrick
went to London, the first of his family to go there, and a stream

of letters back and forth between London and Leicester testify
to the love that held the family together.

Nicholas became an apprentice in the Goldsmiths' Company,
an ancient, rich and powerful organization that could make special demands on the young men who came to it for training.
Even in the Middle Ages the goldsmiths had refused to accept
candidates who could not read, and there was a property qualification also which attracted the younger sons of country gentlemen into the Company. The standards of the craft were kept
rigorously high, and any article of gold or silver which failed
to win the necessary stamp of approval, the Hall mark, was
broken to pieces by the wardens of the Goldsmiths' Company.

Robert Herrick's father passed his term of apprenticeship successfully, set up in business for himself and became one of the
most prosperous goldsmiths in London. As soon as he could, he
sent for his younger brother William to come and be his apprentice, and the twelve-year-old William was as much missed by
the family in Leicester as his elder brother must have been.
When young William, suddenly grown tall, came home for a
visit, his father wrote a letter of gratitude to Nicholas for sending him; "for your mother and I did long to see him, and so did
his brothers and sisters."

Two of the sisters had gone up to London already and found
themselves husbands there. Probably each of them had gone
originally to keep house for Nicholas, who could not have taken
an apprentice unless he were a householder. Their mother, Mary
Herrick, sent knit hose and jersey gloves to London, the two
married sisters sent marmalade and pomegranates to Leicester,
and young William, the apprentice, sent his parents such a
lavish gift of oysters that his father suggested mildly that a
quarter as many would have done as well.

A third daughter, named Mary, arrived in London to keep
house for her brother Nicholas, and then the unexpected happened. Twenty-six years after he came to London, and long after
the normal time for an Elizabethan marriage, Nicholas Herrick

finally took himself a wife. Her name was Julian Stone, she came
of a prominent London family, and he married her in the parish
church of St. Leonard's on the eighth of December, 1582.[1]

Since it was winter and the roads were clogged with mud and
snow, John and Mary could not take the long trip to London to
see their son married. Mary had a pain in one of her knee bones
so that she had to walk with a staff, and John was so troubled
in his right shoulder that he could not put on his gown without
help. But they prayed for the "joy and comfort" of Nicholas and
their new daughter, and they sent some supplies "to make merry
withal in Christmas." A great deal of meat went to London from
Leicester that Christmas—"Everybody's piece hath their names
written on them"—and John's letter ended on a hopeful note.
"I trust we shall see your wife and you at Leicester this next
summer to make merry with us."

Now that Nicholas was a married man, he no longer needed
his sister Mary as his housekeeper. Her father wanted her to
come home, but she wished to stay in London and paid no attention to his wishes. Any normal Elizabethan parent would have
ordered his daughter home with peremptory finality but John
wrote her a very gentle letter. He pointed out how many times
he had "desired and prayed" her to return and promised she
should have a room of her own and very little to do. Mary did
not obey him even then, and in the end she made a highly successful marriage with a London man of business. Old John could
not have foreseen this gratifying end to the matter but he bore
her no ill will for her disobedience. He wrote his son Nicholas
a letter the following year in which he thanked him for the
many kindnesses he had shown his brothers and sisters and "especially" Mary.

Nicholas Herrick is rather a shadowy figure except as he is
reflected back through the love in his father's letters. He was not

[1] This was Robert Herrick's mother, and he speaks of her in one of his
poems as Julia. But her signature is extant on a document, and she herself
spelled it Julian.

a good correspondent, and his father once remarked plaintively
that paper must be very scarce in London since the family had
not heard from Nicholas for three months. But he obviously
loved his family deeply and showed them many kindnesses.

One of the qualities that Robert Herrick, the poet, inherited
from his ancestors was this love of family. He wrote poems to
his brothers and his sisters, his nephews and his nieces, his
brothers-in-law and his cousins; and in his judgment he had
the finest and most remarkable set of relatives in all England.
His was a spontaneous affection that was prepared to embrace
all his kindred, the uncritical love that comes of being brought
up among people who enjoy each other.

Herrick also shared the family gift for having a good time.
He wrote some of the happiest poetry in the English language,
and his delight in wine and feasting and flowers seems to have
been a direct legacy from the Herricks of Leicester. He owed
his long life to them too. He was eighty-three when he died,
which was a great age for the average Englishman of the period
but not for a man whose uncle William lived to be over ninety
and whose grandmother was ninety-seven.

Herrick was born in the city and he loved London. But his
best poems reflect the flowers and fields and country ways that
his ancestors knew, and they echo the old, innocent delight that
the Puritans were destroying in England. He is usually called
an Elizabethan poet, although he was only twelve years old
when Queen Elizabeth died and Joseph Addison had already
been born before Herrick's life came to an end. But he remains
truly an Elizabethan, for he was deeply rooted in an older England through his "dear ancestry" in the town of Leicester.

CHAPTER SIXTEEN

R OBERT HERRICK WAS BAPTIZED ON THE TWENTY-FOURTH OF
August, 1591, in the parish church of St. Vedast in Foster
Lane, where his six older brothers and sisters had been christened
before him. His uncle Robert of Leicester was named as his godfather and must therefore have been in London that day, to stand
beside the baby at the font and to assume the obligations that
were laid upon him by the Church of England.

Around the corner from the church was Cheapside, the hand-
somest and most prosperous business street in London, and here
Robert's father had his home. Nicholas Herrick lived in what
was called Goldsmiths' Row, a series of houses just east of
Foster Lane and so magnificently decorated that they were one
of the main tourist attractions of London. A wealthy goldsmith
named Thomas Wood had built them a century before to glorify
his trade and his name, and they consisted of "ten fair dwelling
houses and fourteen shops, all in one frame, uniformly built four
stories high, beautified towards the street with the Goldsmiths'
arms, and the likeness of woodmen . . . riding on monstrous
beasts; all which is cast in lead, richly painted over and gilded."
Within the fourteen shops an array of gold and silver was for
sale, and when Robert Herrick referred to the place of his birth
he rightly called it "golden Cheapside."

Nicholas Herrick was one of the most prosperous goldsmiths
in London, with a clientele that included several noble families.
Apparently the only grief he had encountered was the death of
his first-born, William, who would have been seven in 1592 if
he had lived. The youngest, Robert, was fourteen months old
by then and another baby was coming, when Nicholas Herrick
made his will on a November day in 1592. It was a short will,

witnessed by his unmarried brother William and his married sister, Helen Holden. He estimated that he possessed about three thousand pounds, and he left it all to his wife and children.

When Nicholas Herrick made the will he described himself as "sick in body." Two days later, on the ninth of November, he made his way to the fourth floor of his house and fell from the window. Perhaps it was an accident, but the evidence seems to indicate that it was suicide.

No one knows what could have driven Nicholas Herrick to such a thing. He had been brought up by devout parents, and even the worst of physical pain did not permit a good Christian to take his own life. Moreover, he must have known that if he killed himself the will he had just made would be useless, since a suicide's goods were forfeit to the Crown. Perhaps he was prey to the same inexplicable agony that made a rich Londoner, eight years later, throw himself from the parapet of St. Sepulchre's steeple. Or perhaps, as many people must have hoped, it was not suicide after all.

The Privy Council thought otherwise. On the thirteenth of November the lords of the Council wrote the mayor of London not to permit the coroner to render a verdict in the case of Nicholas Herrick until his death had been thoroughly investigated. If it were suicide, "as it is credibly thought," all his goods were forfeit to the Queen's Almoner.

The Almoner was Richard Fletcher, the courtly and extravagant Bishop of Bristol. He had some influence in London, where his brother Giles was the City Secretary, but the widowed Julian Herrick had influence also. Her husband's younger brother, William, was now a man of property, so much in favor at court that Queen Elizabeth had sent him on a special mission to the Turks; and his sister Mary had married in Thomas Bennett a wealthy Londoner who later became a baronet and mayor of the City. On Julian's own side of the family there were equally useful connections; her brother was a well-known lawyer and her sister

Anne had married into a prominent London family named Soame.

Within the month the Almoner accepted defeat and renounced his claim to the goods of Nicholas Herrick, "being moved with charity and for divers other good causes and considerations." The estate was worth over five thousand pounds, a large sum in those days and much more than Nicholas had estimated, and its administration was put in the hands of three Londoners—an alderman named Sir Richard Martin, Nicholas' brother William and the Almoner's brother, Giles Fletcher.[1]

Julian Herrick was evidently a woman of property in her own right, for she made over her share of the inheritance to the children. She was entitled to about thirteen hundred pounds, and the following May she put her name to the document that gave it to her sons and daughters. Her two brothers-in-law, Robert and William Herrick, were the overseers of the will and she signed in their presence.

Julian Herrick was in the same position that Magdalen Herbert found herself in four years later, carrying a son in her womb after the sudden death of her husband. The plague was raging in London and Julian went to the house of her married sister, Anne Campion, who was living in the village of Hampton fifteen miles away. There she gave birth to a child she named William, after a fashion of the time to use again the name of an older child who had died.

There were seven children in the family now, all of them less than eight years old. The two eldest were girls, Martha and Mercy, and after them came Thomas, Nicholas, Anne, Robert and the new baby, William. They were surrounded by relatives (on the father's side alone they had four aunts and uncles in London and seven in Leicester) but the chief responsibility for

---

[1] Giles Fletcher was considered "an excellent poet," and so were his two sons, Giles and Phineas. The Almoner's son, John Fletcher, was also a poet, and he wrote the plays that Robert Herrick called "incomparable."

their welfare lay with the two overseers of the will, Robert Herrick of Leicester and William Herrick of London. The two brothers were conscientious men, well fitted to work together, and they had the added advantage of loving each other. Two decades later, William wrote Robert that a letter from him was as welcome as "eighteen trumpeters" and Robert replied with equal grace.

Since Robert was the godfather of his small namesake, he may have assumed a special responsibility for the future poet. He and his wife Elizabeth had eleven children of their own and could easily have taken one more into their large house in Leicester. But the town had relatively few business opportunities, and when young Robert Herrick reached a suitable age it was his uncle William who took him in hand. William Herrick was an important member of the Goldsmiths' Company, and it was decided that young Robert should become his apprentice and be trained in the same profession.

From that time forward, the relationship between Robert Herrick and his uncle William was a close one. Under the law, an apprentice lived in his master's house almost as though he were a son; and the master, in addition to giving him his training, assumed full responsibility for his physical and moral welfare. William had once been an apprentice himself in the house of his elder brother Nicholas, and he now had an opportunity to return the care he had received.

William was Sir William Herrick now, but he had changed very little from the days when he was a tall young apprentice sending home a lavish gift of oysters. He remained a typical Herrick, with a strong sense of responsibility for the members of his family. When his nephew Toby went to Cambridge, William sent him gifts and did him various services, and when Toby tried to rise in the Church his uncle pulled strings vigorously. He felt the same sense of responsibility for his home town, serving in Parliament and helping to finance the local hospital, and

he was so valued in Leicester as "the town's special good friend"
that one of its residents burst into song in his praise.

Canticles for your sake the people sing,
Kyrie Eleison: this from our heart doth spring.

Although his business was in London, William's roots remained
in Leicestershire and not long after his marriage he bought a
place in the country. About eight miles from Leicester and on the
east side of Charnwood Forest was the ancient manor house of
Beaumanor, formerly in the possession of the Earl of Essex,
and when William bought it in 1598 he became lord of Barrow,
Woodhouse, Quorndon, Woodthorpe and Mountsorrel, with tenants to bring him "one red-rose garland" on Midsummer Day
and fat turkeys and claret wine at Christmas. There were fish in
the moat at Beaumanor and fallow deer in the park, and William
Herrick even had the right to keep his own flock of swans,
marked with his initials, on the river Soar. His brother Robert
built up the orchard at Beaumanor with peach and pear stocks
from his own grounds in nearby Leicester and received reports
on the state of his brother's timber and game when Sir William
was away.

In London, Sir William Herrick lived in the big house on
Wood Street that had once been Lady Allett's. He had married
in 1596, on a day in May, and on the page where he noted his
wedding he made the characteristic Herrick addition, "Much
joy together!" He added the birth of his first son William to the
same record and hoped soberly that God would bless him "with
long life and make him a good man."

When sixteen-year-old Robert Herrick came to live with his
uncle William and his aunt Joan on Wood Street, six of their
twelve children had already been born. One of them had been
named Robert also, after his uncle in Leicester, and another
was named Henry at the request of Prince Henry himself. By
this time Sir William Herrick owned land in thirteen counties
and had living quarters in both Richmond and Westminster; but

his social life still centered in Beaumanor and his business life in Wood Street.

Robert Herrick became his apprentice on the twenty-fifth of September, 1607. He and his uncle went to Goldsmiths' Hall, which was a short distance to the west in Foster Lane, and there Robert Herrick was entered in the books and was presented to the Master and the Wardens with the indenture he had signed. The wealth and dignity of the Goldsmiths' Company were reflected in the gardens and courtyard of the Hall, in the bay window with its armorial bearings and in the Flemish tapestries that were costly enough to have financed the whole of a smaller building. They depicted the life of St. Dunstan, patron saint of the goldsmiths, and had been woven to order in Brussels, with four artists working sixteen days to create the design and a boy at twopence a day to sharpen their pencils.

In time, if all went well, Robert Herrick would take his place as a member of the Company, eligible to wear the livery of violet and scarlet and to be as much at home in the Hall as his father had been. But a long time had to elapse before this could happen, since Herrick's term as an apprentice stretched for a decade from the feast of St. Bartholomew. The average London apprenticeship lasted seven years, but the art of the goldsmith was so difficult to learn that the Company required ten. The time could be shortened by a special arrangement if the apprentice were related to his master, but Sir William Herrick evidently felt that his nephew needed the full ten years. He himself was a brilliant craftsman, and it was said that he had been given his knighthood because of the special skill with which he had drilled a hole in a large diamond belonging to King James.

Young Robert Herrick made the usual promises that were required of an apprentice, not to marry or play cards or haunt taverns or "commit fornication." He was expected to work twelve hours a day in summer and as long as the light held in winter, and he was not supposed to wear silks or jewels or go to dancing school. His life was to be sober, virtuous and hard-working, and for his guidance there was the letter his grandfather wrote his father when Nicholas was beginning his own apprenticeship in London. "We do pray to God daily to bless you, and to give you grace to be good, diligent, obedient to your master both in word and deed. . . . It is a great part of the fulfilling of God His commandments, to do as we would be done unto."

Robert Herrick probably embarked upon his profession with the best of intentions, eager to be a credit to his dead father and his important London uncle. But love of a craft is born, not made, and the affection for metals that made his uncle Robert rejoice was omitted from the make-up of his godson. The enthusiasm of a good workman existed in young Robert Herrick but it did not find expression in the manipulation of solders and alloys and hammers and in the control of furnaces. His tool was the pen and his love was poetry, and if Robert Herrick had spent half a century at his bench in Wood Street he would still have been no true goldsmith.

It is not possible to say when Herrick first discovered poetry. He lived in an age when boys learned to write Latin verse in grammar school and many of them carried the trick over into English. There was a great deal of versifying, as there was of singing, and the London air was filled with music however soberly an apprentice might try to shut his ears.

Yet the love of poetry came in a special way to Herrick. Most schoolboys had a cautious bowing acquaintance with the Roman poets and forgot them as soon as they left the classroom, but Herrick greeted them like a wanderer come home. Throughout his long life he was their lover, and the Roman customs and phrases wound themselves around his Englishness until they could not be separated. He knew Horace and Martial as well as he knew his own brothers; and under their influence the apprentice who did not care what shapes were taken by that most malleable of metals, gold, began to struggle joyfully with that most refractory of substances, words.

Anyone who knew the Augustan poets also knew the works of

Ben Jonson. He was the great English champion of all things
Roman—in his masques, his plays, his lyrics and even his quarrels
—a magnificent and self-elected autocrat who was determined to
turn his fellow countrymen back to the great days of the Augus-
tans. Herrick probably did not know Jonson personally during
this period of his life; but he had read some of his work in
manuscript and the first of Herrick's poems that can be dated
uses Jonson as a model.

In 1610, when Herrick was nineteen, his brother Thomas left
London to take up farming in Leicestershire and Herrick wrote
a poem for the occasion. He called it "A Country Life" and
modeled it on Jonson's unpublished verses, "To Sir Robert Wroth
in Praise of a Country Life." Jonson had sketched the classic
portrait of an ideal English gentleman in a life of rural peace,
and behind it stretch the long shadows of Vergil and Horace and
Martial. Herrick loved all four, Jonson and Horace especially,
and yet for all that he is a young man speaking clearly in his
own voice.

Never did any English poet more completely build a world of
his own to live in, and the achievement shows as clearly in Herrick's first poetry as in his last. Paganism lodged beside Christianity in his mind as affably as flowers in a field, and there is
an innocent certainty about his Roman customs that makes them
contemporary. It was not really probable that his brother Thomas
would rise at dawn in Leicestershire to sacrifice to Jove in salt
and meal. Yet it seemed so to Herrick as a poet, and therefore
it is so to the reader also.

Another characteristic that stayed with the poet all his life
was his pleasure in small things like fairies and insects and mice,
and the domesticity that Herrick offers his brother has a snug
delight in small, furry objects that remained his own.

> Yet can thy humble roof maintain a quire
>   Of singing crickets by thy fire:
> And the brisk mouse may feast herself with crumbs,
>   Till that the green-ey'd kitling comes.

Also characteristic of Herrick is the language in which he addresses his brother. To call Thomas the other half of his soul might seem extravagant to an outsider but not to a member of so loving a family as the Herricks.

Thomas Herrick was three years older than Robert and had been apprenticed to a London merchant named Massam. He apparently decided that he could not endure a life of business, and in 1610 Mr. Massam was paid off with a hundred pounds which was delivered by Sir William Herrick as his nephew's banker. Thomas retired into Leicestershire to take up farming and in 1611 he married a local girl named Elizabeth.

In the same year that Thomas Herrick married Elizabeth Stanford of Loasbey, his elder sister Mercy married a Suffolk gentleman named John Wingfield. Robert Herrick had written a poem to Mercy before her marriage as a blessing "to my dearest sister," and he extended his affections to include his new brother-in-law. Wingfield was a Cambridge graduate who was eventually knighted, and Herrick admired him

> For being comely, consonant, and free
> To most of men, but most of all to me . . .

One by one the members of the family were settling down, and as Robert Herrick watched them he had reason to think about his own future. Above all, his brother's flight from the bonds of apprenticeship must have made him question his own position in London. For Robert Herrick did not want to produce ornamental buttons and silver-gilt cups. He wanted to produce poetry.

CHAPTER SEVENTEEN

B Y THE TIME ROBERT HERRICK WAS TWENTY-TWO IT WAS
apparent that he would never be a goldsmith. He had spent
six years as an apprentice and his term of service had four more
years to run, but it was clear that the profession in which his
father and uncle had distinguished themselves was not for him.
Three years earlier his brother Thomas had left London, and
in 1613 Robert made an equally drastic move. His uncle William
released him from his contract, and Robert went to the University of Cambridge.

Herrick was much older than the average undergraduate, or,
as he himself rather elegantly put it in a letter to his uncle,
"Time hath devoured some years." Although boys of thirteen
and fourteen sometimes went to Cambridge, George Herbert
was about the normal age when he entered Trinity College at
sixteen and Herrick was off to a very late start when he entered
the rival college of St. John's at twenty-two.

St. John's was just north of Trinity, with only a garden wall
between them, but the two Colleges did not live together in the
brotherhood that might be expected of such close neighbors.
The College heads wrangled over the use of the meadows on
the other side of the river Cam, and the students pursued a
permanent feud that sometimes exploded into riots. Two years
before Herrick entered, there had been a magnificent fight
among the undergraduates, started by Trinity College but entered into with the greatest enthusiasm by St. John's.

The feud may have had something to do with the fact that
St. John's had been the largest and richest College in the University until it was eclipsed by the founding of Trinity. It was
still an impressive place, built of red brick and with perhaps

the most beautiful gateway in Cambridge. A student, who entered St. John's shortly after Herrick, has left a rather touching account of the excitement of moving into his rooms and meeting new friends. "I was much delighted with variety of acquaintance and settling in my new chamber . . . with viewing the Colleges abroad, and our own walks, bowling-ground, and tennis court in St. John's, and with other like toys, which began to breed in me a serious delight and marvelous content." What chiefly shocked this young man was the drinking and swearing, but since Herrick was one of the most enthusiastic drinkers of his generation this could hardly have counted against the College in his estimation.

The one real charge that could be brought against St. John's at this period was the rather low state of its learning. The current head of the College was a Welshman named Owen Gwyn and he had not acquired the office through scholarship. He had slipped in through good connections, and in particular through the pressure that had been exerted by his influential cousin and fellow Welshman, John Williams.[1]

Apart from his love of books Herrick does not give the impression of being an ardent student, and he was probably quite happy in the unscholastic atmosphere of St. John's. He entered as a fellow-commoner, which was an arrangement reserved for the sons of wealthy families who were willing to pay double fees, and his position gave him certain perquisites. He dined, for instance, on the dais in the College hall, while George Herbert did not attain that privilege until he became a fellow.

---

[1] Bishop Williams was a graduate of St. John's College, and since he was an "immense reader" it was suitable that he should present the College with a new library. It was begun in 1623, the year before he gave his first gift to George Herbert, and when it was finished had his arms over the door and his portrait within it.

Williams was also kind enough to help Leicester with its own library, when the town was trying to obtain larger quarters for its collection of books. In those days Leicester was within the diocese of Lincoln, and Williams, as Bishop of Lincoln, interceded with the local earl on the library's behalf and headed the subscription list with a gift of ten pounds.

Herrick had put himself into a rather expensive position for a young man whose inheritance amounted to only about eight hundred pounds, and he found also that there were a great many incidental expenses. He had to pay five pounds for the ten-ounce silver goblet that was the price of his admission as a fellow-commoner to St. John's, and there were tips to the butler and porter, fees to the lecturer, payments to the barber and laundress and, of course, the much larger sum to his tutor. When Herrick arrived at St. John's he had not even made arrangements for his bedding, and like most Cambridge undergraduates he was astonished to find how quickly the money melted away.

Herrick's money was held for him by his uncle William, who acted as his banker and sent him a quarterly allowance. If he needed anything he had to write his uncle for it, and a steady stream of letters flowed from Cambridge to Wood Street. They all dealt with the same subject and nothing was altered except the method of approach. Sometimes Herrick tried pathos: "Did you but know how disfurnished I came to Cambridge . . . you would . . . better your thoughts towards me." Sometimes he tried rhetoric and wrote with a scholarly flourish of Apelles and Arcisilaus before he brought up the delicate question of finances. Sometimes he was aphoristic and seemed to be thinking only of his uncle's happiness: "Generous minds still have the best contentment, and willingly help where there is an evidency of want." But the intent of the letters is always the same and they all echo what Herrick wryly admitted to be his single chant. "*Mitte pecuniam.*" Send me money.

The first letter, written in the same month he entered Cambridge, does not ask for money for his own needs. Herrick wanted fifteen pounds for his brother Thomas, whose efforts at farming had not been successful. But after that it was his own college expenses that filled Herrick's anguished horizon. He fell behind on his tailor's bill, he ran into difficulties with his "chamber room," and on one occasion his tutor became so openly dissatisfied with his payments that Herrick seriously considered a special trip to London to get the money.[2]

Sir William has been reproved by some of Herrick's admirers for not being more lavish with his talented nephew. Yet it was obviously to Herrick's own advantage to be given a set sum of money and made to keep his expenses within bounds. Actually, Sir William seems to have been a patient man. In the year in which his nephew was exhorting him to be a "true Maecenas," he had been forced to lend King James a huge sum of money without interest, and three years later he was imploring the government to repay it, "that I may not sink under a greater burden than I am able to bear." He was also ill part of the time, which made his nephew "honestly sorrowful" but did not stop him from writing letters.

Robert Herrick himself seems to have felt that his uncle was good to him. In one of his letters he mentions "the large extent of your favor and kindness," and he speaks also of Lady Herrick and the "kindness shown by my lady to my unworthy self." He was also of the opinion that his own demands were "importunate," but this did not prevent his pursuing the subject with skill, tenacity and vigor. The money was handled through a London bookseller, and the receipted letters kept by his uncle are proof that the bills were paid.

Sir William Herrick was no stranger to college bills, since his eldest son, William, was at the University of Oxford the same time that Robert was at Cambridge. William also was living beyond his means, as a cautious letter from William's tutor admitted.

---

2 The Cambridge tutors seem to have had a hard time collecting from their charges. Simonds D'Ewes, a fellow-commoner at St. John's, was an earnest young man who worked hard with his tutor over the moral philosophy of Pickolomineus and admired the rhetoric lectures of George Herbert. But he fell so far behind on his payments that "my loving and careful tutor . . . accompanied me home, not only to perform the last loving office to me, but to receive some arrearages due to him upon his bill."

When Robert Herrick had been two years at Cambridge there was a plan for his cousin William to visit him. King James was planning a gala visit to the University in 1615, and the two cousins arranged it between themselves that William would attend the festivities and lodge with Robert. But William's tutor asked permission to keep his charge tightly by his side, and it may be that Robert was not considered an especially good influence.

The King's visit was a great success except for the weather. March was a cold month that year, and "the world was nothing but air and snow" when all the Cambridge scholars, including George Herbert and Robert Herrick, were brought together by the ringing of bells to stand respectfully in their hoods and gowns until the royal procession had passed by. The only impropriety was committed by the Public Orator, Sir Francis Nethersole, who made a spectacular blunder in his Latin. But this gave a great deal of pleasure to the Oxford men who had come up for the occasion, and since Nethersole was a Trinity man his error may also have pleased the rival college of St. John's.

Herrick's social life at Cambridge was an important part of his education, since one of the duties of an undergraduate was to make the kind of friends who would help him in his future life. When Henry Peacham wrote his book, *The Complete Gentleman,* and gave advice on the way a young man should comport himself at the University, he remarked firmly, "Your first care, even with pulling off your boots, let be the choice of your acquaintances and company." When Simonds D'Ewes entered St. John's, his tutor saw to it that he was at once introduced to a member of the great Manners family; and "he, being a fellow-commoner of the same College, did me the favor to bring me first not only into the hall but into the chapel also."

The most influential friend that Herrick made at St. John's was Clipseby Crew, a fellow-commoner who was knighted a few years after he left Cambridge. He was eight years younger

than Herrick and son of the distinguished judge, Sir Randall
Crew, who had a beautiful estate in Cheshire. His mother, like
Herrick's, was named Julian, and she brought a great deal of
money into the family as well as giving her son Clipseby her
family's name.

Herrick wrote several poems to his friend, calling him "my
Clipseby" and "my dearest Crew," and the friendship lasted for
many years. When Sir Clipseby married, Herrick wrote a nuptial
song for him and his bride, who came of a Leicestershire family.
When their baby died Herrick wrote its epitaph, and when Jane
Crew herself died at the age of thirty he wrote six lines to be
carved on her tomb.

An even closer friendship was the one that Herrick formed
with John Weekes, who became a fellow of St. John's College
the same year that Herrick entered. Weekes was apparently
about Herrick's own age, and the two men became so close that
nothing parted them for long. In one of the poems Herrick dedicated to Weekes he tried to describe the love that united them.

> Say, we must part . . .
>   Can we so far
> Stray, to become less circular,
>   Than we are now?
> No, no, that selfsame heart, that vow,
> Which made us one, shall ne'er undo,
> Or ravel so, to make us two.

The whole of Herrick's biography supports the truth of what
he wrote there, since in most of the major events of his life John
Weekes was beside him. Weekes was "a cheerful man that was
good at making a jest," a man of many friends and highly gifted
in the art of enjoying himself. The spirit of play that was so
strong in Herrick was equally strong in Weekes, and they would
no doubt have been delighted to rollick around Cambridge with
vine leaves in their hair, carolling suitable lines from Anacreon
to a sympathetic moon.

> . . . For when
> We two are dead,
> The world with us is buried.
> Then live we free
> As is the air, and let us be
> Our own fair wind . . .

Such a plan might be suited to poetry, but it was not a practical one for two young men who had to earn their livings. Weekes was planning a career in the Church of England, and he left for Oxford in 1617 with the idea of taking a degree in divinity. By this time Robert Herrick also had changed his way of living, for it was becoming increasingly clear that he was wasting his time at St. John's and spending more money than he could afford. He wrote a cautious letter to his uncle William inquiring whether it might not be better to enter a less expensive college and take up the study of law. Herrick admitted that this new plan might be "to a lesser end and smaller purpose" than the one he had originally formed, but it was one that might be more hopeful of success.

In actual fact, Robert Herrick was no better suited to the life of a lawyer than he was to the life of a goldsmith. But he seems to have held the optimistic belief that whatever he was not currently doing was the thing to do, and so he moved his bedding and baggage over to Trinity Hall.

Trinity Hall had no connection with Trinity College. It lay south of it, facing Mill Street, and was usually called "the Hall." It had been founded by a Bishop of Norwich who was an eminent diplomat and wished to produce men skilled both in civil and canon law. In general the College was not ecclesiastical, although its first master, a probate judge who was a distant kinsman of Herrick's, left it to become a bishop.

Trinity Hall was the smallest college in Cambridge and its surroundings were less lavish than those of St. John's. There was no tennis court in Herrick's new college, and no bowling green. But it was a lively and well-run institution, full of intelligent men, and a future lawyer who applied himself to his studies could go far.

After Herrick arrived at Trinity Hall, he sent a letter to his uncle that was unusually full of noble sentiments. He announced that he intended to live as a recluse, vowed to a life of the most stringent economy and with nothing but "upright thoughts" for company. And he ended with the final and inevitable request: will his uncle please send ten pounds?

CHAPTER EIGHTEEN

R OBERT HERRICK GRADUATED FROM TRINITY HALL WITH A B.A.
in 1617 and received his M.A. three years later. But the
training was wasted on him, as his six years' attempt to be a
goldsmith had also been wasted, for Herrick did not become a
lawyer. Instead, three years later, he turns up in the company
of his close friend, John Weekes. Weekes had been in training
for the ministry, and when he entered the Church Herrick entered it with him.

On the twenty-fourth of April, 1623, Robert Herrick and John
Weekes stood in the presence of Thomas Dove, Bishop of Peter-
borough, and by him were ordained deacons in the Church of
England. It was a solemn ceremony, the same ritual in which
George Herbert took part a few years later, and it testified that
Herrick and Weekes were "inwardly moved by the Holy Ghost
. . . to serve God, for the promoting of His glory and the edify-
ing of His people."

Their next step was to be ordained priests. The Church of
England had originally decreed that a full year must elapse
before a deacon could receive this ordination, so that his fitness
for his vocation could be fully tested. It was four years at least
before George Herbert took this final step and assumed the cure
of souls. But so scrupulous a conscience was not usual, and the
Church had modified its original rule. There was now a waiting
period of only three months, and Herrick and Weekes were
free to return during the next Ember week if they were "faithful
and diligent" as deacons.

In flat disregard of this rule, Herrick and Weekes presented
themselves before the Bishop on the twenty-fifth of April, the
day after they had become deacons. And the Bishop of Peter-

borough, with a cheerful disregard to equal their own, ordained them both as priests in the Church of England.

For the rest of his long life Herrick was in holy orders, serving for over half a century and apparently quite unperturbed by the weighty responsibilities of his office. He and Weekes heard the same words that Herbert listened to later, but they made no difference to him. "You have heard, brethren . . . of what dignity and of how great importance this office is. . . . We have good hope, that you have well weighed and pondered these things with your selves, long before this time, and that you have clearly determined, by God's grace, to give your selves wholly to this vocation, whereunto it has pleased God to call you, so that (as much as lieth in you) you apply your selves wholly to this one thing."

Robert Herrick had already chosen his vocation. He had given himself wholly to the desire to write good verses, and it was to this he brought his patience, his dedication and his whole mind. He had no gift for any other vocation.

Nevertheless, Herrick could not earn his living by writing poetry, and if he were not to be a goldsmith or a lawyer there was no reason why he should not enter the Church. Perhaps he was especially attracted to the idea because his friend Weekes was entering the ministry and Herrick could not forget "that vow which made us one."

Weekes had been studying divinity for some time and Herrick probably had not. But the Church did not set up rigid qualifications, and Herrick could have fulfilled them easily enough. It was considered sufficient if the candidate was twenty-four years old, possessed of a university degree and some testimonials as to his virtuous behavior and had taken the Oath of Supremacy.

A much more difficult problem than qualifying for the ministry was the question of finding employment. The bishops were under strict orders not to ordain any candidate who did not already have, to put it crudely, the offer of a job; and if a bishop broke this rule he was responsible for the financial support of the newly ordained priest until he obtained a church living.

Getting a benefice was a highly competitive matter, since Oxford and Cambridge were full of well-trained young men industriously writing letters to influential people in the hope of getting some kind of ecclesiastical preferment. Some of the livings were controlled by the colleges themselves, and a graduate of St. John's might become the rector of Lilly-Hoo in Hertfordshire or Thursford cum Snoring in Norfolk if he could wait long enough and if none of his fellow graduates was ahead of him. Some of the benefices were controlled by the Crown, some by the Church, and an enormous number were in the hands of laymen. But whatever the circumstances, getting such a position was chiefly a matter of the endless, skillful and tenacious pulling of strings. Testimonial letters flourished, and even in Queen Elizabeth's day Hooker had been obliged to defend the Church for permitting "ambitious suits and other oblique ways" by which pressure could be exerted.

The problem can be illustrated in the case of Herrick's cousin Tobias, whom the family called Toby. This was the only surviving son of Robert Herrick of Leicester, and since Robert held the patronage of the church at Houghton on the Hill he was able to install his son there as rector. Toby was not content with this, although his father pointed out in a letter to Sir William Herrick, "If I had not preferred him to it, by Abram's father, it might have been that he had not got so much." Toby wrote his own letters to his uncle William, long, explicit letters in which he suggested various ways his uncle might work on his problem. What he wanted was either a wealthier parish or a prebend, and Sir William did his best. But for all his letter writing, Toby lived and died the rector of Houghton on the Hill and never achieved anything better than the office his father had given him.

In his younger days Toby had been a chaplain and he sometimes thought of becoming one again, chiefly because a patron was much more likely to bestow a vacant living on one of his own chaplains than on an outsider. But he told his uncle William not to pursue this aspect of the problem too vigorously. "I have been chaplain to one or two great personages already and received little commodity by it." By commodity he probably meant advancement, but it was equally true that the average chaplain was not very well paid. As one observer remarked, "Their allowance is good if it be 20 mark and their diet." Moreover, their social position was equivocal. They were not servants but neither were they equals, and in a great house the chaplain would sit at the "parlor table" with the steward and the secretary, in a lesser position than the "lord's table" but higher than the others. In addition they were expected to report disorders among the servants, an obligation which could cause a great deal of trouble.

A chaplain who found himself in a sympathetic household could have a happy if somewhat unclerical life. Bacon's chaplain was closely involved with his writing, acted as his secretary and became for all practical purposes his literary executor. The chaplain of the Countess of Pembroke spent much of his time reading aloud to her, for she loved books so much she used to memorize quotations pinned to the furniture of her bedroom while she was dressing. Sir John Wynn, on the other hand, was fond of bowling, and so in his case the chaplain played bowls with him. Few were as versatile as John Williams when he served as chaplain in a great house, for he delighted his master with his learning, the ladies with his courtliness, and all strangers with his courtesy, while "he interposed gravely, as became a divine, against the disorders of the lowest servants."

Sometimes, especially in free and easy households, the chaplains had been known to supply their own disorders. Sir John Wynn would not permit his chaplain to visit the local alehouse, but a contemporary admitted that there were many chaplains who "love the strong beer cellar, or wine tavern, more than their studies; whose ambition is to be conversant with the gentlewomen, and now and then to let an oath slip with a grace, whose acquaintance and familiarity is most with the butler, and then

care to slip to an alehouse unseen." The author describes such
chaplains as "imitating their masters' faults," and in general it
would seem that a wise chaplain modeled himself on his em-
ployer, saying prayers twice a day and catechizing the servants
if he lived in a godly household, and adding as many extracur-
ricular activities as were required of him.

When Robert Herrick makes his next traceable appearance,
four years later, he is serving as a chaplain, and it is quite possible that he became one as soon as he was ordained. There is
no record of his having received a benefice anywhere; and if
some nobleman had agreed to take Herrick into his household
that would help to explain the rather unseemly haste with which
the day-old deacon became a priest.

If it is true that Herrick spent these intervening years as a
chaplain, it is to be hoped that he did not find himself in an
intensely godly household. He belonged to a happy little band
of hard-drinking clerics which included Richard Hinde, James
Smith, Martin Nansogg and, of course, John Weekes—

> . . . friends of mine
> Loving the brave Burgundian wine . . .
> Whose fortunes I have frollickt with. . . .

Most of them became vicars without ceasing to frolic and they
all remained Herrick's dear companions, drinking wine and giving "applause to verse" when their thoughts should doubtless
have been on holier things.

Many years later, when Herrick was preparing his poetry for
publication, he was aware that his drinking songs and his love
songs outnumbered what he called his "pious pieces" by three
to one. He did not wish to suppress them, but he wrote a little
prayer asking forgiveness

> For those my unbaptized rhymes
> Writ in my wild unhallowed times. . . .

During this "wild unhallowed" period, as he calls it, he was
serving both as a chaplain and as a vicar in the Church of Eng-

land, and it is perhaps an odd way for a cleric to describe his career. But what Herrick called his "wanton wit" was quite un-affected by his entrance into the Church of England and no one knew it better than himself.

Occasionally he had his brief moments of repentance, in which he felt that some sort of absolution would no doubt be desirable, but in general his relationship to God was untroubled by any inward questioning. When Herrick was not being purely pagan in his writing he usually showed a kind of innocent medievalism, with a pleasant respect for his Maker but no real worries. His was not a difficult God, and at the back of Herrick's mind it seemed probable that He would enjoy poems about daffodils and wine and pretty girls.

It is certain that Herrick's own interest in these and kindred subjects remained quite undiminished when he entered holy orders. Five years earlier, for instance, he had written an epithalamium to celebrate the marriage of Sir Thomas Southwell, and he makes it a jubilant glorification of the joys of the wedding night. Two years after he entered the Church, Herrick wrote another wedding song, this time to celebrate the marriage of his friend Sir Clipseby Crew, and again he is the delighted and delightful pagan, dwelling with open affection on the bride's garters and the "proud plump bed."

This kind of enthusiasm was not quite what the Church of England had envisioned in its ministers. But it was indigenous to Herrick, as much a part of him as the love of metals in his uncle Robert, and he saw no reason to change his point of view merely because he had knelt down before the Bishop of Peter-borough one April day.

CHAPTER NINETEEN

IT IS NOT KNOWN WHEN ROBERT HERRICK FIRST MET BEN JONSON. But it was apparently some time during the twenties that he became an informal member of that hard-drinking, scribbling, reverential crew of disciples known as the Tribe of Ben.

By 1623, the year in which Herrick entered holy orders, Ben Jonson had attained a public eminence that no one could have dreamed of in his unpromising youth. He started life as a slum boy and his longing for a university education was blocked by poverty. Instead of going to college he was apprenticed to a bricklayer, a project which failed as completely as Herrick's attempt to become a goldsmith. Jonson had no intention of spending his life laying bricks. He wanted to write, and he fought his way up in the world of the theatre until he became the most talked-of dramatist in London. In and out of prison, in and out of debt, he surged on to an increasing success both in court circles and with the general public, until he emerged in 1616 in the full glory of his collected works, with a forest of learned notes to decorate the pages and an engraving of his laurelled head as a frontispiece.

Success meant more to Ben Jonson than to most men, since he was not only a poet but a prophet. Back in his school days his mind had been lit by a vision of the glory of Rome, and he spent the rest of his strenuous life trying to bring literary England to the same vision. He argued, he harangued, he wrote vociferous introductions to his plays, and he quarreled fiercely with those of his fellow writers who did not agree with him. But he brought an increasing number of younger men under his spell, and by 1623 he was the most influential writer in England.

Part of Jonson's success with young men came from the fact
that he was so openly an idealist. Sir Lucius Cary, who signed
himself Jonson's "son and servant," spoke of the crowd of young-
sters who gathered around him, hoping to achieve something
worthy of his praise. Jonson's dream of bringing back the Augustan Age was a magnificent one, and young men are roused
by magnificence even if they do relatively little about it afterwards.

Moreover Jonson was wonderful company, a gargantuan
drinker and talker who led the Sons of Ben through the taverns
of London in a glorious series of drinking parties. By 1624 he
had acquired what amounted to a permanent clubroom in the
Devil Tavern. And here, in the Apollo room, Jonson sat on a
raised seat near the bust of the god, with his "rocky" face and his
spreading belly and his youthful enthusiasm for good talk and
good wine.

Herrick does not mention the Devil Tavern and perhaps he
knew Jonson earlier. But certainly he attended some of the drinking parties; and not even Francis Beaumont, with his glowing
tribute to Jonson's wit and the wine of the Mermaid Tavern,
could match the verses Herrick wrote in praise of the master
and some of his London haunts.

> Ah Ben!
> Say how, or when
> Shall we thy guests
> Meet at those lyric feasts,
> Made at the Sun,
> The Dog, the Triple Tun?
> Where we such clusters had,
> As made us nobly wild, not mad;
> And yet each verse of thine
> Out-did the meat, out-did the frolic wine.

Herrick had admired and imitated Ben Jonson since the days
when he was a goldsmith's apprentice, and he knew very well
what a privilege it was to be in the great man's company.

Herrick did not possess either Jonson's intellectual vigor or his scholarship, and since he was a wise man he did not try to change himself into something he was not. Herrick gave thanks in the only way a good poet can, by entering the door Jonson had opened to him and making the territory beyond it his own.

For instance, Jonson had once written a song for one of his plays in which he praised the art of "sweet neglect" in a woman's attire. Herrick borrowed both the idea and the metre, and the result is his own brilliantly original lyric, "Delight in Disorder." For Jonson's moral approach he substituted his own pagan sense of play, and he let his imagination flow over the details of a woman's dress with a most affectionate eye for detail.

> A winning wave (deserving note)
> In the tempestuous petticoat . . .

was duly noted by Herrick, who was not only well informed on petticoats but knew how to link them to the most accurate of adjectives.

Once again, some years later, Jonson wrote another poem that Herrick used as the model for a small masterpiece. Jonson wrote some verses on magic and the moon for one of his court masques and used a curious but effective five-line stanza. His good friend Richard Corbet borrowed the metre and in his hands it became doggerel; but when Herrick used it the result was the famous "Night-Piece to Julia."

> Her eyes the glow-worm lend thee,
> The shooting stars attend thee;
> And the elves also,
> Whose little eyes glow,
> Like the sparks of fire, befriend thee.
>
> No will-o'-th'-wisp mis-light thee;
> No snake, or slow-worm bite thee:
> But on, on thy way
> Not making a stay,
> Since ghost there's none to affright thee.

Let not the dark thee cumber;
What though the moon does slumber?
    The stars of the night
    Will lend thee their light,
Like tapers clear without number.

Then, Julia, let me woo thee,
Thus, thus to come unto me:
    And when I shall meet
    Thy silv'ry feet,
My soul I'll pour into thee.

Herrick reverenced the art of poetry—what he called "the holy incantation of a verse"—and he reverenced equally the man who had helped him to enter that sacred ground. In Herrick's eyes, Jonson was both priest and saint in an ancient and enchanted land, and he wrote a set of verses that he called "His Prayer to Ben Jonson."

Close as the two men were in their devotion to poetry, there is nothing to indicate that there was a similar closeness in their lives. Herrick was not one of the young protégés whom Jonson took formally under his wing and he was never "sealed of the Tribe of Ben."

Of all Jonson's "sons," the one who most resembled Herrick was Thomas Randolph, who wrote light, erotic verse full of nymphs and shepherds and Phrygian pipes and adaptations of Horace and Martial. Randolph had been encouraged from childhood to be a poet, and when he composed, at the age of nine, a versified history of the Incarnation, his brother preserved the manuscript with fraternal care. When he went to Cambridge he was equally admired, praised by his elders for his "wit and learning" and loved by his contemporaries for his good fellowship.

When Randolph was formally accepted as one of Jonson's sons, he wrote an exultant poem to express his gratitude.

I am akin to heroes, being thine,
And part of my alliance is divine.

He goes on to say that since Jonson is his father all the poets of
Greece and Rome are his uncles and the nine Muses his aunts.
It was an opinion in which his admirers would have concurred,
since Randolph's head was full of the usual clutter that passed
for classical learning and his contemporaries felt he could well
have been born in "old Rome, or Athens." But it was an unwise
boast for a glib versifier like Randolph to make; Ben Jonson
might adopt him but he could not transmit his own vision.

It was Robert Herrick alone, of all these poetical Londoners,
who could fairly claim to have entered ancient Rome. Since he
had none of Jonson's stern dogmatism, he was quite unable to
take an uncompromising stand beside his master on the Capitol
steps. But he roamed about in the Augustan Age among the
flowers and the girls, and in his own fashion he was the kind of
nephew that some of the Roman poets could have had.

Horace, for instance, would surely have been willing to accept
Herrick into the family. That easygoing, civilized bachelor, who
described himself as "little of stature, early grey, fond of the
sunshine," shared with Herrick an enthusiastic interest in girls
and a real affection for country customs. If there were many
aspects of Horace that Herrick could not approach, that was
equally true of his relationship to Ben Jonson, and Herrick did
not worry himself trying to reach for the unobtainable.

One quality that Horace and Jonson both had was a profound
respect for the art of poetry and a pronounced tendency to dog-
matize on the correct way to write it. Both of them were teachers
by instinct, and Herrick was an ardent pupil. He excelled particularly in an art that the facile Randolph found impossible, the
art of revision. Horace recommended a rigid standard of good
craftsmanship: "Cut out the ill-turned lines and bring them to
the anvil again," and Jonson echoed his advice: "Bring all to the
forge, and file, again; turn it anew." The care with which Herrick followed this advice may be traced in every case where a
manuscript copy survives and can be compared with the printed
version. All these poems are reworked and all for the better.

Herrick loved his verses as a father loves his child, but he would ruthlessly eliminate whole sections that no longer pleased his ear. In the manuscript version, for instance, of his wedding song to Sir Clipseby Crew there are sixty-seven lines that Herrick removed before he was ready to have the final version appear in print. This pride in the work for its own sake made him as truly akin to Horace as the verbal echoes of the great Roman that fill so many of his pages.

Oddly enough, considering the scrupulous way that Herrick thanked Ben Jonson, he never publicly acknowledged his debt to Horace. In his lively song, "To live merrily, and to trust to good verses," Herrick lists the classical poets he wishes to honor—Homer, Vergil, Ovid, Catullus, Propertius and Tibullus—but he does not mention Horace. It is not a reliable list, since Herrick had only a bowing acquaintance with Homer, respected Vergil more than he loved him and was sometimes ill-advised when he tried to follow the heartbreaking ardor of Catullus. His temperament was alien to the melancholy emotionalism of Propertius, and Horace's gentle friend Tibullus was the only one on the list to whom Herrick was really related.

As for failing to mention Horace, Herrick does not list Anacreon either, and that happpy Greek was another of his favorite models. It was not the real Anacreon that Herrick knew, for the fragment of his work that has survived was not available in Herrick's day. What he knew was the collection of odes written by later Greeks in imitation of the poet, which had been published in France during the previous century along with a popular Latin translation. Herrick apparently trusted the Latin more than the Greek but he recognized a kindred spirit immediately. Some of his poems are direct translations of the odes in the *Anacreontea*, and dozens of others are filled with their flowers and perfumes and their delight in wine and girls. Herrick's joy in living was very like Anacreon's, and the fact that "Death will come and mar the song," only gave an extra sheen to the delight of being alive and singing.

Like Anacreon's poetry, Herrick's songs glitter and flow with wine, and by his own account, at least, he was forever carousing. Thomas Randolph, who makes little mention of liquor in his verse, drank himself to death by the time he was thirty, while Herrick lived to be eighty-three. One of Randolph's friends remarked that "without moderation few men reach old age," and if this is true Herrick was perhaps not quite the drinker he said he was. On the other hand he came of a long-lived family, and he looked upon wine with such kindly affection that in his case it may have acted as a preservative.

Next to wine and song, Herrick's chief delight was, of course, women, those lovely ladies who flit so amorously through his verses. When he was grey-haired he was still writing about his "fresh and fragrant mistresses," and they fill his poetry with their white arms and their pretty ways—Perilla and Electra, Anthea and Diamene, Lucia, Perenna and over and over again his beloved Julia.

Never were mistresses better suited to a poet, and whether they bore any resemblance to the women Herrick encountered in real life it is impossible to say. With the exception of some young ladies with whom he went junketing up the Thames, none of them seems to exist in London or even in English air. "My girls," as he calls them, were as fragrant as roses and as lovely as daffodils; but none of them is rooted in earth and men seldom encounter such thoroughly satisfactory mistresses except in their dreams.

On the other hand, when Herrick wrote songs to demonstrably real women the tone is not unlike his addresses to Julia. He calls Susan Herrick his "dearest" and compares her to flowers, and when he addresses three poems to his uncle Robert's daughter, Elizabeth Wheeler, she is his "dearest love" and they kiss in the flowery meads. His Valentine to Margaret Falconbrige is also to "my dearest," and the reader would have no way of guessing that Margaret was at the time less than nine years old.

The poems to Julia are more erotic than these, and yet there is no fundamental difference in tone. Herrick is a poet of surfaces, and all beautiful surfaces had a certain resemblance for him. The whiteness of a woman's thigh could stir him to poetry, but so could the sheen of a petticoat or a bough of whitethorn in May, and they all have a kind of innocence that Herrick somehow retains even in his most mischievous verse. If there is a real woman beneath the petticoats he gives no indication of it, and certainly Herrick was no Catullus to report in agonizing reality the progress of an actual love affair.

Herrick's mistresses belong to the light-hearted tradition of Horace with his Chloe and his Lydia, or of Anacreon whose troops of ladies were (he says) as numerous as the waves of the sea. As a poet Herrick was equally willing to bestow his affections wholesale, and he celebrated the pretty things with the same affectionate skill he lavished on violets and primroses. The ladies had reason to be equally grateful to him in return; and the least they could have done, as Herrick once suggested, was to make a yearly pilgrimage to his tomb so that he could cast on his "girls" a final affectionate eye.

CHAPTER TWENTY

ROBERT HERRICK WAS GIVEN HIS FIRST PUBLIC COMPLIMENT, OR at least the first that has survived, when he was thirty-four years old. This was the year in which King James died, and the writer of an elegy called *The Muses' Dirge* felt that England's monarch should have been praised while he lived by some prominent poet,

Some Jonson, Drayton, or some Herrick.

Michael Drayton had never been an influential poet but he was always quietly respected, while Ben Jonson was by now the most important writer in England. It must have been very gratifying to be bracketed with two such men, and in fact it was the highest compliment that Herrick received during his lifetime.

It was not really true that King James had gone unpraised by the poets. Ben Jonson, for one, had written many lines in his honor and called him the "best of kings." But it was true that James was chiefly interested in poets who wrote on religious themes and that the men who wrote light, secular lyrics had more encouragement under his successor.

It is curious that this should have been so, since King Charles was a much more devout man than his father. James was a poor churchgoer, with a deplorable habit of talking and making jokes during the services, while Charles was a most "attentive hearer" at sermons. During his reign there were private prayers in the court both morning and evening, readings from the liturgy before dinner, and services in the royal chapel both Tuesdays and Sundays, "all good signs that God hath set him over this kingdom for a blessing."

Since Charles was so dedicated a member of the Church of

England, he approached the great religious ceremony of his coronation with much more gravity than his father had shown. He really believed, with all the force of his passionate, secretive heart, that he was King of England by God's grace, and that when he was anointed with the holy oil on Candlemas Day he became a ruler with whom it was treason to disagree.

Charles would not permit the Dean of Westminster to take his usual part in the coronation, for this was John Williams, his father's Lord Keeper who had been retired in disgrace. Instead the duties of the Dean were taken over by the Bishop of St. David's, whose name was William Laud. It was Laud who stayed with the King the night before the coronation, who found an ancient crucifix among the regalia of Edward the Confessor and had it placed on the Abbey altar. And it was Laud who for all practical purposes managed the commission that added a new prayer to the ceremony: "Hold fast from henceforth the place . . . now delivered to you by the authority of Almighty God, and by the hands of us and all the bishops and servants of God."

Charles later told his son that "the chiefest particular duty of a king is to maintain the true religion," and he added that "the dependence of the Church upon the Crown is the chiefest support of royal authority." He and Bishop Laud shared the conviction that this was a holy and immovable authority, consecrated by God to preside over a reverent and obedient kingdom, and they worked together, with tragic results, to superimpose this impossible vision on the fermenting and violently changing land that Charles had inherited.

Laud's first move was characteristic of him. He felt the Church of England had been damaged by the slackness of the bespectacled old Archbishop of Canterbury, and he drew up a list of prominent divines which he labeled O and P. O stood for orthodox, or what Laud believed to be orthodox, and P stood for Puritan.

By this time the meaning of the word "Puritan" had grown so confused that one churchman, six years earlier, had suggested

King James should either define the term himself or appoint a committee to do it for him. Most Englishmen were still hoping that some kind of a middle ground could be reached in the controversy, and if Laud had been a more cautious man he would have added a third category, M for moderate. But Laud's mind was as tidy as it was dedicated, and he really believed that the whole turbulent subject of Puritanism could be tied up and deposited outside the Church door.

In all this Bishop Laud had the full support of the Duke of Buckingham, who had in fact suggested the list of O and P. Laud owed his rise to Buckingham, whom he called "my dear lord," and these two men were by now the closest friends that young King Charles possessed.

Robert Herrick wrote a poem to the Duke of Buckingham in which he spoke of the "cloud of glory" that surrounded him. It was a glory that had increased in the new reign, for nothing happened in the kingdom now unless the Duke willed it. James had loved him in a fatuous, fatherly way, delighting in his good looks and his smooth, deferential charm. But Charles loved him with the whole of his lonely heart, giving him "the most entire confidence . . . that ever king had showed to any subject."

In the King's eyes Buckingham could do no wrong. His enemies in the House of Commons were a pack of vicious malcontents as far as Charles was concerned, trying to overthrow the processes of orderly government, while in return the men of Parliament had convinced themselves that Buckingham was the source of all their troubles. Everything that went wrong in England was blamed on that jewelled and glittering figure, with his beautiful hands and his arrogant ways and his absolute hold over the King.

Nor was this position altogether unjust, for the Duke was a very incompetent statesman who confused public interest with his own whims. The war he had helped to start with Spain may have had some justification, but the war he then proceeded to start with France was based on little more than a private grudge.

Since Buckingham was both admiral and general, he decided to direct the war personally on both sea and land, and he combined these functions in the spring of 1627 by gathering together a fleet to sail for the Isle of Rhé.

On this expedition Robert Herrick was one of the Duke of Buckingham's chaplains. It is the first office that can be definitely assigned to him since his ordination, and he must have had good friends at court to be a member of the great Duke's household on so important an occasion.

The expedition to Rhé took a long time to get started, and all through the spring there was unkind gossip about the series of delays. Finally, in the middle of May, the Duke gave a farewell dinner at York House, where a masque presented "open-mouthed dogs' heads" to represent the barking of the populace until they were dispersed by Fame and Truth. After this nothing happened and the barking increased, with some heartless wits maintaining that the Duke had scheduled his departure for the nonexistent date of June 31.

However, on the twenty-seventh of June there was a surge of activity. Six thousand men were put aboard the ships, with a special vessel for the cows and poultry and the Duke's magnificent coach. The next day was Sunday and the Duke went aboard to hear a sermon, for he was always conscientious about such things; and the following Wednesday, at four in the morning, the fleet at last set sail.

Robert Herrick was not, apparently, a good sailor. He wrote some verses called "His Sailing from Julia" in which he speaks feelingly of "watery desolation" and "dreadful passages," and in another poem, addressed to Neptune, he promises the god a tunny fish as an offering if he gets safely to shore. In still another poem he characterizes the true Christian as one who "fears not the fierce sedition of the seas," and it seems reasonable to deduce that Herrick did not enjoy the voyage across the Channel.

At least he had a friend making the same crossing. John Weekes, by whose side he had been ordained, was also serving

as a chaplain in the expedition to the Isle of Rhé. Weekes was
a Devonshire man and had a rectory there, but anyone who
served as a nobleman's chaplain could always get a dispensation
from his bishop to leave his benefice.

The Duke of Buckingham kept his chaplains busy. There were
sermons on the ships at the time of departure "for the blessing
of the journey," and there were prayers after the bloody landing
on the Isle of Rhé to give "thanks to the God of Hosts." There
were also daily services in camp by the Duke's order, although
he wrote home apologetically to the Countess of Buckingham,
"Dear mother, I am so full of business as hardly have I time to
say my prayers."

The Duke had need of prayers, for his undoubted courage
and good intentions were no match for bad luck and bad management. The landing on the island was bungled and "all things
were done in confusion and tumult." The provisions had not been
properly planned, and although wheat had been brought over in
the heavily laden ships there was no way of grinding or cooking
it. Nor was there any normal forage on the island, since it was
inhabited only by fishermen and growers of grapes and there
was nothing for the English soldiers to gather except the "shreds
of vine stalks."

By early fall Buckingham was still vainly attempting to capture the fort of St. Martin and finding it more and more difficult
to maintain his role of an intelligent and chivalrous commander.
His unhappy troops were bitterly aware of the cold in the inadequate trenches they had dug with such difficulty, and the
rains became so heavy they "had no ground but mire to do
their duties in." Sickness and hunger increased, and the badly
disciplined men talked of mutiny.

The mismanagement in England was equally gross and the
promised reinforcements failed to arrive. After frequently changing his mind, the Duke of Buckingham was forced to retreat to
his ships and there the final catastrophe occurred. The line of
march led across a tidal creek spanned by a narrow wooden

bridge without rails, and for some reason the causeway that led to it was left undefended. The French cavalry came down from the rear and slaughtered the trapped Englishmen almost at will, and over forty English flags were displayed in triumph in the Paris Cathedral of Notre Dame.

A vicious storm caught the survivors after they finally set sail and some of the smaller ships were wrecked. Robert Herrick lived through all this, but two-thirds of the men who went out to the Isle of Rhé did not return.

George Herbert's brother Edward wrote an account of the campaign at Buckingham's request, using the notes the Duke had taken. Edward naturally attempted to exonerate his own side and informed the French firmly: "Our victories were masculine, glorious and due to our virtue . . . yours were only opportune, obnoxious and momentary." But most Englishmen were appalled by the disaster, and the fact that Buckingham had been trying to help the cause of the French Protestants made no difference to a general conviction "that either the Duke of Buckingham miscarried affairs purposely to undo the Church there, or that God cursed and blasted all the enterprises of so irreligious and profane an instrument."

A lieutenant on the Isle of Rhé, whose name was John Felton and whose captain was killed in the retreat, believed he himself should be promoted to the captain's place. Buckingham refused and Felton left the army to give himself over to brooding. The following summer he bought a tenpenny knife, made his way down to Portsmouth and murdered the Duke in broad daylight in a room full of people. So ended the tragicomedy of the great Buckingham's reign. The King, rigid with grief, lacked the money to raise a monument to his beloved; the vast library that the Duke had promised Cambridge went unbuilt; the foreign wars he had instigated ceased, and his followers found places for themselves elsewhere as best they could.

The suggestion was made that some sort of a reward ought to be given the men who had "served as chaplains in his Majesty's

ships and ventured their persons in the action at the Isle of Rhé."
In the case of Robert Herrick, at least, such a reward was forth-
coming; for the King had the right to bestow the vicarage of
Dean Prior, in Devon, and in September of 1629 he gave it to
Herrick.

Herrick was not able to take over the vicarage immediately.
The previous incumbent was Dr. Barnaby Potter, one of the
King's chaplains, who would normally have vacated it in early
spring when he became Bishop of Carlisle. But Potter held the
Dean Prior vicarage *in commendam,* a device which had originally been intended to prevent a living from remaining empty
until a worthy successor could be found but in practice was
usually a way of collecting extra tithes.[2] Herrick could hope to
obtain his vicarage fairly soon, but in the meantime all he could
do was to wait.

It was during this year of 1629 that Herrick's mother died. She
had been living with her married daughter, Mercy Wingfield, in
Suffolk, and she died there in August. Julian Herrick's will was a
careful one, itemizing even her saddlecloth and her "lesser cut-
work handkerchief" and not forgetting her coachman or the boy
in the kitchen. Most of the property went to Mercy, except for
the hundred pounds that Julian left William, her youngest. William's wife was left a ring worth twenty shillings, and the same
bequest was made to Robert and Nicholas. By this time Nicholas
Herrick was a prosperous London merchant who had grown rich
by trading in the Levant, and since Robert was in holy orders
their mother may have felt that neither one needed her help.

Robert Herrick wrote no epitaph for Julian. The first member

---

1 Or at least such was the opinion of a lawyer whom Herrick greatly admired, the learned John Selden. Selden remarked with his usual briskness,
"There was some sense for *commendams* at first; when there was a living void,
and never a clerk to serve it, the bishops were to keep it till they found a fit
man; but now 'tis a trick for the bishop to keep it for himself." Walter Curll
held the Bemerton rectory in this fashion as long as he was Bishop of
Rochester, and it did not become available to George Herbert until Curll
was made Bishop of Bath and Wells.

of the family to receive that honor was his niece Elizabeth, who died the following year when she was eleven. Her family lived in Westminster, and she was buried in the ancient and beautiful parish church of St. Margaret's where she had been christened. Most of the memorials in St. Margaret's were couched either in pious Latin prose or doggerel English rhyme, and Herrick's verses in the north aisle shine out like a lullaby to a good child.

> Sleep, while we hide thee from the light,
> Drawing thy curtains round: Good night.

Elizabeth was William Herrick's daughter, and of all his brothers Robert seems to have loved William the best. When William himself lay dying, Robert wrote a poem of real anguish, and a second poem "upon his brother's death" apparently refers to William also.

> Sunk is my sight; set is my sun;
> And all the loom of life undone:
> The staff, the elm, the prop, the shelt'ring wall
> Whereon my vine did crawl,
> Now, now, blown down . . .

Yet even such a tragedy as this could not make Herrick unhappy for long, for his was a temperament that did not harbor grief. The full title of the poem is "An Ode to Master Endymion Porter, upon his brother's death," and the general idea is that Porter's comforting hand has made it possible for Herrick to stand upright once more.

Endymion Porter had been a good friend to many poets. He was that most gratifying of combinations—a rich man who really admired writers—and since he was easygoing and affectionate he did not value himself too highly. He admitted that when he wrote verse he would spend an hour searching through "the whole kennel of the alphabet" to find a rhyme, and he felt a wholehearted admiration for anyone who could do better. The poets in return gave him a special gratitude. It charmed Herrick that so many poets paid tribute to his friend and he surveyed the

throng of his fellow writers with real satisfaction. "We are thy
prophets, Porter; thou our king."

Endymion Porter was a close friend of both Charles and Buckingham, and when the Prince and the Duke had gone on their
rather collegiate expedition to Spain, Porter was one of three
young men who went with them. He married the Duke of Buckingham's niece and to the end of his life worshipped his friend's
memory. In fact, he left a special request to his heirs that "all
of them observe and respect the children and family of my Lord
Duke of Buckingham, to whom I owe all the happiness I had
in the world."

A successful courtier like Endymion Porter could do a great
deal for his friends, and he did it willingly. Porter was extremely
kind to that irresponsible poet, William D'Avenant, and be-
friended him with more patience than most people were willing
to show; and he was apparently very good to Herrick, who called
him "my chief preserver." It may very well have been Porter
who recommended Herrick to Buckingham as a chaplain, and
he may also have been responsible for the small commissions
that Herrick was now getting.

At about this time Herrick wrote several songs which were
set to music and sung in the King's presence at Whitehall.
Charles had an expert and cultivated ear for music, and the best
musicians in England all held court appointments. Henry Lawes,
for instance, was a Gentleman of the Chapel Royal and Nicholas
Lanier was Master of the King's Music. Both of them set Herrick's songs to music to be sung before the King, and Herrick
was grateful both to "rare Lanier" and to that closer friend he
called "my Harry."

Most of Herrick's court songs were written for use in the
Chapel Royal and were therefore devotional in nature. Herrick
was in holy orders but he was not primarily a religious poet, and
some of these Whitehall songs are not altogether successful. In
two cases, Herrick turned his pictorial imagination to the subject of circumcision, and the best that can be said is that the

poems are no worse than one on the same subject by the much-admired William Cartwright, which was also set to music by Henry Lawes.

A much better example of Herrick's art is "A Christmas Carol," which was also set by Lawes and sung in the presence of the King. Herrick had a youthful approach to religion and he did best when he combined it with children. To Herrick, Jesus is the "darling of the world" and also an excuse for innocent revelling, and he produced a charming carol which must have been made all the lovelier by the beautifully trained male voices that sang it.

The same quality of innocence shows in a pastoral that Herrick wrote to celebrate the birth of the King's son. Prince Charles was born on the twenty-ninth of May, 1630, when "the star Venus was visible all day long," and with no thought of blasphemy this led Herrick's imagination to "God's sweet babe, when born at Bethlehem." The song is a pretty thing, full of shepherds and flowers and the love that Herrick had for children. The little prince was baptized by Bishop Laud in June, with the Gentlemen of the Chapel Royal in full attendance, and since Herrick's song had been set by Nicholas Lanier it may have been one of those they sang as they escorted the baby through the palace, "making excellent harmony . . . to the nursery door." [2]

Four months after the christening of Prince Charles, Herrick made a request to the King. Bishop Potter's tenure at Dean Prior expired at Michaelmas, and Herrick at once wrote out his "humble petition." He reminded His Majesty of his service as a military chaplain and that he had been promised the vicarage as soon as the *commendam* expired. There was no reason to refuse the request and at the end of September, 1630, Herrick officially became the vicar of Dean Prior, during the same month in which Herbert was ordained rector of Bemerton.

---

[2] The royal children were born into an atmosphere as devout as any Puritan's. When Princess Anne lay dying she was told to say her prayers, and she answered apologetically that she could not manage her "long prayer." She was not quite four years old.

George Herbert, who served for three years, was exactly the
kind of holy, dedicated minister that King Charles and Bishop
Laud longed to see in every parish church in England. Robert
Herrick, who served ten times that long, was not. He was once
reported, in fact, for failing to do his duty, and the welfare of
his parishioners' souls does not seem to have caused him much
concern. Yet he was a happy man and an affectionate one, and
the inhabitants of Dean Prior were not wholly unfortunate in
their new parson.

CHAPTER TWENTY-ONE

W HEN GEORGE HERBERT BECAME A RECTOR IN WILTSHIRE HE merely moved south, surrounded by friends and relatives, to settle near a large city and a kinsman's country estate. When Robert Herrick became a vicar in Devon he travelled the width of England, away from court and city and into a county as alien and self-contained as another land.

A seventh-century traveller spoke of "grim Devon," and even as late as the nineteenth century its inhabitants had a reputation for dourness. They mistrusted "foreigners," whom they defined as anyone from another neighborhood. Perhaps this was so in part because it was not an easy land for travelling. Every seventeenth-century traveller in Devon mentions the difficulty of getting about on the narrow, hilly roads, and even a hundred years after Herrick's arrival there were no carriages there. All the freight was carried on horseback—hay and corn and fuel and even stones—and the plowing was done by oxen. In the winter the mire was deep, and the wary inhabitants wore special boots attached to the saddle to keep their legs dry.

In the middle of south Devon was Dartmoor, a waste of land almost as lonely and strange as the great Salisbury Plain that lay near George Herbert's parsonage. Salisbury Plain had its Stonehenge, which the tourists looked at with awe, but no one visited Dartmoor except for turf or tin and to pasture cattle there in the summer. The granite tors of south Dartmoor were a special haunt of the pixies, and there grew up in that barren place a tribe called the gubbings, men and women who lived like savages and would not even bring their children for baptism.

Yet for all that, Herrick had come to a "goodly province." Devon was full of excellent farms, and its wool and mutton were famous. So were its orchards, for the men of Devon were skilled at grafting and produced magnificent cider. Wild strawberries grew on the northern banks of the roadways, to be gathered by passing horsemen and eaten with cream or wine. It was a land of many rivers making their way towards the sea, and it was a land also of small country gentry rather than a few great land-owners.

Herrick's own parish of Dean was made up of about four thousand acres on the southeastern slopes of Dartmoor. The parish was made up of three villages, Dean Prior, Dean Combe and Dean Church. Dean Prior was the largest, and about a mile and a half from it was Dean Church, where Herrick conducted the services and had his little vicarage.

The soil was the good red earth that covers marble in Devon, not the grey and grudging earth that covers slate, and in that fertile district the flowers and wheat and apple trees flourished. As Herrick stood in his churchyard he could look out at the wild moorland from the beautiful green countryside at his feet, but he does not mention the Devonshire scenery in his poetry and speaks of the river Dean only to insult it.

According to the episcopal register, Herrick was installed as vicar of Dean Prior on the twenty-ninth of October, 1630. He was probably inducted in the same fashion as George Herbert, with the bell rope in his hand, since this was "the most common and usual way, and therefore the safest." For Herbert, this day was the climax of his life; to Herrick, its chief importance was more probably the fact that as vicar of St. Mary's he now received an income of twenty-one pounds a year.

The income was not a large one. Even in Elizabethan times it was felt that a parson could not be expected to live on less than thirty pounds a year and prices had been rising ever since. But Herrick's expenses were small and he seems to have been able to live comfortably, for he was a man of simple tastes and easily contented.

Ever since he was a young man Herrick had been writing

poems on the joys of the simple country life, patterned on Horace
and Martial and repeating the same things that a great many
other English poets had been saying. But the poems he wrote on
this theme after he came to Dean Prior seem to come from the
heart rather than from a book. He really enjoyed his small farm
and his little country household, contemplating them with such
innocent pleasure that he was able to write a poem like "A
Thanksgiving to God, for his House."

> Lord, Thou hast given me a cell
>   Wherein to dwell;
> And little house, whose humble roof
>   Is weatherproof;
> Under the spars of which I lie
>   Both soft and dry . . .
> Like as my parlor, so my hall
>   And kitchen's small:
> A little buttery, and therein
>   A little bin,
> Which keeps my little loaf of bread
>   Unchipt, unflead:
> Some brittle sticks of thorn or briar
>   Make me a fire,
> Close by whose living coal I sit,
>   And glow like it.
> Lord, I confess too, when I dine,
>   The pulse is Thine,
> And all those other bits, that be
>   There plac'd by Thee;
> The worts, the purslane, and the mess
>   Of watercress,
> Which of Thy kindness Thou has sent;
>   And my content
> Makes those, and my beloved beet,
>   To be more sweet . . .

Herrick's religious mood is usually that of a good child, and he
had no difficulty in finding joy in little things.

When Herrick listed his "private wealth" at Dean Prior, he
included an orphan lamb which he had personally reared. He

also had a cat, a very reliable hen, a somewhat noisy goose, and
a spaniel. The spaniel was named Tracy and well-loved, and
when Tracy died Herrick wrote a poem in mourning. He also
wrote two poems in honor of his pet sparrow, whose name was
Phil, and they might be called literary exercises in a long tradition that dates back to Catullus if Herrick were not so obviously
the kind of man to surround himself with pets. In fact, it was
still remembered of him in Dean Prior a century later that he
kept a pet pig.

Since Herrick was a bachelor he needed someone to run his
house for him, and this raised a problem the delicacy of which
he was evidently not aware. When George Herbert wrote his
book of advice to country parsons, he suggested that it was wise
for an unmarried minister to have a male cook and send his
laundry out. Herrick, unperturbed by appearances, had a housekeeper named Prudence Baldwin. She must have been younger
than he was, for Herrick died old and Prudence outlived him;
and he never attempted to conceal his pleasure in having her
about. In his list of reasons for rural happiness he includes "my
Prue, by good luck sent," and in a set of verses called "His Content in the Country" he proclaims the joy of "my Prue and me."
He wrote her epitaph once, probably because she had asked him
to, and prophesied that violets would spring from her grave; and
when she was ill he offered up a cock, in the approved Roman
manner, for the recovery of his "dearest maid." She stayed by him
loyally, in good times and bad, and he called her "kind Prue"
when he thanked her for her faithfulness.

Herrick seems to have been on somewhat less affable terms
with the farmers who made up the bulk of the congregation.
The average countryman of the seventeenth century was a fairly
primitive individual, and even George Herbert did not ask for
very high standards when he discussed the matter of making
the responses in church. All he asked was that it should not be
done "in a huddling or slubbering fashion, gaping, or scratching
the head, or spitting." A remote parish like Dean Prior was prob-

ably even less civilized than the one at Bemerton, and some of Herrick's most scurrilous epigrams seem to be pointed at his own parishioners. Or perhaps it is only a coincidence that some of the names he used, Scobble and Mudge, Dundridge and Coone, appear also in the Dean Prior register.

There is no doubt, at any rate, that Herrick was seriously displeased with his parishioners the year he left, for he departed with a vociferous insult which he entitled "To Dean-Bourn, a rude river in Devon, by which sometimes he lived." In the long run at least his flock was rather flattered than otherwise, and an eighteenth-century antiquarian noted that "The Farewell to Dean-Bourn is still remembered by some old people of that parish . . . it never having been committed to writing but . . . passed down, from father to son by oral instruction." The story was also passed down, from generation to generation, that Herrick "one day threw his sermon at the congregation, with a curse for their inattention." His relationship with his parishioners might occasionally be unorthodox but it was evidently not dull.

If Herrick and his congregation agreed over nothing else, they may have met in their mutual fondness for country festivals. Herrick came of a family that knew how to enjoy itself and he encountered the same approach in Devon. Three years before Herrick arrived, there had been an attempt to suppress the wakes, which the Devon authorities felt were degenerating into rowdy drinking parties, but the "people desired their continuance." In his poem on the subject of wakes, Herrick speaks of the happy rustics "drencht in ale or drowned in beer" with the enthusiasm of a man who knew exactly how it felt.

For a man like George Herbert, the calendar of the year was illumined by the great religious festivals, Palm Sunday and Easter, Whitsunday and Christmas. Herrick's heart moved to a more pagan rhythm and when he thought of Christmas it was of the Yule log and "the rare mince-pie." Twelfth Night is plum cake and joy-sops, with plenty of nutmeg in the ale, and the following day is dedicated to St. Distaff and a series of practical

jokes between the maids and the plowmen. The first of February brings Candlemas Eve, when the holly and mistletoe must
be taken down, and in another poem on the same subject Herrick
warns that for every leaf left behind, "so many goblins you shall
see." In the same way, part of the Yule log must be saved on
Candlemas Day to tend next year's fire or the fiend will mischief
the house. Mid-Lent Sunday brings simnel cakes, and Herrick's
spring leaps to its triumphant climax with that most pagan of
symbols, the Maypole. The next great festival is Harvest-Home,
when the last sheaves of wheat in the fields are made gay with
flowers and ribbons and borne triumphantly in a cart through the
village streets to the sound of pipes and tabors. Herrick has an
especially loving and brilliant description of this, down to the
pies and custard and "stout beer" of the festival supper, and he
brings the year to full circle on Christmas Eve with the ceremony
of guarding the Christmas pie.

The new vicar of Dean Prior also took an interest in witches,
and he supplies some useful rhymed advice on keeping them
away. A crust of bread is recommended, a knife with the point
up or a wafer cake; dough should have the mark of the cross
upon it, and washing water should be thrown as far away as
possible. Herrick may very well have believed in witches and
goblins, as the country people around him certainly did. Or he
may have been like that other city poet, Horace, who returned
to share with the tenants of his farm the ancient superstitions
of the land and of his own childhood. Herrick was the poet of
youth and play, and he rejoiced in the ancient customs that were
still a normal part of English country life.

Even within the confines of his duty as vicar there were opportunities for judicious merrymaking. There was, for instance, Rogation Week, when it was the minister's duty to lead his congregation around the bounds of the parish so that no one would
forget where the landmarks lay. The English parish had no legal
boundary, only the traditional one that lay within the memories
of its own parishioners; and both Herbert and Herrick had the

annual duty of leading the people through the farms and the
fields, invoking a blessing on the young crops and repeating the
Mosaic formula: "Cursed be he that removeth his neighbor's
landmark." These had been called Gang Days in the canons of
Cuthbert in the eighth century, and they were held on the three
fast days before Holy Thursday. But the fasting did not prevent
a good deal of drinking, and the parish expenses usually included eight or nine shillings "spent upon the parishioners for
wine at the perambulation."

Herrick had other duties. It was up to him to cooperate with
the churchwardens in the management and policing of the parish
and to make sure that the alms chest in the church had three
locks and three keys. Another chest held that important document, the parish register, whose tough parchment pages contained the record of all the weddings, baptisms and burials in
the community. Whatever armor the parish possessed was frequently kept in the church, and in general it served as a focus
for the life of the community.

In return for services rendered, there were a number of extra
fees that could be collected—a shilling for a peal of bells at a
wedding, two shillings and eightpence for a burial if the coffin
were included, twopence for Easter offerings at communion.
Some of these fees went into the parish fund, some went to the
clerk or the sexton, and some were the prerogative of the minister himself. Herrick, for instance, had the right to supply dis-
pensations to his parishioners so that they could eat meat during
Lent, at a standard rate of six shillings and eightpence.

Most of a minister's income came from the tithes, that tenth
part of the land's increase which had once been a voluntary
offering but was now a compulsory payment made twice a year.
Since Herrick was only a vicar and not a rector he did not receive all the tithes in Dean Prior, and collecting them was probably not always easy. Country parishioners had the reputation
of being "bad paymasters and narrow-hearted contentious
chuffs," and George Herbert, who could find excuses for anyone,

explained this by saying that "country people live hardly . . . feeling their own sweat and consequently knowing the price of money."

Even if there was good will on both sides, the question of the tithes was a complicated one. A farmer clearly owed the parson a tenth of his peas if he used them to feed the hogs, but what about the peas eaten by the family? What happened to the parson's share of the lambs if the farmer had only nine that year? Did a tenth of the apples include windfalls? Should an egg be considered tithable if the parson had already collected on the chicken? These were knotty questions and sometimes gave rise to a good deal of argument. John Earle characterized the ideal minister as one who would not "wrangle for the odd egg," but the average parson lived on so narrow a margin that he needed everything he could get.

Herrick's only epigram on the subject is relatively mild—a reproof to the parishioner who will not "justly pay his tithes" and hoards like an ant. But Herrick took a light-hearted view of the subject and he apparently did some of his collecting in less ecclesiastical areas. As he once pointed out to a bride:

> If nine times you your bridegroom kiss,
> The tenth, you know, the parson's is.

"Pay, then," added Herrick enthusiastically, "your tithe."

CHAPTER TWENTY-TWO

N OT ALL THE MEMBERS OF ROBERT HERRICK'S CONGREGATION were farmers. Among the names that appear in the parish register for baptisms and weddings and burials are those of the Giles family and the Northleigh, the Lowmans and the Yards.

The most distinguished member of the gentry in Dean Prior was Sir Edward Giles, lord of the manor. Sir Edward was a baronet, having been knighted by King James, and when he returned to Devon in all the glory of his new title his father was inclined to tease him a little about it. The family seat was at Bowden, where Sir Edward had been born, but since he was childless he made one of his relatives his heir and moved his own household to Dean Prior. When Herrick knew him he was about fifty years old, a country gentleman who had served faithfully in Parliament during two reigns and was now living peacefully in retirement with his wife Mary. His handsome house, Dean Court, stood in its walled park about half a mile from Herrick's vicarage, with a fireplace that was large enough for the most magnificent of Yule logs.

Sir Edward died at Christmastime, seven years after Herrick became vicar of Dean Prior, and he was buried in the parish church on the twenty-eighth of December, 1637. His wife continued to live in Dean Prior and her death is recorded five years later, but his house went to the relatives that Sir Edward had made his heirs. They had married into the Yard family and it was Edward Yard who moved into Dean Court, with the carved plaster ceiling in the hall and the family coat of arms so prominently displayed. He was evidently already a resident of Dean Prior, for the year before Sir Edward died Herrick had baptized

211

"Giles, the son of Edward Yard, Esq." and in the next two years he baptized two more of Yard's sons.

Edward Yard had a sister a year younger than himself whose name was Lettice, and whom Herrick calls "the most witty Mistress Lettice Yard." When she was thirty she married Henry Northleigh, a Devon man who was an Oxford graduate. Herrick celebrated the occasion with a poem to be sung at the bride-groom's door, and it echoes the wedding songs he wrote for earlier friends. Like the advice he gave to Sir Clipseby Crew fourteen years before, he bids the happy couple reproduce like fishes, and like the epithalamium to Sir Thomas Southwell he ends with the gentle hope that they will die together. The North-leighs settled down in Dean Prior, and the children who were born to them are recorded in the parish register.

Lettice had two half sisters, Amy and Grace, of whom Herrick was very fond. They were the daughters of Dr. Barnaby Potter, Herrick's predecessor as vicar, who had married Lettice's mother, Elizabeth Yard, after she had been three years a widow. All his children were born at Dean Prior before he became Bishop of Carlisle, and his youngest daughter, Grace, was baptized on a day in May, 1624. She grew up to be an exceedingly pretty girl and Herrick wrote a poem on the perfect proportions of her face. Grace Potter's sister, Amy, was the subject of an even more amorous approach on Herrick's part.

> . . . Give him your hand to kiss
> Who both your wooer and your poet is . . .
> Dear, can you like, and liking love your poet?

Another charming young lady of Dean Prior was Bridget Lowman, a niece of Sir Edward Giles. Herrick wrote two poems in her honor when she was crowned queen of the flowers in the Devon meadows one spring. He calls her "princess of the feast" and "lady of this fairy land," and he promises that in all future springtimes, if he lives, "Herrick shall make the meadow-verse for you."

It was later said of the vicar of Dean Prior that he "became much beloved by the gentry in those parts." He seems to have loved them in return, with that free affection that Herrick gave to so many people, and their presence lightened a rural atmosphere in which most of the parishioners saw no further than the ends of their own plows.

Moreover his parish was not isolated, for the high road linked it with Exeter some twenty miles to the north. Exeter was the largest and busiest city in the West Country and its admirers called it, quite truly, "a little London." It was an extremely busy port, with excellent shipping facilities and markets and shops, "a round city on a rising hill" that was ringed with ancient walls and battlements and yet was highly vigorous and modern. In the suburbs there were walks and bowling grounds, and the city's prosperity rested on a solid mercantile foundation of woolen cloth and serges. The finest kerseys in England were made in Devon and some of its inhabitants could think of nothing else, like the man named Lusk in Herrick's epigram who wished to be buried in woolen cloth since he had made all his wealth that way.

Exeter was the ecclesiastical center of Devon and had as its bishop the learned and literary Joseph Hall. Hall was a native of Leicestershire who had been installed as Bishop of Exeter three years before Herrick's arrival, and in his youth he had achieved a special place in English literary history by being one of the lively young satirists of the 1590's whose work was banned by the Archbishop of Canterbury. His later works were of a more sober nature, and it was to these that Herrick was referring when he addressed a poem to Hall as "my learned diocesan." Herrick requested him to sanctify at least one of the poems with his approval, and since the Bishop was a good-natured man he probably obliged. Unlike the previous Bishop of Exeter, Hall got along well with the city authorities, signing himself "your much devoted loving neighbor," and his chief fault was a tendency to plant his relatives in Cathedral positions.

The church revenues were not what they had been in the
Middle Ages, and part of the Bishop's great palace was left
unused or rented out as a warehouse. But the Cathedral itself
was a splendid one, famous for its huge and beautiful organ.
A lieutenant from Norwich who visited the city in 1635 said that
the organ combined with the choir to produce a "heavenly
harmony," and the music that could be had in Exeter must have
been one of its chief attractions for Herrick. He loved music
deeply, and the four poems he addressed "To Music" make it
clear that the enchantment it possessed for him was almost as
pure and as powerful as that of poetry itself.

The young lieutenant from Norwich had a thoroughly good
time in Exeter, and he spoke approvingly of the excellent ale he
had enjoyed in the Cathedral close along with the "honest organist and some of the merry vicars." This was another aspect of the
city that Herrick must have appreciated; the local divines were
excellent drinkers and some of Herrick's most convivial friends
were his fellow parsons in Devon.

When Herrick wrote an early draft of the poem he called "His
Age," he singled out Martin Nansogg as one of his drinking
companions. Nansogg came of an old West Country family near
Exeter which had produced a vicar as far back as the days of
Edward the Third, and although Bishop Hall found him unsatisfactory as a chaplain this would not have affected Nansogg's
qualifications as a companion for Herrick.

Another Devonshire parson, James Smith, is listed in the same
poem. Like Herrick, Smith served as a chaplain in the abortive
expedition to the Isle of Rhé, and apart from being a notable
drinker he was also a fairly talented writer of light verse. He
and another friend of Herrick's, Sir John Mennes, produced a
series of anthologies in which their own verse was sensibly included, and the volumes were sufficiently off-color to sell very
well.

A friend of theirs, and a very close friend of Herrick's, was
that other Devonshire parson, John Weekes. Herrick and Weekes

had gone to college together, they had been inducted into the ministry together, they had gone to the Isle of Rhé together, and now they both served country parishes in Devonshire. Weekes held the rectory of Sherwell in the northern part of the shire, but the year in which Herrick was presented with his vicarage Weekes tried to get one in the south. He wanted Diptford, which was only a few miles from Dean Prior and within easy walking distance, and wrote to ask the help of Endymion Porter. The two were close friends, judging from the tone of Weekes' letter, but for once Porter was not able to be of use and Diptford went to one of the King's chaplains instead. Nevertheless Weekes was given at various times a rectory in Cornwall, a prebend in Bristol Cathedral, a chaplaincy to Laud, a deanery and a post as licenser of books, so that his petitions in general did not go unheard.

Weekes was a widower when Herrick first came to Devon. His wife Bridget had died in 1627, only a few months before the expedition to the Isle of Rhé. She was a most distinguished lady, for her father was the great Sir Richard Grenville of the *Revenge* and her first husband was a Devon knight who had been one of Raleigh's closest friends. Weekes remained a widower for nearly a decade and then in 1636 he married again. His new wife was Grace Cary, sister of the Dean of Exeter, and he married her on the first of August in Exeter Cathedral.

Next to Herrick's fellow divines, most of his friends in Devon seem to have been lawyers. Devon was famous for its lawyers— no county in England except Norfolk produced more—and Herrick paid honor to two of them in his poetry. One was Sir George Parry, who had been trained at the Inner Temple and who became Recorder of Exeter. The other was John Were, also of the Inner Temple and a famous Exeter alderman, whom Herrick respected for his civilized attitude towards the law.

The most interesting of Herrick's lawyer friends was Thomas Shapcot. His home was in the middle of Devon in the lonely parish of Knowstone, but Shapcot preferred to spend most of his

time in the busy, lively city of Exeter. Herrick valued him for his
interest in "things that are curious and unfamiliar," and he dedicated to Shapcot two poems that describe the court of the fairies.
They are named "Oberon's Feast" and "Oberon's Palace," and
a third poem, on Oberon's temple, was dedicated to yet another
lawyer, John Merrifield.

These three fairy poems are an account in octosyllabic verse
of the way that King Oberon and Queen Mab conduct their
court. All Herrick's precise, delicate art as a miniaturist and all
his brilliant control of detail combine to picture with a painter's
vividness the life of his small, odd folk. They are court beings,
tiny fantastics of the Old Religion, who spend their miniature
lives feasting and making love while Herrick examines them in
affectionate detail.

In Herrick's fairyland the kernels of a dried apple core are
rattled to sound the call to evensong, the stewed thigh of a newt
is laid on a mushroom table, and a cave is paved with the nicest
care by Herrick and the fairies.

> Squirrels' and children's teeth late shed
> Are neatly here enchequered
> With brownest toadstools, and the gum
> That shines upon the bluer plum.

This gift for precise detail may have been developed in part
by Herrick's youthful training as a goldsmith; Nicholas Hilliard,
that brilliant painter of miniatures for the courts of Elizabeth
and James, was trained as a goldsmith also. But most of it Herrick owed to an alert eye and a remembering heart. He noticed
everything—the silver shine of a snail's track on wheat straws,
the small knobs that are "the horns of papery butterflies," the
pattern of a trout fly's wings—and he envelops them in a curious
atmosphere that is half mockery and half delight as he describes
the life of his fairy beings and their intent, ceremonial ways.

It is not known when the poems were written, and therefore it
cannot be said whether Herrick was starting a fashion or follow-

ing one. A friend of his, Sir Simeon Steward, wrote some verses on the same subject and gave it a title almost as detailed as a laundry list: "A description of the King of Fairies' clothes, brought to him on New Year's Day in the morning, 1626, by his Queen's chambermaids." [1] Describing the fairies was a popular game among poets in the twenties and early thirties and most of the verse was not of very high quality. Next to Herrick, the most skillful poet in this field was Michael Drayton, whose "fairy court" was admired even by Ben Jonson.

Jonson himself, during the last year of his life, was working on a play that brought in glowworms and beetles and "span-long elves" and "giddy flitter-mice with leather wings." It was characteristic of him to be working on so sunlit a play after having endured nearly a decade stretched on a paralytic's bed. But his lively spirit was undimmed, and so was his attraction for the young men who still lit their candles by his light. When Jonson died on an August day in 1637, he left behind him an emptiness that no one else could ever fill.

A memorial volume was planned in honor of his memory, and Herrick evidently believed that he would be asked to contribute to it. There is in existence a stiff and formal poem written by him which repeats the same routine references to Jonson's art that are found in the memorial volume. But Herrick's poem was not printed with the rest and perhaps he was never asked to send it in.

In any case, it is the other poems which Herrick wrote in praise of Ben Jonson which express much more truly their relationship: the six-line epitaph to his master as the best of poets, the ode to "my Ben" and the drinking parties, and above all the lovely lyric that Herrick named "His Prayer to Ben Jonson."

---

[1] Sir Simeon Steward was a fellow-commoner in Herrick's college of Trinity Hall, and he lived there so long that he had his coat of arms carved over the chimney piece. Three years after Herrick received his M.A., he sent as a yuletide gift to Sir Simeon a "jolly verse crowned with ivy" on the joys of Christmastime.

When I a verse shall make,
Know I have prayed thee,
For old religion's sake,
Saint Ben to aid me.

Make the way smooth for me,
When I, thy Herrick,
Honoring thee, on my knee,
Offer my lyric.

Candles I'll give to thee,
And a new altar;
And thou Saint Ben, shall be
Writ in my psalter.

Jonson's death in London must have deepened Herrick's sense of exile. He had many friends in Devon, but it seemed a grey sort of life after the color and excitement of London.

More discontents I never had,
Since I was born, than here;
Where I have been, and still am sad,
In this dull Devonshire . . .

Yet there was a compensation, and a great one. A country minister who did not take his religious duties seriously had time on his hands, and the sin of sloth was usually considered to be his chief temptation. Herrick had no inclination to sloth, not as long as there was a blank sheet of paper in front of him and lines of poetry running through his head. He therefore had to admit that there was at least one advantage in dull Devonshire, and so he ended his verse.

Yet justly too I must confess;
I ne'er invented such
Ennobled numbers for the press
Than where I loath'd so much.

CHAPTER TWENTY-THREE

SINCE THE DAYS OF HIS APPRENTICESHIP, THE WRITING OF POETRY had been the chief thing in Robert Herrick's life. And with this had come, in time, the idea of a single book in which all his work would be gathered together. The dream had come to him relatively early, for in the 1620's he was already talking about "my Book" in the same excited terms he used two decades later.

The book was to be his memorial as a poet—"a laurel, to grow green for ever." It was to be a memorial also to all the people who were fortunate enough to be mentioned in it. Over the years Herrick had written a large number of tributes to friends and relatives and public personages, or, as he put it in one of his more stately moments:

> . . . I've travell'd all this realm throughout
> To seek, and find some few immortals out
> To circumspangle this my spacious sphere . . .

Sometimes he thought of his growing collection of poems as a mighty town—"a city here of heroes I have made"—and sometimes he thought of the inhabitants of his book as "a stock of saints" or as jewels in an "eternal coronet." But whatever the wording the idea is always the same. The fortunate individuals who have stepped into his book are worthy of immortality and he has assured them of it.

> Stand by the magic of my powerful rhymes
> 'Gainst all the indignation of the times . . .
> While others perish, here's thy life decreed
> Because begot of my immortal seed.

This idea of the poet's ability to confer immortality has been a poetic commonplace ever since the first rhymer tried to bribe his first patron with a vision of the approval of posterity. But in this case the men and women whom Herrick honors are not always influential people from whom he might expect something in return. He hymns the wonders of his friends and relatives, not with any idea of payment or return, but out of sheer innocent enthusiasm for their attainments. He really believed that Dr. William Alabaster, who had done a commentary on the *Apocalypse,* was a great seer who understood the secrets of eternity; and, when a nephew of Herrick's took up painting, his admiring uncle was sure that he had only to continue as he had begun to outdo both Rubens and Titian. The advantages of the situation are twofold in Herrick's eyes. He is fortunate to have so many remarkable friends and relatives, and they are fortunate to be included in this deathless memorial of the poet's love.

It was perhaps because Herrick's eyes were fixed so strongly on this vision of "my Book" that his poems were not published separately during all these years. His work must have been well liked; it was passed around freely in manuscript and there are twenty-four copies of one of his poems. And yet by the time Herrick was forty-nine and had been writing poetry for at least thirty years, only six of his poems were in print and none of the six was attributed to him.

The first of Herrick's poems to appear in print reached the public in the revised edition of Stow's *Survey of London* that was published in 1633. The book contained a discussion of the monuments in St. Margaret's church, and among the epitaphs that were quoted was Herrick's memorial to his niece Elizabeth. A year or so later an early draft of the poem that Herrick called "Oberon's Feast" was published, also anonymously, in a collection of five poems on fairy lore. In 1640 a book called *Poems by Thomas Carew, Esquire* made its appearance, and within its pages were two of Herrick's poems. One was the little love song called "The Primrose," and the other was a pastoral verse in honor of his uncle Robert's daughter.

"The Primrose" was printed twice in 1640, for it appeared not only in the Carew collection but also in *Poems written by Wil. Shakespeare, Gent.* Three of Herrick's poems were included in the Shakespeare collection, and none of them was credited to him. He was merely one of the "other gentlemen" whose poems followed Shakespeare's to make weight in the volume.

When this particular book was announced for publication in the Stationers' Register of November, 1639, Herrick was identified as one of the poets who would be in it, along with Jonson, Beaumont and others. The two men who licensed the volume were also identified—a Mr. Featherstone who was one of the wardens of the Stationers' Company, and John Weekes who was Herrick's close friend. It is quite possible that Weekes passed along the news of the book to Herrick, and it may have been this that made Herrick finally decide to publish his own poems under his own name.

Herrick must have gone to London, since it would have been difficult to arrange for publication from the other end of England. There he negotiated with a London publisher named Andrew Crooke who kept a shop at the Sign of the Green Dragon in St. Paul's Churchyard. The result of these negotiations appeared in the Stationers' Register for the twenty-ninth of April, 1640, where it was announced that Crooke would publish as one of his forthcoming books "Poems written by Master Robert Herrick."

Andrew Crooke probably had the best of intentions but the book was evidently never published. Certainly there is no record of it anywhere. By this time Herrick had written a vast number of poems and perhaps Crooke felt incapable of publishing them all. Or perhaps he could see no market for them and abandoned the project before too much money had been invested in it. The times were troubled, and even a very enterprising publisher could not be blamed for a reluctance to invest in hundreds of poems by a comparatively unknown writer. If they had been religious poems it might have been different, since there was always a market for religious work, but very few of Herrick's verses were religious in nature.

Crooke's failure to publish the book must have been a real blow to Herrick. But he had a resilient nature and this was not the first disappointment he had known in his life. He had once cherished the hope, for instance, that Bishop Williams would do something for him. Even during the years of the Bishop's disgrace he had enough money and power to assist his fellow clerics, and particularly someone like Herrick who had been a member of his own college of St. John's. When Williams was imprisoned in the Tower of London in 1637, Herrick wrote a poem to express his sympathy, adding his hopes for the Bishop's quick release.

> This, as I wish for, so I hope to see;
> Though you, my lord, have been unkind to me:
> To wound my heart, and never to apply
> (When you had power) the meanest remedy . . .

Williams was released from the Tower during the same year in which Herrick had hoped to have his book published. The date of his release was the sixteenth of November, 1640, and Herrick was one of those who publicly rejoiced. He wrote as a New Year's gift a carol for Bishop Williams that was clearly intended to be sung at a public gathering by the friends of that effervescent prelate.

> Come then, great lord,
> And see our altar burn
> With love of your return.
> And not a man here but consumes
> His soul to glad you in perfumes.

Herrick was not supposed to be lingering about London even for so worthy a purpose as saluting a dignitary of the church. According to ecclesiastical law a vicar could not leave his parish unless he had a dispensation from his bishop, and Herrick had no such dispensation. Once, when John Weekes was being per-

suaded by his friends to come to London, they suggested that
the trip would be worth the risk.

> A London goal, with friends and drink,
> Is worth your vicarage, I think.

Herrick may have felt the same. He had never taken his pastoral
duties very seriously, and he probably believed that his presence
in London was thoroughly justified.

The officers of the Church of England thought otherwise and
the vicar of Dean Prior was duly reported for nonresidence. The
report is not dated but it is believed to have been made in 1640,
the year in which Herrick was hoping to get his book published.
It states that Herrick had no license to leave Dean Prior but that
he nevertheless was living at Westminster in the Little Almonry.

The Little Almonry was a street near Westminster Abbey and
lay in St. Margaret's parish. This was the parish in which Herrick's brother William had lived for many years, and the street
was near the church where his eleven-year-old niece had been
buried.

It was a musical district, for Herrick's street stood at right
angles to the Great Almonry, where the gentlemen who sang in
the Abbey choir had their residence. Living in the Little Almonry
itself was Henry Lawes, the distinguished composer who had
set some of Herrick's court songs to music. Herrick's poem in
praise of "my Harry" speaks of his admiration and his love, and
having Lawes as a neighbor must have added to the attractive-
ness of the district for him.

Many men loved Henry Lawes, and they loved his brother
William also; for both men were delightful human beings as
well as distinguished musicians. They had been born in Wiltshire and came of a musical background, for their father was
one of the singing men of Sarum, and Herrick was only one of
many poets who knew them well.

Henry Lawes enjoyed a special popularity with poets since
he was willing to subordinate his music to their words, and

writers like Milton and Waller united to praise so exemplary a
point of view. Lawes himself remarked that the ability to "shape
notes to the words and sense is not hit by too many," and this
courteous aspect of his art is evident in the settings he made for
some of Herrick's poems. When Herrick writes a word like
superabundantly, Lawes fits his notes to the syllables with self-
effacing grace, and when Herrick describes a kiss flying about
like a honeyed bird, Lawes' music follows as lightly as the bird
itself.

Herrick had other friends in St. Margaret's parish, and many
of the names that are found in his poems are to be found also in
the parish registers. Margaret Falconbrige, the little girl to
whom he wrote such a charming Valentine, was christened in
St. Margaret's, and so was Katherine Bradshaw, now in her
twenties, whom Herrick calls his "sweet mistress" in another
engaging rhyme.

There were two girls in St. Margaret's parish whom Herrick
knew especially well. These were the Parsons sisters, Dorothy
and Thomasin, whose father, John Parsons, had been the church
organist. Later he was promoted to be the organist of Westminster Abbey, which stood almost next door, and when he
died in 1623 he was survived by his wife Jane and their three
children. The older girl, Dorothy, was the object of one of Herrick's most affectionate lyrics.

> If thou ask me, dear, wherefore
> I do write of thee no more:
> I must answer, sweet, thy part
> Less is here than in my heart.

The younger daughter, Thomasin, was christened in St. Margaret's church in 1618, and she was probably still a child when
Herrick wrote this couplet in her honor.

> Grow up in beauty as thou dost begin,
> And be of all admired, Thomasin.

Thomasin Parsons would have been twenty-two in 1640, when Herrick was in London, and the report which cites him for non-residence also implies rather strongly that he was the father of her illegitimate child.

Thomasin Parsons hath had a bastard lately. She was brought to bed at Greenwich.

Mr. Herrick, a minister possessed of a very good living in Devonshire, hath not resided thereon, having no license for his non-residence and not being chaplain to any noble man or man qualified by law, as I hear. His lodging is at Westminster in the Little Almonry at Nicholas Weilkes his house where the said Thomasin lives.

There is no way of knowing whether the charge of fornication was true, as the charge of nonresidence certainly was. The report was made by "Mr. Dell's man," whose business it was to supply information of this kind to William Dell, secretary of the Archbishop of Canterbury. It was not Dell's business to investigate the charge. This was the function of Herrick's local diocese and the information should have been sent to Bishop Hall in Exeter.

There is no record in Exeter that bears on the charge and it may have been pursued no further. Perhaps Herrick was not the father of the child, as Mr. Dell's man seemed to feel that he was, and if he returned to his Devonshire parish with reasonable promptness the change of nonresidence could have been dropped.

Or it may be, if the conjectural date of 1640 is correct, that it was not possible to conduct the vigorous kind of investigation that William Laud, Archbishop of Canterbury, would have liked. That mighty edifice, the Church of England, was in serious trouble, so serious that there was little time to pursue the question of a misbehaving vicar in Devon.

CHAPTER TWENTY-FOUR

WILLIAM LAUD, ARCHBISHOP OF CANTERBURY, WOULD HAVE BEEN acting quite in character if he had concerned himself with the case of Robert Herrick even in this time of threatening catastrophe. No detail had even seemed trivial in Laud's eyes if it involved the welfare of the Church of England or the behavior of any of its ministers. For he was driven by a dream of perfection, and no change in outward circumstances could keep him from trying to do his duty.

Laud began his career with a single lapse from this high ideal, and the memory of it tormented him ever afterwards. When he was chaplain to Lord Mountjoy he performed the ceremony that united his patron to a divorced woman, and he marked the day by an annual fast in which he prayed to be forgiven for this one sin of expediency. "Behold I am become a reproach to Thy holy name, by serving my ambition and the sins of others. . . . Much more happy had I been if . . . I had suffered martyrdom, as did St. Stephen, the first of martyrs."

Laud's unrelenting determination to do right found very little scope under King James, who once remarked of him: "I keep Laud back from all place of rule and authority because I find he hath a restless spirit, and cannot see when matters are well, but loves . . . to bring things to a pitch of reformation floating in his own brain." When Laud was Dean of Gloucester, for instance, his restless spirit sent him to see what was wrong with the Cathedral and he found that the communion table was being moved about in the usual Protestant fashion instead of remaining fixed at the east end of the chancel. Laud believed ardently that the Church of England should be "kept up in uniformity and decency, and in some beauty of holiness," and he had the communion table set permanently in what he felt was the correct position. Since this was also the location of the altar in Roman Catholic churches, the people of Gloucester believed that Laud was trying to introduce popery into the Cathedral. They protested violently and "severe proceedings" were taken against them. For Laud considered them Puritan malcontents and would not let public pressure interfere with his duty to the Church of England.

When Charles came to the throne, Laud discovered that the new king was a man after his own heart. Laud's advance was extremely rapid, from one bishopric to another, until by 1629 he had become Bishop of London and a member of the Privy Council. This was the year in which King Charles decided he would reign without Parliament, and even that foolhardy decision was no more frightening to the average conservative Englishman than what Laud had been trying to do in the Church of England. Matthew Sutcliffe died that year, a distinguished churchman who had helped King James organize a theological college for "the righting of errors and heresies," and Sutcliffe wrote in agony that Laud's party was moving "towards popery and Babylonian slavery, endeavoring to make a rent in God's church and a peace between heresy and God's true faith."

What chiefly frightened Sutcliffe was Laud's endeavor to get rid of the doctrine of predestination. In spite of the rigidity of one side of Laud's nature he was a liberal in theological matters and like his friend Lancelot Andrewes he preferred to believe in something more humane than the iron Calvinist doctrine which divided all mankind, beyond hope of appeal, into the saved and the damned.

Predestination had always been a thorny subject in England, and trouble had been avoided up to now by a kind of gentleman's agreement not to discuss it. Queen Elizabeth's religious settlement was worded so ambiguously on this point that no one could openly disagree with it; and when Archbishop Whitgift tried to clarify matters with the Lambeth Articles, which came out flatly in favor of predestination, Elizabeth was furious with him and had the articles "quasht." She knew that nothing but trouble would come from arguments within the Church on so difficult a point, and she was quite right.

William Laud did not object to trouble. In fact, he went out of his way to welcome it. For it was his announced conviction that anyone who believed in predestination was really a Puritan at heart, a "doctrinal Puritan." As an admirer of his wrote in 1630, "Predestination is the root of Puritanism and Puritanism is the root of all rebellion."

It was true that the Puritans, being the most intense and literal-minded group in England, talked about the "elect" more than most people did and that they carried the doctrine through to its ultimate savagery. But it was also true that most orthodox English Protestants, from King James down, believed in the doctrine of predestination and that Matthew Sutcliffe was echoing conservative religious opinion when he called Laud's position a "heresy."

It is difficult to realize, in the twentieth century, why Laud's gentler doctrine seemed so dangerous to the average Englishman; but the matter was clear enough in the seventeenth century. In its long battle with the Roman Catholic church, the strongest single weapon that Protestantism possessed was the dogma that salvation came through God's absolute decree and had nothing to do with the work of churches. Predestination was the rock upon which militant Protestantism had been built, and now that the movement was fighting for its life on the Continent it was doubly important that its basic doctrine should not be betrayed from within.

To many Englishmen, Laud's attempted reform looked like such a betrayal. Like his equally well-meaning attempt to alter the services in Gloucester Cathedral, it seemed to be a sinister attempt to move the Church of England towards the Church of Rome. Laud and his supporters were called Arminians, after a somewhat similar movement in Holland, and the men who met in the Parliament of 1629 fought an anguished last-ditch battle against Laud's obvious favor with King Charles. "An Arminian is the spawn of a Papist; and if there come the warmth of favor upon him, you shall see him turn into one of the frogs that rise out of the bottomless pit."

For his part, Laud prayed daily for the welfare of the Church of England. "Gracious Father . . . fill it with all truth, in all truth, with all peace." The short, bright-eyed, quick-tempered little churchman knew that he had many enemies, but he was working for the glory of God and not the approval of man.

After the death of the Duke of Buckingham, Bishop Laud became for all practical purposes the King's chief minister. His opportunity for making enemies increased, whether it was among the members of the gentry whose grip on church offices he was trying to loosen and whose morals he was trying to improve, or whether it was among his fellow bishops whose views he suspected. George Herbert's bishop, John Davenant, was not normally a troublemaker, and neither was Herrick's bishop, Joseph Hall. Yet both men were forced on their knees before the Privy Council to answer the charges that Laud brought against them, and Bishop Hall said that he would vacate his office if Laud's spies would not leave him in peace.

Above all, of course, Laud was hated by the Puritans, the men who wanted to rid the land of bishops entirely. He had two strong weapons against them, the civil court of Star Chamber and the ecclesiastical Court of High Commission, and to the Puritans he became "the Arch-wolf of Canterbury . . . persecuting the saints and shedding the blood of the martyrs."

Laud became Archbishop of Canterbury when he was sixty years old, and a lesser man might have thought of resting from his labors. He moved into Lambeth Palace along with his cat and pet tortoise and noted with pleasure the songs of the thrushes and nightingales along the palace walks. Next year the birds did not return and Laud took it as an omen that he might have "a troublesome time" as Archbishop. It proved worse than troublesome. Yet even if he could have known that a violent death lay at the end of it he would not have swerved from his course.

"His error was . . . that he considered not the unreasonableness of the times." Laud had a touching faith in the power of reason, and since he knew that his reasons were good he was sure that the results would be satisfactory. He was like that other good man, Herbert's friend Nicholas Ferrar, who was trying to build a perfect community at Little Gidding in the same way that Laud was trying to build a perfect commonwealth. Ferrar had the advantage of working with a small, handpicked group, but even so he had difficulty in applying reason to emotion. His brother John had taken for his second wife a London woman named Bathsheba, and Nicholas attempted to deal with her in a spirit of godly reason over such matters as when the children should go out of long coats and into breeches. He quoted Scripture at Bathsheba, he wrote out long, careful statements which she refused to read, he and his brother prayed anxiously over her. And poor Bathsheba, deprived of any normal emotional outlet and expected to be wholly obedient, took refuge in hysteria.

For a time the Puritans had a safety valve. If Laud's paternal, tormenting attention became unendurable they could migrate to New England. But by 1637, when Laud had been Archbishop four years, it was clear that these mass migrations were upsetting property values and beginning to depopulate certain sections of England, to say nothing of the fact that the Massachusetts settlement was becoming a "receptacle of discontented, dangerous and schismatical persons." King Charles issued a proclamation in 1637 that no one would be allowed to migrate unless he had a certificate of conformity to the Church of England. At this worst of all possible moments Archbishop Laud decided to make an example of three prominent Puritans, a lawyer, a doctor and a clergyman, by having them publicly punished, and London rocked with such fury that even Laud could not fail to notice the intensity of "this malicious storm which hath lowered so black upon me."

The storm was born in part of real religious emotion but it was also in part the result of a skillful manipulation of public opinion by the Puritans. The cropping of ears and the use of brands for disturbers of the public peace were a normal part of seventeenth-century legal machinery and Laud was not the bloodthirsty monster that his enemies made him out to be. There was no tragedy in his regime to compare with that of John Penry, the brilliant young Welshman who attacked the bishops during the reign of Elizabeth and was hanged in spite of his agonized question, "What have I done, and what is mine sin, that I should die this day at the hands of these prelates?" Penry's death went almost unnoticed as a routine act of self-protection by a popular government. But Charles' government was not popular, and in the face of such fury the Archbishop of Canterbury should have trimmed his sails.

Instead Laud steered straight into the teeth of the gale and in this same year made up his mind to force the liturgy of the Church of England on Presbyterian-minded Scotland. When the news came out, Archie, the King's fool, inquired who was the fool now and was formally banished from the court by order of King Charles and seventeen Privy Councillors. But it was more difficult to deal with the inconvenient question itself. It forced Charles into two wars with Scotland, from which he retired ingloriously, and it forced him also into the expedient he had avoided for eleven years. At last he had to call Parliament into session.

Parliament met in 1640, the year in which Herrick had hoped to have his book published, and he could hardly have chosen a time when men's minds were less on poetry. The quarrel over religion had merged into a greater quarrel over the constitutional rights of the King's subjects and the fundamental question of who really possessed sovereignty in England. A mighty battle was fought between the King and his Parliament, the product

of huge, subterranean forces in England's social and economic
life which had been developing for a long time. But the wind
that troubled the waters and finally whipped them to open fury
was religion, the dominant emotion of an age so deeply troubled
by the problem of salvation.

Most of the men in Parliament did not want an open break
with the King. All they intended was to follow the lead of earlier
Parliaments and impeach his ministers, and within six weeks
after the Long Parliament opened those "terrible reformers" had
sent both Archbishop Laud and the Earl of Strafford to the
Tower. Strafford was a brilliant administrator whose vigor and
efficiency had earned him almost as much hatred as Laud, and
the two men had worked together in a close partnership, "joining
hearts and hands" and even sharing little jokes in their letters.
The Earl was beheaded the following May, and Laud blessed
him from his Tower window.

King Charles had himself signed Strafford's death warrant,
in one of those suicidal moments of weakness by which he was
sometimes visited. He turned from this to an equally suicidal
stubbornness, and his refusal to consider any sort of compromise
gave a free hand to the radicals, the men who were resolved
to remove all grievances by "pulling up the causes of them by
the roots." Finally the split grew so wide that it became a chasm
nothing could bridge, and on the twenty-second of August, 1642,
England entered upon the final tragedy of civil war.

The following year Parliament acquired its own Great Seal,
as an outward sign that it was now in its own eyes the government of England, and two months later it made clear to the
world what kind of a body it considered itself to be. On the
twenty-fifth of September, 1643, meeting "with great solemnity,"
the entire Parliament gathered in St. Margaret's church and took
the oath that was called the Solemn League and Covenant, "for
the preservation of ourselves and our religion from utter ruin
and destruction." This end was to be achieved by honoring the

King, remembering the rights of Parliament, and by the "extirpa-
tion of popery, prelacy . . . superstition, heresy, schism, pro-
faneness and whatever shall be found contrary to sound doctrine."

After fighting for three reigns, the Presbyterians had at last
triumphed. In a Parliament full of differences of opinion they
had managed to get unanimous consent to the Presbyterian
point of view, that "the Lord may delight to dwell in the midst
of us." They consolidated their position with the assembly of
"godly divines" which had been meeting for the past two
months in Westminster Abbey, and this Westminster Assembly
labored to build in England the city of God that had been
dreamed of ever since the days of Calvin. There was no thought
of demolishing the idea of a national church. This was as vital
to the Presbyterian way of thinking as it was to Laud's, and in
fact they hoped to establish a church more rigidly all-embracing
than anything Laud himself had conceived.

Now that the Presbyterians were in power, the Archbishop
of Canterbury could not expect to keep his life. With the usual
English respect for legality, Parliament gave him able lawyers
and a long trial, but the end was a foregone conclusion as it
usually was in the political trials of the seventeenth century. In
December of 1644, William Laud was found guilty of high
treason, and on the tenth of January he was beheaded on Tower
Hill.

According to the Puritans, Laud died "an impenitent and
desperate death" after a "godless" life, but a more impartial
observer would have seen an old man of seventy-one ending
his career with the same earnest regard for order that he had
lived it. He wrote out his last words with great care, fashioning
them like the sermons he had known in his youth with quotations
and subdivisions, and he apologized to the people gathered
around the scaffold because he trusted to the paper instead of
his failing memory. When he had finished he was still worrying

that he might not have followed the text exactly. Then he knelt in prayer, and when he reached the words, "Lord, receive my soul," the axe descended.

Once, long ago, Laud had decided that it was better to endure a martyr's death, like St. Stephen, than to fail to do what seemed to him to be right. If his wisdom had equalled his dedication he would have been a great man. He was in any case a brave one. He died as courageously as he had lived, and the civil war he had helped to bring into existence raged on without him.

CHAPTER TWENTY-FIVE

THE CIVIL WAR HAD ITS FORMAL OPENING ON A STORMY DAY IN August, 1642, when the royal standard was set up outside the castle walls in Nottingham. The herald read a declaration on the causes of the conflict and had trouble with the manuscript, because King Charles had called for pen and ink and made some last-minute alterations in an effort to have everything quite clear.

The King might feel he knew what the war was about, but few other people did. Thomas Knyvett wrote bitterly to his wife, "The best excuse that can be made for us must be a fit of lunacy," and Sir John Oglander echoed his bewilderment when he spoke of "our unnatural wars, no man understanding the true grounds of it." Oglander was a royalist with a dearly loved brother on the side of Parliament, and he had special reason to hate the cruelty of a civil war.

Each man had to make up his mind where his loyalties lay, and only a few extremists found the task easy. The King's standard-bearer was a typical case as he stood on that windy hill in Nottingham, for Sir Edmund Verney believed that the bishops were the cause of the war and it was against his conscience to fight for the bishops. Yet it was equally against his conscience to fight against the King. "I have eaten his bread and served him near thirty years and will not do so base a thing as to forsake him." His eldest son was on the Parliament side, a tragedy that made no difference to his father's love for him. "He hath ever lain near my heart, and truly he is there still." But as a result Sir Edmund almost welcomed the death he met that year at the battle of Edgehill.

The same split, if a less heartbreaking one, showed in the

Herrick family. Sir William Herrick, Robert's uncle, was "conformable to the church established." His two eldest sons were ardent royalists and his third son, Richard, was an equally ardent Puritan, so fanatical in his Presbyterian zeal that he was able to say, "Cruelty for Christ is godliness."

Robert Herrick, vicar of Dean Prior, was a royalist, and it apparently never occurred to him to be otherwise. He wrote two briskly approving epigrams on the cropped ears of Puritans and several verses in praise of "adored Caesar," as he called the ineffectual Charles. Yet he was well aware that there were two sides to the question, as he shows in the five-line stanza called "Liberty."

> Those ills that mortal men endure,
> So long are capable of cure,
> As they of freedom may be sure:
> But that denied, a grief, though small,
> Shakes the whole roof, or ruins all.

Herrick wrote a pastoral for King Charles in which he describes the cold shadow that had been creeping over the sunny, flowery life of the court, and he thought of the war as a kind of frost that had spread over England. He found it difficult to write poetry in what he called "the untuneable times" and said that he was "lost to all music now." Yet he went on writing, since it was not in his nature to do otherwise, and in fact admitted that he admired a man who dared to sing

> When as the roof's a tottering.

Herrick had his own private tragedy the year after the war began, when his sister-in-law, Elizabeth Herrick died. She had been living in Dean Prior, and he buried her on the eleventh of April, 1643. In his poem of mourning he speaks of "how I love thee," using the present tense although she was dead, and in that time of many burials he took his leave of her with special tenderness. "Dear, farewell."

Of the bright throng who died in the King's service, the one

Herrick knew best was probably William Lawes, the brother of
"my Harry." Because the King admired his music, Lawes was
given a protected position when he joined the army. But he was
too adventurous to be safe and was killed by a stray shot during
the siege of Chester. Herrick wrote a dirge in his honor, and
another for the young hero, Lord Bernard Stuart, who was killed
in the same engagement. The second one in particular has the
stately, tapestry-like quality that exists in so many of the Cavalier
war poems, and it would be difficult to deduce from it that
Herrick had known war at firsthand in the bloody, useless expedition to the Isle of Rhé. He was less gifted in describing war
than in writing about flowers, and his most characteristic term
for the disaster was that it was an "inconsiderate frenzy."

Rumors of war had been arriving in Devon as early as May of
1642; and when a new and absent bishop was consecrated in
the Cathedral of Exeter the sermon struck an ominous note. "The
waters are risen, O Lord, the waters are risen." Three months
later the King raised his standard at Nottingham, and Devon
was taken over by the Earl of Bedford, Lord Lieutenant of the
shire and owner of that show place of Exeter, Bedford House.
He was strongly on the side of Parliament, like several English
earls and most of the inhabitants of Devon, and since Exeter
was a vital port he fortified it strongly against the King.

The King's most valuable asset in the West was that brilliant
officer and good man, Sir Ralph Hopton. He was the "darling"
of his soldiers and loved even by his enemies, and he was so
devout a commander that there were prayers before each battle
and "a solemn thanksgiving to Almighty God" for each victory.
After Sir Ralph was made a baron in 1643, Herrick wrote a poem
in his honor, cheering him lustily for his military successes in
the neighboring county of Cornwall.

In the same year the royalists succeeded in capturing Exeter;
and although the city had already spent the huge sum of nearly
eighteen thousand pounds in the Puritan defense, it managed
to scrape together another five hundred as a present to the new

governor. This was Sir John Berkeley, who managed the city with his usual hard-working efficiency for the next three years. Herrick wrote a poem in his honor also, announcing that Sir John had at last delivered weeping Exeter from her widowhood.

Exeter was now the chief royal stronghold in the West, and it became a kind of small court which was frequently visited by royalty. Queen Henrietta gave birth to her baby in the city, and a canopy of state was reared in the Cathedral for the elaborate baptism of the little princess. The child was left in the care of Lady Dalkeith, the beautiful niece of the Duke of Buckingham, and Herrick was sure that she would like his poetry.

> Permit my book to have a free access
> To kiss your hand, most dainty governess.

When King Charles arrived Herrick wrote a poem to him also, on the joyful note suitable to this triumphant time of 1644 when nearly the whole of the West was in the hands of the King.

The following year Herrick wrote another poem of rejoicing when the King captured Leicester. "This day is yours, great Charles!" Herrick might have been a little less enthusiastic if he had actually been living in the town of his ancestors instead of getting the news by report, for the soldiers were out of control and the town was brutally sacked. King Charles had intended to have a highly religious and virtuous army and had earnestly issued proclamations that the soldiers were to stay out of taverns, avoid "profane swearing and cursing," and go to church every Sunday. But bad leadership, lack of pay and the death of many of the best officers in three years of war had brought about a steady deterioration of the King's forces just when the Puritan army was having a rebirth under the genius of Oliver Cromwell and becoming an instrument of single-minded dedication. "Those under the King's commanders grew insensibly into all the license, disorder and impiety with which they had reproached the rebels," while the rebels of the new army fought as though they were the hosts of the Lord. On the fourteenth of June, 1645, two weeks after the capture of Leicester, the royalists faced Cromwell and his New Model army at the village of Naseby and met defeat. A year later the war was over, leaving the King to try to salvage by negotiation what he had failed to win by force of arms.

The Presbyterian party experienced a defeat of its own at the battle of Naseby. Its attack on the bishops had been so successful and the support for its Solemn League and Covenant had been so unanimous that it never occurred to the Presbyterians that they did not represent all the Puritans in England. They possessed an absolute majority in the Westminster Assembly and saw no reason to worry about the handful of "dissenting brethren" who also attended the meetings. These dissenters, who were variously called Congregationalists or Independents, were just as much heretics in the eyes of the Presbyterians as they would have been in Laud's, for they did not believe in a state church at all. The Independents believed that each congregation should be self-governing and they had been able to put their theories into practice in the forest clearings of New England. Once the war began and the Church of England was demolished, the Independents came pouring back into the mother country and found waiting for them a generation that had been reared on the Bible and on the appeals to individualism that had been made by the Puritan preachers. Their theory of church government was more attractive to the average Englishman than the rigid theocracy that Calvin had bequeathed to the Presbyterians, and Cromwell began to find his best and most determined soldiers in the ranks of the Independents. If Cromwell's army had been defeated, the reins of government would have remained in Presbyterian hands. But instead the army triumphed; and the men of the Covenant, who had hoped to extirpate "heresy, schism . . . and whatever shall be found contrary to sound doctrine" suddenly found a very unsound doctrine flourishing in their midst. The royalist who spoke bitterly of "Congregational insects" would have had the warm approval of the Presbyterians in that at least, even though they agreed with him in little else.

Nevertheless, the Presbyterians remained in technical control of the religious life of the country. They had the advantage of a clear program and a compact organization, while the Independents had to struggle with the splinter sects that their more liberal approach tended to encourage. Moreover, the Presbyterians still had a majority in Parliament. There the recommendations of the Westminster Assembly had been thoroughly debated and a series of measures had been passed which turned England into a Presbyterian nation.

When Exeter finally surrendered to the Puritans in the spring of 1646, it seemed clear to the mayor and the other Presbyterians in the city that the services in the Cathedral were intended by the Lord to be conducted in the Presbyterian fashion. But the soldiers who had captured the city were Independents, and it seemed equally clear to them that the services should follow the Congregational pattern. Neither side would submit to the other, and it was finally necessary to erect a brick wall and divide the Cathedral in two. The Independents worshipped in the eastern part of the building, the Presbyterians in the west, and the cloth making that was the basic trade of the city flourished as before.

The Puritans might disagree among themselves over forms of worship, but they agreed on the fashion in which the people of Exeter should behave. The waits were no longer permitted to play in that once-musical city, an oath brought a five-shilling fine, and a man could be punished in the stocks for letting his child play on Sunday. Devon had been a Puritan stronghold even in the days of Queen Elizabeth, but there had been nothing like the pall of organized respectability that now descended on the shire. The spirit of play that Herrick had found when he first came to Dean Prior had vanished as completely as the "merry vicars" in the Cathedral close.

It is doubtful if Robert Herrick could have endured such an existence for long, and it is remarkable that the authorities permitted him to stay in his vicarage as long as they did. Ever since the beginning of the war the royalist ministers in Devon had been steadily ejected from their parishes, and in 1647 a member of the Westminster Assembly came down to hasten the work. The Presbyterians faced an impossible task in trying to impose a rigid ecclesiastical pattern upon a divided and uncooperative country, and they were reasonably successful only in London and Lancashire. But they did their best, and the year in which Thomas Ford arrived in Devon to organize the county on strict Presbyterian lines was the same year in which Robert Herrick was ejected from Dean Prior.

It must have been hard for him to leave. He had lived in his little house for seventeen years, along with his succession of pets and his faithful Prue, and when he was forced to abandon it he wrote a sober poem of farewell, like any proper Roman, to the household god he had left behind.

> No more shall I, since I am driven hence,
> Devote to thee my grains of frankincense;
> No more shall I from mantle-trees hang down
> To honour thee, my little parsley crown:
> No more shall I (I fear me) to thee bring
> My chives of garlic for an offering:
> No more shall I, from henceforth, hear a quire
> Of merry crickets by my country fire.
> Go where I will, thou lucky Lar stay here,
> Warm by a glit'ring chimney all the year.

Herrick no longer had a chimney of his own to keep him warm, although he apparently stayed a short time with John Weekes in his friend's parish in the northern part of Devon.

What Herrick really wanted was to return to his beloved London. He longed to be once more what he called "a Roman citizen," and after he arrived in the city of his birth he wrote a triumphant poem called "His Return to London." It is one of his worst, with the false elegance that afflicts him sometimes when he tries to be impressive, but the joyfulness is unmistakable.

> Ravisht in spirit, I come, nay more, I fly
> To thee, blest place of my nativity!

Herrick's income must have stopped when he left Dean Prior. The Puritans tried to be fair to the ejected royalist ministers and paid them one-fifth of the tithes. But this was collected by the minister's wife for the support of the family, and Herrick was of course a bachelor.

On the other hand, he possessed a large collection of distinguished relatives and so affectionate a man could not have lacked family support. The Stones, his mother's family, were prominent people, and when his first cousin, Richard Stone, was knighted in 1641 Herrick wrote a poem in his honor. His mother's sister Ann had married into an equally prominent family named Soame, and Herrick wrote poems to his first cousins, William and Thomas Soame, who also were knights. Sir Thomas Soame's daughter received a poem from Herrick after she became Lady Abdy, and a second cousin on the same side of the family whose name was Stephen Soame also had the honor to be enrolled in what Herrick called "my eternal calendar."

Now that he was back in London, Herrick was still searching out various individuals, relatives and otherwise, who were worthy to be immortalized in his book. The year he arrived he found a suitable candidate in twenty-year-old John Hall, whose facile verses had created a stir at Cambridge the previous year. Herrick hailed him as his "worthy friend" and announced with his usual enthusiasm that Hall was the greatest poet of the age.

Literary London, for its part, was not wholly unaware of Robert Herrick. In this same year of 1647 the plays of Beaumont and Fletcher were published in a huge folio edition, and Herrick contributed a commendatory poem. He was not, however, singled out for any special honor since there were nearly forty of these commendatory poems in the front of the book. The publisher had neglected nothing to make his venture the publishing event of the season, and Herrick's lines "upon Master Fletcher's incomparable plays" were only one small chord in a chorus of praise.

In a way Herrick was moving back into somewhat the same position he had occupied before he left London, and even the golden days of writing songs for the King were returning. King Charles arrived at Hampton Court on the twenty-fourth of August, 1647, and Herrick prepared a welcome for him. It was set to music and sung in the royal presence, as Herrick's earlier songs had once been presented to a younger and happier monarch at Whitehall.

Charles was a defeated ruler but he was still a powerful one, engaged in playing off the Presbyterian party against the Independent and still heir to the devoted respect that was his legacy from the great Tudors. He was treated like a king during his stay at Hampton Court, "having the nobility about him, his chaplains to perform their duty, the house amply furnished, and his services in their accustomed form and state." Many of his courtiers were in attendance on him, and among them was the Duke of Lennox, whom Herrick hailed as a "right gracious" nobleman even though he got his first name wrong.[1]

England was still shadowed by political and religious controversy, but with his usual optimism Herrick was sure that the good days were not far away. King Charles had returned to his "longed-for home" and Herrick himself was back in his beloved London. He had with him the collection of manuscript that represented nearly forty years of writing poetry, and surely there could not be a more auspicious moment for his beloved book to appear at last in print.

---

[1] Herrick called him Ludovick, which was the name of his uncle, George Herbert's patron. The name of the present Duke of Lennox was James, and his brother was the Lord Bernard Stuart whom Herrick had also honored in his poetry.

CHAPTER TWENTY-SIX

R OBERT HERRICK'S BOOK OF POEMS WAS PUBLISHED IN 1648. HE
was fifty-seven years old and had waited a long time for the
event, as the climax of a lifetime's devotion to the art of writing
poetry. Only a fraction had already been published—what Herrick called "a little-peeping-part"—and nothing under his own
name. Now it was to be unveiled as a glorious whole, and the
long delay only made the event more magnificent.

Like to a bride, come forth, my book, at last. . . .

The fortunate printers were John Williams and Francis Eglesfield. Williams had a shop called the Crown in St. Paul's Churchyard, and Eglesfield had one called the Marigold in the same
location. There was also an arrangement made with a Devon
printer named Thomas Hunt, who had a press in Exeter in the
Cathedral churchyard. Hunt took a certain number of copies
and put his own imprint upon them, since it seemed reasonable
to suppose that Herrick would have friends and admirers in the
West Country.[1]

Herrick called his book *Hesperides*, after the nymphs of the
West who guarded the golden apples; and if Devon was not precisely what the Greeks had in mind, Herrick seems to have felt
that the analogy was close enough for his golden poems. The
subtitle explained that these were "the works, both humane and
divine, of Robert Herrick, Esq." but it was found expedient to
give the "divine" poems a separate heading at the end of the
book and entitle them *His Noble Numbers*.

It may be that this plan was the suggestion of Frances Egles-

---

[1] When George Herbert's book of poems was published, a similar arrangement was made with Francis Green, a bookseller in the town of Cambridge.

field, who specialized in religious books and made most of his money from them. Religion was the staple of the London book trade, and the religious convulsions of the last few years had only increased the number of purchasers at the bookstalls. It would clearly help the sale of Herrick's book to be able to isolate "his pious pieces, wherein (amongst other things) he sings the birth of his Christ, and sighs for his Saviour's suffering on the cross." There were not many of these pious pieces. They make up only 79 pages as opposed to 398 for the rest of the book, and there is some evidence that even this percentage was achieved in part by a last-minute effort. Two years earlier a book had been published called *Notes and Observations upon some passages of Scripture* by the learned John Gregory, and nearly a score of Herrick's pious pieces are nothing more than rhymed versions of Gregory's notes.

It is probable that his publishers saw a great deal of Herrick while his book was going through the press. He probably read proof, and along with the list of errata in the front of the volume there is a reproving little verse on the sins of the printer. It may also have been Herrick who arranged for the engraving that was used as a frontispiece, although a portrait from the hand of the fashionable and prolific William Marshall was a familiar object in any new book of poetry. Marshall usually worked in ovals and most of his work was harmlessly conventional. His likeness of Shakespeare in the 1640 edition of the poems shows him clutching a laurel wreath, and his portrait of Fletcher for the 1647 folio has him crowned with laurel and with the usual figures of comedy and tragedy to prop up the printing.

Marshall's design for the frontispiece of Herrick's book is so confused, however, that the author may have been helping him with too many suggestions. A heaving landscape is ornamented on the right by Pegasus, who seems to be about to throw himself, shrieking, from a hill, while to the left a clutter of cupids dance industriously in a ring. Two more cupids, impaled against a stormy sky, are equipped with wreaths from which rigid roses

are falling, and in the center foreground is a large profile bust
of Robert Herrick, hook-nosed, double-chinned, bull-necked,
with a look somewhat between a minor Roman emperor and a
prosperous English butcher.

Very few seventeenth-century artists worked in profile, since
most sitters preferred the three-quarters view, and Herrick must
have thought well of his nose to wish its outlines handed down
to posterity. Leicestershire had once been Roman country, and
it may have been from some remote ancestor that Herrick acquired so beaked and classical a curve. There was a family resemblance in the Herricks, to judge by the portraits of Uncle
Robert and Uncle William and their equally handsome, bright-
eyed mother; but none of them looks in the least like Robert
Herrick himself. As his bust rears up from its leafy base in
Marshall's drawing, it looks like nothing so much as the family
crest—"a bull's head argent, issuing forth of a laurel garland."
It may be that it was after he looked into a mirror that he wrote
the line,

Herrick, thou art too coarse to love.

Herrick may have been more delicate-looking when he was
younger. His friend, Henry Lawes, had a very sensitive and
luminous face in his twenties, while by the time he was Herrick's age he had acquired a double chin, heavy jowls and the
suffused, beefy look of a heavy drinker. But at least Lawes' curls,
like his mustache, are the regulation equipment of the average
Cavalier, while Herrick's, winding in strange profusion over his
head, are most decidedly not.

At the bottom of Marshall's drawing, flanked by two more
cupids, are eight lines in Latin apparently written by Herrick's
friend, John Hamar. There are fourteen lines of praise to Hamar
in *Hesperides* and this would be a return of the compliment.
A seventeenth-century book of poetry was usually freighted with
commendations, and when William Cartwright's poems were
published three years later they carried nearly a hundred pages

of poetical offerings in his praise. Yet Herrick's book was otherwise bare, and in this, if in nothing else, it resembled George Herbert's, which came from the press "free and unforestalled to every man's judgment."

When Herbert designed *The Temple* he worked with architectural precision, and the less than two hundred poems it contains are arranged by a man who had a profound respect for order. Herrick has more than fourteen hundred poems in *Hesperides* and most of them are in no detectable order at all. Herbert's book has a careful index of titles, and the reader can quickly find what he wants in its 192 pages. There is no index for the 477 pages of Herrick's book. If anyone should wish to reread, for instance, that lively and lovely song in praise of miniature things, "A Ternary of Littles," he would have to work his way through the whole volume to find it again.

Perhaps this was what Herrick intended. He did not wish to deprive his readers of the pleasure of encountering all his poems, and the best way to achieve this was to make it impossible to do otherwise. As he said,

> Full is my book of glories . . .

and it was desirable that the reader should not miss any of them.[2]

The effect of jumble in *Hesperides* is increased by the way Herrick scattered his epigrams through the text, sprinkling them about with such judicious care that even the most wary reader cannot avoid them. Between Oenone and Electra are Blinks with his pimples and Adam Peapes picking his teeth, and a tender epitaph on a child is followed by Scobble whipping his blubbering wife for being a whore.

Many editors have solved this difficulty by omitting the epi-

---

[2] Even if the disorder in the book is intentional, it must be admitted that Herrick did not have a tidy mind. A poet with a sense of order would not have used the classical line, "Hence, hence, profane," as the opening of a dirge for Lord Bernard Stuart and then permitted the line to reappear on the next page in a comic connotation.

grams, but they have achieved an effect of order at the risk of
being haunted by Herrick's ghost. He thought well of his epigrams, and of course the form has a long and honorable history.
Herrick's savage little couplet on toothless Bridget is an almost
direct translation from Martial, and his attack "Upon Gut" is no
worse than Ben Jonson's on the same subject. Most of the poets
of the day tried their hand at the epigram, from George Herbert's
brother Edward with his "Epitaph to a Stinking Poet" to an
otherwise gentle soul like William Cartwright. The form was a
fashionable one and does not shed much light on the man who
used it.

In Herrick's case, the emphasis on scatology is normal for
the period and no one pursued this with more vigor than Ben
Jonson. What is most individual about Herrick's epigrams is
their real, ruthless hatred of physical ugliness. He cannot hide
his fury at the existence of bleary eyes and sweaty feet, toothless
gums and bad breath. His delight in the surface of things—
silks, flowers, perfumes, crystals, the softness of a woman's flesh
—made him feel a sense of betrayal when they disappeared; and
he turned on the pitiful victims of poverty and old age with the
slingshot pebbles of his epigrams.

It is a childish reaction, and most of Herrick's epigrams are
juvenile enough. Yet it is this same youthfulness in Herrick that
produced the innocence of his famous prayer, "Another Grace
for a Child."

> Here a little child I stand,
> Heaving up my either hand;
> Cold as paddocks though they be,
> Here I lift them up to Thee,
> For a benison to fall
> On our meat, and on us all. *Amen.*

The small hands, cold as frogs, come from the same mind that
gave Luke Smeaton thirty-two corns and that welcomed the
jewel and the pebble alike. As a result, *Hesperides* is an extraordinary jumble of poems that are good, bad and indifferent,

presented to "the generous reader" in the serene conviction that he will surely find something in it to love.

This attic-like quality of Herrick's mind may have been one reason why he was so devoted to Robert Burton, whose *Anatomy of Melancholy* was now in its fifth edition. Herrick seems to have had no interest in abnormal psychology and the serious base of Burton's book escaped him. What delighted him, as it has delighted readers ever since, was the omnivorous reach of Burton's mind, its vigor, its liveliness and the wild enthusiasm with which he packed the results of his vast reading into a happy conglomeration of opinions and ideas.

Both men had some tricks of style in common, a fondness for portentous Latinisms and for piling up words because of the sound of them. Herrick was not such a "devourer of authors" as Burton was, but the quotations that Burton amassed would sometimes lodge in Herrick's mind until they became a poem. Burton collected, for instance, the remarks of a great many authors on the subject of virgins and roses and the evanescence of youth. Herrick took the miscellaneous heap and gave them perfect shape in one of the loveliest of his lyrics, "To the Virgins, to make much of Time."

> Gather ye rosebuds while ye may,
> Old Time is still a flying;
> And this same flower that smiles today
> Tomorrow will be dying. . . .

Herrick had read so much, seen so much and enjoyed so much that the least of his poems usually has a long root. One of the most beautiful is his "Corinna's going a-Maying," with its many echoes of Burton who is himself a resounding echo. That famous evocation of youth and springtime reaches back through all the English boys and girls who ever went out to pick hawthorn in May, back to all the ancient poets who ever mourned the passing of youth and love. The wonderful cry of loss at the end is from Catullus.

> All love, all liking, all delight
> Lie drown'd with us in endless night.

Nevertheless the poem is purest Herrick, with the happiness outweighing the sadness because it could never be otherwise for him.

Unlike most men of the seventeenth century, Herrick had a temperament that turned away, almost instinctively, from self-questioning and grief. He was that odd phenomenon, a happy man, and when he tries to comfort a woman whose husband has died he turns out some verses that are very nearly absurd.

> Your storm is over; lady, now appear
> Like to the peeping springtime of the year. . . .

He sees the three Fates as three pretty girls, and a dead child is merely one who has been "sung asleep with lullabies." When he wrote of burial, a subject which fascinated his contemporaries, it was usually to picture Robin Redbreast tossing leaves upon his grave or one of his numerous ladies, Julia or Anthea or Perenna, performing the last rites in a suitably Roman manner. Only once does Herrick sound like a man of his century when he writes of death and that is in the sombre and witty masterpiece, "His Winding-sheet," which bears witness to the strong, dark current in Robert Herrick that flowed underground and came so seldom to the surface.

Herrick was not a simple man. No good poet is. But there is in general a consistent climate to his poetry. There is no winter of the mind, as Donne and Herbert knew it, but there is a kind of spring they never knew. Herrick is a poet that any April could appreciate, and his fellow feeling for daffodils is exceptional. There was never a man who wrote lovelier flower pieces, as teasing and affectionate to violets as to a pretty girl, as loving to a primrose as to a baby.

Herrick knew very well what kind of a poet he was, and he opened his book with a description of himself that could not be bettered.

> I sing of brooks, of blossoms, birds, and bowers:
> Of April, May, of June and July-flowers.
> I sing of May-poles, hock-carts, wassails, wakes,
> Of bridegrooms, brides, and of their bridal-cakes.
> I write of youth, of love, and have access
> By these, to sing of cleanly wantonness.
> I sing of dews, of rains, and piece by piece
> Of balm, of oil, of spice and ambergris.
> I sing of times trans-shifting; and I write
> How roses first came red, and lilies white.
> I write of groves, of twilights, and I sing
> The court of Mab, and of the fairy king.
> I write of Hell; I sing (and ever shall)
> Of Heaven, and hope to have it after all.

It is all there, the country customs and the sensuous perfumes, the fairies and the flowers, the girls he loved in the springtime. And at the end are Hell and Heaven, in what may be a climax or what may equally well be an afterthought.

Herrick's religious poems, as has been said, were given a separate place at the end of the volume and entitled *His Noble Numbers*. To adjust the reader's mind to the sudden change in mood, Herrick closes the first section of the book with a quotation from Ovid,

> Jocund his Muse was; but his life was chaste,

and it is a sedate and virtuous poet who opens the second section with an apology for his "wanton wit" and a prayer for absolution.

Yet if any reader turns to *His Noble Numbers* with the hope of finding religious enlightenment he has come to the wrong place, for Herrick was perhaps the least meditative Christian that the seventeenth century produced. He was aware of the fearful problem of salvation with which his contemporaries were wrestling, but he personally expected, in his sunny fashion, to go to Heaven "after all." He attempts to portray the Christian soul tormented by sin, but his poetic attention is so little engaged that the result is merely doggerel.

Thy scourge of steel,
(Aye me!) I feel,
Upon me beating ever:
While my sick heart
With dismal smart
Is disacquainted never.

Even when the idea is orthodox the phrasing is not, as in Herrick's statement that no "comfort peeps" in Hell. And when he describes the entombment of Christ, the Saviour is "sweetly buried" in almost the same tone of voice that the poet uses for Robin Redbreast.

Herrick was of course a good Christian, but he was a Christian in the medieval manner rather than in the more tense and personal fashion of the seventeenth century. In the same way that an early painter of Madonnas might welcome a cucumber or a fly as part of his picture, so Herrick saw no reason to change his habits of thought when he wrote of holy things. When he wrote a poem on the infant Jesus he knew that any baby would have a bib and corals to play with, and he sends a child to Jesus with a gift of a new whistle in the same spirit of innocence with which he wrote of his own small buttery or his hen.

Since Herrick is a true poet he can sometimes combine innocence and Christianity with complete success. "A Thanksgiving to God, for his House" has all the sweetness of a child's speech and the simplicity of a primitive Christian, and "His Litany to the Holy Spirit" is a wonderful combination of folk wisdom and Christianity in the dark house of dying. But in general the vicar of Dean Prior did not write well of either Hell or Heaven. His "Eternity" is a beautiful thing but it is not particularly Christian, and "The Goodness of his God" is Christian enough but very poor verse.

By virtue of his profession Herrick knew the Bible well. In fact, he once pictured himself spending his last days on earth with "a little piggin, and a pipkin" beside him, reading nothing but Holy Writ. Some of *His Noble Numbers* are based on verses in the Bible, but the result is not one that Lancelot Andrewes and his fellow translators would have recognized. Herrick bases one poem on the verse in *Judges* where "the daughters of Israel went yearly to lament the daughter of Jephthah the Gideonite," and he blithely equips the daughters of Israel with laces and ribbons and cowslip balls. He was incapable of keeping the Bible in a special compartment of his mind and was quite willing to interlard a pagan piece with quotations from *Isaiah* and the *Psalms*, just as he was equally willing to end a religious poem with a quotation from Horace. He can write a truly theological and effective line like

Redemption comes by thee

and address it to Julia, while a poem on matins and evensong is addressed to Jove. The line between the sacred and the profane was almost nonexistent in Herrick's mind and sometimes it is only his purity of intention that keeps him from blasphemy.

Herrick himself had no doubt that he could handle any religious theme successfully, and the final poems in *His Noble Numbers* are an account of the Passion of Christ. These are singled out on the title page, which informs the reader that the poet "sighs for his Saviour's suffering on the Cross," and possibly the publisher, Francis Eglesfield, hoped to find the same market for Herrick's poems that Herbert's had already achieved. Many English poets had been influenced by *The Temple*, and some of Herrick's poems show clearly that he had been reading it. He uses the device of Herbert's remarkable "The Sacrifice" in his own poem, "His Saviour's words, going to the Cross," and the difference between the two men can be seen even in the prosody —in Herbert's intricate and haunting rhythm and Herrick's cheerful amble. If they resembled each other at all it was in a gift for concrete detail and a real love of proverbs, and of course they shared a deep respect for the art of poetry.

Herbert and Herrick both included in their books an example of shaped verse. It was a fashion of the period to arrange a poem on the page in such a way that the lines formed a pattern, and both poets happened to choose the same shape—a classical altar. Herbert calls his poem "The Altar" and uses it to describe his dedication to God. Herrick calls his "The Pillar of Fame" and uses it to proclaim the imperishable nature of his poetry.

Herrick's outspoken approval of his book is unusual in an Englishman, but it is nevertheless just. For all its oddities and its many failures, *Hesperides* is one of the most beautiful books ever written.

Here in green meadows sits eternal May. . . .

Within its pages the aging poet kept safe the spirit of youth and of springtime, and the book he published with such pride was worthy of his devotion.

CHAPTER TWENTY-SEVEN

R OBERT HERRICK MUST HAVE HAD HIGH HOPES FOR THE SALE OF
Hesperides. Even if it found its first customers only among
the people mentioned in the book there should have been a
fair number of purchasers, from the Earl of Westmoreland, who
had two poems addressed to him, to a Mr. Thomas Herrick who
asked rather tardily to be included.

In addition, it was reasonable to expect a good sale among
Herrick's fellow royalists in London, and it was perhaps to encourage such purchasers that the type in *Hesperides* becomes
abnormally large whenever royalty is addressed. The relatively
brief dedication to Prince Charles trails over two pages, and
whenever the King himself is addressed the type expands again.[1]

Towards the end of the century Anthony Wood reported that
Herrick's book was "much admired" at the time of publication,
especially by the royalists. But if they admired they did not
buy, for there was no second edition for a hundred and seventy-
five years. It may be that the first printing was too large, so
that the publishers could not get rid of it, but it seems more
probable that the book simply could not find a market.

The apparent failure of *Hesperides* cannot be explained by the
fact that this was a time of political turmoil when poetry could
not be expected to thrive. A great deal of poetry was being published in London, and most of it did well. Nor can it be argued

---

[1] An effort to increase sales may also have influenced one change that
Herrick made in the text. When he originally wrote "The Apparition of his
Mistress calling him to Elysium" he had a description of Shakespeare and
Beaumont reading their plays to their admirers in the Elysian fields. When
Hesperides was published Fletcher's name is substituted for Shakespeare's,
and Herrick may have been influenced by the fact that the magnificent Beau-
mont and Fletcher folio had just been published.

that Herrick's kind of verse belonged to an older and simpler age and therefore was no longer in demand. Thomas Randolph's verse belonged to the same genre, with its "flowery pastorals," its nymphs and shepherds, its translations from Horace and its light eroticism. And although Randolph was no longer living and his work had never been anything but second-rate, his book of poems was doing an excellent business at the bookstalls, with three editions already in print and a fourth soon to be issued.

It may be that part of the difficulty in the case of *Hesperides* lay in the fact that the publishers had unwisely aimed it for a religious market. A year after publication, for instance, it was advertised by Francis Eglesfield in a list of books, mostly theological, which was printed at the end of David Dickson's commentary on *Epistle to the Hebrews,* although it should have been clear that readers who were attracted by an elderly Scottish theologian like Dickson would not share Herrick's delight in his Julia. Some twenty years later *Hesperides* was still being offered for sale among "books of divinity" and readers were still, apparently, refusing to buy.

However, there was some interest in Herrick as a poet, and the year after his book was published he was asked to contribute to a volume of memorial verse in honor of Lord Hastings. Various "persons of nobility and worth" contributed to *Lachrymae Musarum,* from eighteen-year-old John Dryden to Robert Herrick, who was nearly sixty. Herrick employed a device he had used before, a dialogue with Charon, and in this case the boatman on the river Styx speaks with the young girl Lord Hastings was to have married. It is a cool, pretty poem, perfectly formed in the classical tradition, and Herrick's good friend, Henry Lawes, set it to music.

Lawes was by now the most prominent music master in London, and when his own long-delayed book of songs was issued four years later it was an immediate success. Many of the admiring poems that introduce Lawes' book call him the "Father of Music," and it was his pride that he had supplied musical settings for the work of the "most and chiefest" poets of his day. Herrick was among them, and Lawes obviously valued Herrick both as a friend and a poet.

There is no indication that the London public agreed with him. No one seemed to feel that Herrick's name on a poem would increase sales, and when anthologists helped themselves to the contents of *Hesperides* they gave no credit to the author. Two years after its publication, the compiler of an anthology called *Wit's Recreations* calmly reprinted seventy-five poems from *Hesperides* and did not see fit to mention their source.

Herrick remarked in one of his poems, "Seldom comes glory till a man be dead," but the treatment he received in the fifties was almost worse than a complete lack of recognition would have been. The climax came in 1657, when a Mr. Henry Bold published an anthology called *Wit a Sporting*. He not only gave Herrick no credit for the forty-four poems he used from *Hesperides* but did not take the trouble to transcribe them accurately, and in one case what he did was really unforgivable. Herrick had written a little piece "To Robin Red-breast," in which he gives the bird instructions for his own burial, and the poem ends:

> Here, here the tomb of Robin Herrick is.

Herrick had often been called Robin in the days of his youth and he was indulging in a pleasant little pun. Mr. Bold inexplicably printed the line so that it read:

> Here, here the tomb of William Ridley is,

and it was a final stroke of cruelty to take away not only Herrick's authorship but even his little joke.

The following year Herrick was given the only compliment in print which he received, so far as is known, during the whole of this decade. Another of those innumerable little anthologies, this one called *Naps upon Parnassus*, printed a verse which said that Herrick wrote as well as Horace. But since the author had just characterized Horace as a "sour ass," it is not likely that the tribute gave Herrick much pleasure.

Herrick had dreamed of his book for a long time. It was to be his temple of fame, his pillar of immortality; and in verse after verse he had expressed his conviction that the book was a green laurel that would never fade. He admitted that his poems might become fatherless when he died and left no one to protect them, but he cannot have expected that they would be unprotected while he lived. *Hesperides* was pillaged by incompetents and otherwise almost wholly ignored; and one of the loveliest books ever written in English lay unsold at the Crown and the Marigold while lesser works went through edition after edition.

In another way also these were difficult years for Herrick, for his optimism in the field of politics had been equally betrayed. Perhaps the last poem he wrote before the publication of his book was the song of rejoicing over the King's return to Hampton Court. Herrick gave him a Roman welcome, calling him Caesar and great Augustus, and he apparently believed that the country would at last be set on a "new foundation" of peace and kingly rule.

King Charles believed this also. He was sure that England would always be a monarchy, and he had been equally sure from the first that the unrest in his kingdom was not the result of legitimate grievances but the work of a few "envenomed spirits" who were plotting to destroy the harmony of the realm. He had a mental picture of what he called the "circle of order" into which Church and State were tucked by the will of God, and everything he had endured throughout the civil war had given him no understanding of the forces that had brought it about. He negotiated busily at Hampton Court; but he never did it in good faith because he never had any real intention of agreeing to a compromise.

King Charles arrived at Hampton Court in August of 1647 and he fled from there the following November. He was convinced that the revolutionists had engineered a plot against his life, and he arrived at the Isle of Wight with a speech to that effect. He was given a polite imprisonment in Carisbrook Castle, with the parade ground turned into a bowling green for his benefit, and there he stayed, reading the sermons of Lancelot Andrewes and the poems of George Herbert and laying plans for a new civil war that would bring blessed harmony once again.

The second civil war was brief, savage and conclusive. Nor could anyone maintain this time that it had been caused by the King's evil ministers. The engineer was Charles himself, the man who could no longer be swayed by an argument and who had never been bound by a promise. Once more his refusal to compromise gave strength to the most radical branch of the opposition, and this time the King went on trial for his life.

It was probably true that peace and order could not be restored to England as long as Charles remained alive. It was also true that religious and political fury was by now at such a height that even the idea of beheading a king had somehow become conceivable. But the court that was set to try him had no real jurisdiction, and the attempt to give the color of legality to a piece of necessary murder only made the act more appalling.

The King's judges did not think of themselves as murderers. Most of them were upright men, and the wife of Colonel Hutchinson expressed quite truly the force that drove them on. "It was upon the conscience of many of them, that if they did not execute justice upon him, God would require at their hands all the blood and desolation which should ensue by their suffering him to escape, whom God had brought into their hands."

Two of the King's judges had once been in his service and therefore faced an even sharper conflict of loyalties. One of these two was Sir John Danvers, onetime Gentleman of the Privy Chamber, once also the young husband of Magdalen Herbert and the beloved stepfather of her son George. The royalists insisted that he had been seduced by Oliver Cromwell's persuasions and the weight of his own debts. But Sir John Danvers had opposed the King on the hotly contested subject of ship money and had held a colonel's commission on the Parliament side during the civil wars, and there is no need to deny him the faithfulness to a principle that is so obvious in the case of Colonel Hutchinson.

Danvers was present on Saturday, the twenty-seventh of January, 1649, when the sentence of death was pronounced on King Charles by the scarlet-robed president in Westminster Hall. Not all the judges could be persuaded to sign the death warrant; but Sir John Danvers' name is there, along with Oliver Cromwell's, among the regicides, and the date of execution was set for the following Tuesday.

It still seemed impossible that the King could die, and prayers went up everywhere for his safety. One of those who sent him a special message was Sir Henry Herbert, former Master of the Revels, who said that his Majesty should read the second chapter of *Ecclesiasticus* for his comfort. A kinsman of Sir Henry's named Sir Thomas Herbert was caring for the King, and early on Tuesday morning he dreamed that William Laud came to the door with a message. The dead Archbishop of Canterbury and the King drew aside to a window where they could not be overheard, and Herbert's dream was so deep that he did not waken until he heard the King calling him.

Charles was as trim on that last morning of his life, and as gravely punctilious, as for his coronation. He put on an extra shirt, lest he shiver for cold on that winter day and the onlookers mistake it for fear. His shirts were of linen, his collar was of lace, his embroidered gloves were fringed with silver, and he wore the jewelled pendant of the Order of the Garter. He was quite calm, almost saintly in his fortitude, for if he did not know how to rule like a king he knew how to behave like one. He carried with him to the scaffold a small piece of paper, about four inches square, on which he had written out the main points of his speech, and he carefully explained for the last time to the assembled people that it was impossible for them to have any share in the government. "A subject and a sovereign are clean different things." He said once that if he could not live like a king he would die like a gentleman and he remained faithful to the end to the stately vacuum of his code. It was with a kind of grace that he laid his head on the block and died, "wickedly murdered in the sight of the sun."

It was snowing when they buried him at Windsor, and the black velvet pall was white. St. George's Chapel had been so mutilated in the wars that it was difficult to find the grave of Henry the Eighth so that the King could be laid in a royal place. Nor were the mourners permitted to perform the last rites as set forth in the Book of Common Prayer, and that most devout of kings was buried without any religious ceremony in a plain lead coffin that bore only his name and the date.

It was a tragedy that could easily have been avoided. But Charles had all the political stupidity of his father, with an additional high-mindedness that made him drive ahead where King James, in his woolly fashion, at least had the sense to retreat. Charles saw everything in a noble simplification of black and white, and anyone who did not agree with him was quite simply a man of evil. As Bishop Burnet said, "He had too high a notion of the regal power, and thought that every opposition to it was rebellion." So it became rebellion in the end, because there was no footing left for the moderates. The gentle, sensitive Charles— kind husband and father, lover of art and music, devoted admirer of Lancelot Andrewes and faithful son of the Church— brought about two bloody civil wars and died in the end a cruel and unnecessary death.

Such a disaster had never been the wish of the Presbyterians. They were loyal monarchists, as they kept informing Queen Elizabeth and King James, and they never intended an attack on the Crown. What they wanted was to get rid of the bishops, and they brought Archbishop Laud to his death. They did this in what they believed was a holy cause, the purifying of the Church, and they did not dream of destroying the King. But the Presbyterian party was impotent now, expelled by force from the Parliament it had once controlled, and the cold steel of a radical Independent army now ruled England. There was nothing the Presbyterians could do but to pray for the King during his trial and weep for him after his death.

A friend of George Herbert's remarked with some truth that the royalists would have settled "for less blood, less loss of honor, less confusion with the Presbyters than with the Independent and Congregational tyranny." Yet it was the new regime that made the only real gestures towards religious toleration, and if it was ruthless it could justify itself in the name of order. In its own eyes it was not a tyranny and it entered the first year of its control with a new Great Seal which proclaimed "this first year of freedom by God's blessing restored."

The young Commonwealth that was proclaimed in 1649 had one great advantage that had been denied the royalists and the Presbyterians; it had the services of a very great man. Oliver Cromwell had been almost unknown at the beginning of the civil wars. He was merely one of the country gentlemen who gathered together for the Long Parliament, a big man in a country-made suit, his linen not very clean, his voice clumsily used and his fervor unmistakable. During the war it became obvious that he was a brilliant cavalry officer with an extraordinary gift for leading men, and in time his great powers as a politician and an administrator grew equally clear. He was driven, like all Puritans, by a profound conviction that he was doing the will of God, but he was nevertheless no theorist. He moved with events as they came and forced them only as he must, and there was not his equal in England.

In the end Cromwell ruled the country, and in everything but name he was its king. When he refused the crown and was reconfirmed as Lord Protector, the Earl of Warwick laid on his shoulders a purple velvet robe lined with ermine and the sceptre he held was of gold. His daughters married men of high rank, their weddings were celebrated at Whitehall "with all imaginable pomp and lustre," and Andrew Marvell hailed him as great Jove in the same way the Cavalier poets had once hailed King Charles. Yet Cromwell remained essentially a country gentleman, and when he dined in state at Hampton Court it was of farming he spoke. "I have been in all the counties of England, and I think the husbandry of Devonshire is the best." He himself had been a Huntingdonshire man who specialized in wheat, and he never forgot it as he moved among the glitter and the glory, just as he never forgot that what mattered the most was his own strenuous, sometimes despairing and always violently personal relationship to God.

The Commonwealth was held together by the strength of one man, and his enemies labored hard against him. The royalists were trying to bring the son of the dead king to the throne, and the Presbyterians, who had once been their bitter foes, had joined in the attempt. Robert Herrick's cousin, for instance, the ardently Presbyterian Richard Herrick, joined in a plot to bring Prince Charles back to England, and when it failed Richard's leader was executed for treason.

There were many executions in England during the Commonwealth. But Cromwell avoided them when he could, and he had relatively little tyranny on his conscience when he died quietly in his bed. It was on the afternoon of the third of September, 1658, after a Monday of such fierce winds that many people claimed the Devil had come to hurry the Lord Protector away. His eldest son was made Protector in his place, and the troopers were pelted with carrot tops when the news was proclaimed.

Neither the well-intentioned Richard Cromwell nor the various army factions had the strength to stop a rising tide of reaction against Puritan rule, and when King Charles the Second arrived back in England it was on a wave of popular approval. As a rector of Exeter put it, his return was a "most distinguished work of God's hand." Charles reached London on his birthday, the twenty-ninth of May, 1660, to the accompaniment of an ex-

plosion of joy that rocked the city, and that night the London
bonfires leaped three and four stories high, with sometimes an
effigy of Oliver Cromwell burning at the top.

When Charles II came ashore at Dover, a large Bible was
pressed into his hands and he accepted it politely. But one of his
churchmen remarked: "He seemed to have no sense of religion. . . . He said once to my self, he was no atheist, but he
could not think God would make a man miserable only for
taking a little pleasure by the way." After so many strenuous
years of government by the elect, a great many of his subjects
felt the same way. On Holy Thursday the people of Oxford put
up a dozen Maypoles merely to show their Puritan neighbors
what they thought of them, and a Puritan vicar noted in his
diary, in open pain, that the old ways were returning in his
parish. "This day I heard and then saw the youth openly playing
at cat-on-the-green." He added a prayer that such sins might
yet be healed, but there was little chance of a continuation of
Puritan austerity in Restoration England.

Charles was crowned on an April day in 1661, the delay having
been caused by the fact that all the coronation regalia had been
destroyed in the late unhappy tumults and had to be recreated
by the London goldsmiths at a cost of thirty-two thousand
pounds. There was the usual pageantry as the King moved in
the traditional line of march from the Tower to Whitehall, and
Rebellion, in a crimson robe with snakes crawling about, was
routed by Monarchy. The coronation anthem was written by
Henry Lawes, who had his court appointments back in spite
of the fact that French musicians were now getting the best
commissions, and it was almost possible to believe that the
long years of war and change had never existed.

Robert Herrick was seventy now, and he had been waiting a
long time. But he had celebrated "the star-led birth of Charles
the prince," he had dedicated his book to him, and he lived to
see him, at last, England's king.

CHAPTER TWENTY-EIGHT

IT IS NOT KNOWN WHAT ROBERT HERRICK WAS DOING DURING THE Commonwealth except for a later report that at the end of the period he was living "in St. Anne's parish in Westminster." There was no St. Anne's parish in Westminster in Herrick's day, and perhaps what was meant was St. Anne's Lane in St. Margaret's parish.[1]

It is not improbable that Herrick was living in St. Anne's Lane. It was near the Almonry, where Herrick is known to have been living on an earlier occasion, and would be a natural place of residence for a man with so many Westminster connections. It seems to have been a pleasant district, and one of Herrick's distinguished neighbors would have been Sir Robert Pye, who had been running Westminster Abbey as chairman of a committee and doing the work normally done by the Dean and Chapter. An enormous number of such committees were at work during the Commonwealth, and they all ceased with the Restoration.

In June of 1660, less than a month after King Charles the Second returned to England, the newly restored House of Lords ordered all the tithes in Puritan parishes to be held by the churchwardens until they could be given to their former owners, the ejected ministers of the Church of England. One of the first royalist ministers to petition the House of Lords under the new ruling was Robert Herrick, who pointed out that he had been

---

[1] The statement comes from Anthony Wood, who was not notable for his accuracy. Wood's little biographical notice of Herrick is included in what is supposed to be "an exact history of all the writers and bishops who have had their education in the University of Oxford," and of course Robert Herrick never went to Oxford.

forced to leave his vicarage at Dean Prior because of his affection for "his late Majesty of blessed memory" and asked to have
the income from the benefice held until he could prove his title
to it.

Herrick was one of a hundred and forty-two Devon ministers
who had been ejected in the past seventeen years, and a hundred
and twenty-one were restored in the first two years of the new
reign. In Herrick's case this meant the ejection of an heroic old
Presbyterian named John Syms, who went on doggedly preaching, sometimes at the risk of his life, in his own house or in the
neighboring villages. It was a bitter time for the Puritans of
Devon, who saw the devoted work of years being swept away
and the county turning to the old ways again.

The city of Exeter hailed the Restoration with enthusiasm.
The conduits ran with wine, the bells sang, the people shouted,
and "at night tar barrels and bonfires capered aloft." The waits
returned, with full pension rights, to bring back the old days of
music, and the Bishop's palace, which had recently been occupied by a sugar broker, was restored to its rightful owner. The
strong Puritan movement went underground, as it did in the rest
of the country, and officially Devon was back in the arms of the
Church of England.

Herrick returned to his old place as though he had never left
it, and the unkind remarks he made about his parish were apparently quite forgiven. In the poem he wrote when he quitted
Dean Prior he described his congregation as rocky, currish,
churlish and rude, and a hundred and fifty years later all the
parishioners were still acquainted with the poem. It seemed
to delight them that Herrick had sworn never to see Dean Prior
again. " 'But,' they added, with an air of innocent triumph, 'he
did see it again.' " The people of Dean Prior had the last word
in the matter, but it was an amiable one.

Even Herrick's Prue apparently returned into his service.
Prudence Baldwin was still living in the parish, and she did not
die until four years after her master. He had already thanked

"kind Prue" for her faithfulness to him in a difficult time, and it is likely that she went on being faithful still.

If Herrick wrote any more poetry it is lost now, with the single exception of his epitaph to Sir Edward Giles, whose body had lain for a long time in the south aisle of the parish church with his wife Mary by his side. Herrick was said to have been "very aged" when he wrote the epitaph, and the last lines sound like his own farewell.

> These two asleep are: I'll but be undrest
> And so to bed. Pray wish us all good rest.

Yet Herrick had said farewell before in his poetry and lived on. Three bishops of Exeter came and went, and the Restoration was in its fourteenth year when a brief note appeared in the parish register of Dean Prior: "Robert Herrick, vicar, was buried the 15th day of October, 1674."

Herrick lay in an unmarked grave, but his lively spirit did not rest there. For the next century there were stories of his haunting Dean Prior, and a visitor who arrived there in 1810 heard "a whole budget of anecdotes about his ghost." Since the visitor was a product of the Age of Reason he did not stoop to record any of these anecdotes; and it is a pity, for the performances of Herrick's ghost would have been illuminating.

The subsequent vicars of Dean Prior tried to put their effervescent colleague in a more dignified light. In 1704 the current incumbent received a request from Exeter for some information on Herrick, to be used in a book that was being compiled on the sufferings of the Anglican clergy during the Commonwealth. The vicar reported that Herrick had been a "sober and learned man," which would seem to indicate that William Pearse knew relatively little about his predecessor. The villagers of Dean Prior, still remembering after a hundred years "that he kept a pet pig, which he taught to drink out of a tankard," had a juster appreciation of Robert Herrick.

They knew also that Herrick had loved God in his own way.

There was an old woman in the village, named Dorothy King, who was nearing her hundredth year in 1810. Her mother had served Herrick's successor in the vicarage, and she had taught her daughter five of the poems from *His Noble Numbers*, including the beautiful "His Litany to the Holy Spirit." Dorothy King "called them her prayers" and recited them to herself in bed when she could not sleep. She had never seen them written down and could not have read them if she had, but in her ninety-ninth year she was still able to repeat them "with great exactness."

Those people of lesser wisdom, the literary critics, dismissed Herrick from their consideration early and with thoroughness. Milton's nephew, Edward Phillips, published a survey of English poets the year after Herrick's death, and he warmly praised such disciples of Ben Jonson as Thomas Randolph and William Cartwright. But he put the best of them all, Robert Herrick, in the same category as an obscure versifier named Robert Heath. The most he was willing to grant Herrick was the possession, now and then, of "a pretty, flowery and pastoral gale of fancy."

In the following decade William Winstanley brought out his lives of the English poets and copied Phillips' judgment on Herrick, including the comparison with Heath. After that, even patronizing attention ceased to exist. The verses Herrick wrote for Sir Edward Giles, which had been set in gold on the black marble, faded in time and could no longer be deciphered. There was nothing left of Robert Herrick in the eighteenth century, except a few stray copies of *Hesperides* and a lively ghost wandering by the river Dean.

Like Herrick, George Herbert had been laid in an unmarked grave, and in his case also the eighteenth century found little to admire. Up to the end of the seventeenth century Herbert's reputation had remained high, and when a Danish scholar visited England after the Restoration and then returned to lecture on English poets at Copenhagen his list was headed by Sidney, Spenser and Herbert. He was still "known and approved" when

Winstanley wrote his *Lives*, read both by the learned and the common people, but his reputation faded swiftly. There were at least thirteen editions of *The Temple* before 1709, and then for the next ninety years there were none.

In a general way it could be said of the eighteenth century that it turned its face away from everything that the seventeenth century had valued. Intensity had led to disaster, ardor had nearly destroyed the country; and it was natural that emotion should become suspect and that the power of reason should be exalted in its place.

The real victors in the civil wars were not the men who fought in them but the men who refused to fight. A man like Lord Herbert of Cherbury, making excuses for not joining the King's army in Scotland, making excuses for surrendering Montgomery Castle to the Puritans, and finally dying "very serenely" after remarking that it made no difference whether or not he received the sacrament, was one of the true fathers of the eighteenth century. The only sign of intensity in George Herbert's elder brother was his hatred of church control and his profound conviction that truth must be tested by reason, and this much intensity the eighteenth century was willing to tolerate.

Men became, on the whole, much less preoccupied with their relationship to God and much more concerned with their relationship to the world around them. When Herbert and Herrick went to Cambridge, all the strength and vitality of that great University was focussed on religious questions and it was the seedbed of the coming Puritan revolution. Mathematics was a stepchild at Trinity College and Sir Francis Bacon an alien. But during the civil wars Trinity began to develop a real interest in the sciences, and when eighteen-year-old Isaac Newton entered it in 1661 it was at last a place in which the men of the new order could flourish.

The prophet of this scientific revolution was Sir Francis Bacon, and when the Royal Society was incorporated in 1662 it accepted him formally as its model and guide. Bacon had promised

that the study of the world from a scientific point of view would
bring a new kind of freedom and that the mind of man would
be able to "exercise over the nature of things the authority
which properly belongs to it." In this way man could retrieve
himself, in part at least, from the disaster of Adam's fall. "For
creation was not by the curse made altogether and forever a
rebel."

Instead of the agonized anatomizing of the soul that had
been going on in the seventeenth century, the visible world was
to be anatomized instead; and from this new way of looking at
things would come a sure salvation. Or at least so it seemed to
the excited historian of the Royal Society, reporting on what its
achievements would be when the organization was less than
four years old. "Opinions will be less violent and dogmatical
but more certain." Men would "be gods one to another, and
not wolves." Man in his calmness and wisdom would conquer
the earth and his own destiny, and all tempests would cease.

The eighteenth century was an improvement on the age that
had gone before, if only because it had at last become clear that
men could differ and still survive. Robert Herrick's Presbyterian
cousin Richard was speaking for a great many Englishmen of
the seventeenth century when he helped to write a manifesto on
the dangers of religious tolerance. "A toleration would be the
putting of a sword into a madman's hand . . . a proclaiming
liberty to the wolves." Such a man would have been appalled
by the state of things in Exeter by the end of the following
century. By then the city had not only a series of nonconformist
congregations but also a Quaker meeting house, a Roman Catholic chapel and a Jewish synagogue. And yet no wolves were
abroad.

In one of the wisest and most beautiful of his sonnets, George
Herbert speaks of prayer as "something understood." For generations the Anglicans and the Presbyterians had been praying
for spiritual peace in England, and both sides had been con-

vinced that it came only through absolute obedience to a single,
all-embracing church. The prayer was answered and the conflict ceased when it became clear that such forcible uniformity
was unnecessary and that there might well be more than one
way to worship God.

Perhaps this discovery came less through conviction than
through sheer weariness. There was certainly a loss of moral
intensity in the eighteenth century, and in its place there grew
a kind of moral smugness. Englishmen were so sure that they
were on the right track at last, with their pursuit of scientific,
provable fact and their reverence for reason, that they forgot
there were other ways which were also available to so infinitely
various a being as man.

The damage that could be done by this new way of thinking
shows especially in a narrowed approach to the act of writing
poetry. When the Royal Society was formed, its members
pledged themselves to write simply and clearly, "bringing all
things as near the mathematical plainness as they can, and pre-
ferring the language of artisans, countrymen and merchants
before that of wits or scholars." If matters could have been left
at that the reform was a reasonable one, but it was decided that
the same principle should be extended to all kinds of writing.
"Now, when men's minds are somewhat settled, their passions
allayed . . . if some sober and judicious men would take the
whole mass of our language into their hands," to decide what
was desirable and what was not, then a vast reformation would
clearly take place in the whole field of writing.

This in itself was not a new idea. For many generations English theorists had been preaching the doctrine of elegance and
correctness in poetry, proclaiming the desirability of following
French and classical models instead of indulging in so much
personal freedom. They had made remarkably little headway
during the turbulent and excitable years that had gone before,
but now a new age was dawning, an age that was weary of

emotions and mistrusted everything that had led to "the passions and madness" of civil war. Self-control was the watchword now, and control of the language was an obvious part of it.

Here there was a real loss. The rigidity of mind and the enforced discipline that had become out-of-date in religious matters were transferred to the field of poetry. Instead of the huge variety that had been known in the sixteenth and seventeenth centuries there was now, in the eighteenth, only one correct way of putting words on paper. Alexander Pope, who was a master of the new way of writing, read George Herbert's poems in private and apparently admired them, but no one was permitted to write like Herbert in public. John Wesley loved Herbert's poems, but he rewrote them to make them suit the polite ear of the eighteenth century, and William Cowper, who loved them also, nevertheless admitted that they were "gothic and uncouth."

The way was very clear to the men of the eighteenth century. And if it was also narrow, with imagination a stranger and the whole spirit of man focussed on only one of his faculties, the contented poets of the age saw no reason to quarrel with that. Only one voice was raised in real fury against this orderly and limited approach and that was William Blake's:

> May God us keep
> From single vision and Newton's sleep!

Poets and the readers of poetry are a hardy race, and they cannot be controlled forever by even the most reasonable of rules. By the end of the eighteenth century there were still readers who enjoyed the unenlightened old poets of whom no one approved, and in 1796 there appeared in the *Gentleman's Magazine* a request for information about five obscure writers of the 1650's: Robert Heath, Robert Herrick, Nicholas Hooke, Edward Sherburne and Martin Llewellyn. The editor of the magazine had been working on an excellent history of Leicestershire and so he happened to know a good deal about the Herrick family. He or some member of his staff had also read *Hesperides,* and in answering the query the magazine remarked that Edward Phillips' opinion of Herrick was "tolerably just. . . . Several of his epigrams possess much point, with a very judicious merit in such compositions, brevity." It was characteristic of a man of the eighteenth century to admire Herrick for his epigrams and to have no real respect for his lyrics.

But the important thing was that *Hesperides* was beginning to be read. The book itself was "very scarce" but selections from it began to appear, and by 1810 the *Quarterly Review* proclaimed that Herrick had been unjustly neglected. More and more readers discovered him, and they found it difficult not to like him. One of the exceptions was the poet laureate, Robert Southey, who remarked snappishly that Herrick was "a coarse-minded and beastly writer whose dunghill, when the few flowers that grow therein are transplanted, ought never to have been disturbed." But Southey was beginning to be in the minority. The literary quarterlies wrote laudatory articles, edition followed edition, and by the end of the century Swinburne was speaking of Herrick's "incomparable genius" and calling him the greatest writer of songs that England had ever known.

It took longer for George Herbert to win approval from the critics. When one of the gentlemen of the *Retrospective Review* singled out a few of his poems for commendation in 1821, he did it only because he considered *The Temple* as a whole unreadable, "a mass of uninviting and even repulsive matter to modern readers of poetry." Even so wise and sensitive a critic as Coleridge read Herbert at first only because his "quaintness" amused him. The more he read the more warmly he admired, but he could not persuade his contemporaries to do the same. Charles Lamb, who agreed with Coleridge in nearly all literary matters, could not agree with him in this and in fact actually disliked Herbert's work.

Coleridge, with his usual acuteness, put his finger on the difficulty. "G. Herbert is a true poet, but a poet *sui generis,* the merits of whose poems will never be felt without a sympathy with the mind and character of the man. . . . For religion is the element in which he lives, and the region in which he moves." The nineteenth century, as its legacy from the eighteenth, was still treating religion as something that could be filed away in the mind, a Sunday observance to be forgotten on workdays, a part of life but not the basis of all reality. To such a generation Herbert was embarrassing, and people could not read him.

A poet like Gerard Manley Hopkins, who felt otherwise, could leave the Church of England but he could not give up *The Temple*. Oddly enough, he linked Herbert and Herrick in his mind as the last of the Elizabethans. He associated them both with the smell of apples and daisies, with country songs, and with the Welsh and Herefordshire landscapes. And he loved them both as they were meant to be loved.

It was left for the readers of the next century to take George Herbert as seriously as he deserved. In many ways the first half of the twentieth century was like the first half of the seventeenth, a violent, passion-ridden time that was bringing to birth new forms which no one quite understood and going in a direction of which no one knew the road. The problem of salvation that had seemed so remote to the Age of Reason suddenly grew insistent again, for Bacon's theory that the world could be controlled by science was now proven to be as much an illusion as the earlier theory that it could be controlled by ecclesiastical organization. Again men began to ask, "What shall we do to be saved?" and if George Herbert provided no final answer he at least gave a sense of companionship.

Moreover, any good poet provides his own kind of salvation. T. S. Eliot once said, in an essay on Herbert, "All poetry is difficult, almost impossible, to write." It consists of imposing an order and meaning on what was formless before; and in achieving so difficult a task it contributes to order without narrowing it, to existence without simplifying it.

George Herbert and Robert Herrick were both somewhat alien to their own century. They were gentle men in an age that was not gentle, and they refused to interfere with their neighbors at a time when interference was almost a duty. They did not try to change the world, but only to write well.

Therefore their two books endured while they themselves lay in unmarked graves. For the word is a durable thing, stronger than fears or beliefs and far stronger than the sword. It is also a lonely thing, the speaking of one individual to another; and yet it may well be through such lonely ways, and not through all the attempts at mass solutions, that salvation in the end will finally come.

APPENDIX

IZAAK WALTON PUBLISHED HIS LIFE OF GEORGE HERBERT IN 1670, when he was in his late seventies and living as a guest in the palace of the Bishop of Winchester. Unlike his earlier *Lives*, which were written on request, this one was "a free-will offering . . . writ chiefly to please myself." His other motive in writing the little book on Herbert was to show the Restoration clergy what the life of a minister in the Church of England ought to be. Walton was troubled when he considered "how few of the clergy lived like him then, and how many live so unlike him now," and he wrote the biography to supply "a pattern of virtue to all posterity, and especially to his brethren of the clergy."

Since this was Walton's intention, he naturally placed his chief emphasis on the three years during which Herbert was a minister at Bemerton. The information and stories about Herbert which he collected with "great diligence" focus on Bemerton, and Walton's account of the last three years of Herbert's life takes up more than half the book.

The period of Herbert's life to which Walton paid the least attention was the time during which he was in politics. All the information that Walton has to offer about this is contained in a few lines, and he does not even mention the fact that Herbert served in two Parliaments. No doubt the information would have been available to him if he had pursued it as energetically as he did the Bemerton material, but Walton was not interested in politics.

Only a serious interest in facts for their own sake would have led a man like Walton to do research on Herbert's political career, and this was a quality that Walton did not possess. The four biographies he wrote are riddled with minor inaccuracies

277

which he could easily have corrected, and his dates frequently contradict each other. As he grew older he became increasingly attached to the fictional device of imaginary dialogues, and he admitted quite cheerfully in his life of Bishop Sanderson: "I have been so bold as to paraphrase and say what I think he . . . would have said."

A modern biographer who wishes to make use of Walton can easily correct his inaccuracies and ignore his obvious reconstructions. A much more difficult problem lies in the fact that Walton was as much artist as biographer, and in order to produce a precise and vivid picture in the reader's mind he will sometimes manipulate his material in such a fashion that it is no longer reliable.

When Walton wrote his life of Richard Hooker, for instance, he had reason to believe that Hooker had been trapped into an unhappy marriage. No one who reads the biography is likely to forget Walton's picture of two of Hooker's former students travelling down to visit him at his country vicarage of Drayton Beauchamp.

> They found him with a book in his hand—it was the Odes of Horace—he being then like humble and innocent Abel, tending his small allotment of sheep in a common field; which he told his pupils he was forced to do then, for that his servant was gone home to dine, and assist his wife to do some necessary household business. But when his servant returned and released him, then his two pupils attended him unto his house, where . . . Richard was called to rock the cradle; and the rest of their welcome was so like this, that they stayed but till next morning, which was time enough to discover and pity their tutor's condition.

One of the students, George Cranmer, expresses his sympathy and is given this noble answer by Richard Hooker: "My dear George, if saints have usually a double share in the miseries of this life, I, that am none, ought not to repine at what my wise Creator hath appointed for me: but labour—as indeed I do daily—to submit mine to His will, and possess my soul in patience and peace."

For centuries, thanks to Walton, Hooker has served as the model of the saintly scholar tormented by family cares, and it was left for C. J. Sisson to discover that the scene was a complete fabrication. Walton believed that Hooker married Joan Churchman in 1581 and that he was therefore a married man when he received the benefice of Drayton Beauchamp in 1584. In actual fact he married her in 1588, when he was living in London, and the record of their marriage still exists in the parish church of St. Augustine's in Watling Street. All the children were born in London, and the scene that Walton records never took place.

A great deal of malicious gossip had been current in Walton's circle about Hooker's wife, all of it apparently untrue. Walton had no special reason to disbelieve it, since some of it came from his own Cranmer relatives, and he passed it on innocently enough. But all the vivid little touches that make the scene come to life, even to the name of the book in Hooker's hand, are Walton's own invention, inserted to give the scene the reality which he believed it already possessed. The whole thing, including Hooker's saintly and resigned speech, is beautifully conceived and executed. The fact that none of it took place does not detract from Walton as an artist, but it does make him suspect as a biographer.

In Walton's life of George Herbert there seems to be a similar case of manipulation, one that adds a great deal to the effectiveness of the story of a saint who forsook the world but one which has no support outside of Walton's pages.

It is Walton's contention, repeated several times, that Herbert went into politics because he was ambitious and tempted by the glitter of a worldly life. For some reason, Walton omits the fact that Herbert had studied divinity at Cambridge. He must have known that Herbert intended to go into holy orders as early as 1618 because he prints at the end of the book, among the collection of letters, the one in which Herbert tells Sir John Danvers that he is "now setting foot into divinity" and laying the platform for his future life. But Walton may have found that this piece of information was impossible to fit into the smooth

flow of his narrative, since it cannot be reconciled with the
subsequent speeches he attributes to Herbert.[1]

When Walton first brings up the subject of a court career he
says merely that George Herbert had "a laudable ambition to
be something more than he then was." But Walton was a picturesque writer and soon he is referring to the "painted pleasures
of a court-life" and to Herbert's having "ambitiously thirsted
for . . . painted pleasures." A friend of Walton's named Charles
Cotton, who knew nothing of Herbert except what he had read
in Walton's book, put the matter even more strongly. In his view,
and in that of most readers since, Herbert was "deeply tainted
with ambition."

It would be interesting to know where Walton got this interpretation of Herbert's behavior. Certainly it was not from the
two accounts of Herbert's life that were already in print. The
first of these was written by Nicholas Ferrar to serve as a biographical introduction to Herbert's poems, and the second was
written some years later by Barnabas Oley to accompany Herbert's little book of advice to country parsons. Walton says that
Oley's preface was "most conscientious and excellent" and Ferrar's preface, of course, was written by a man who knew Herbert
well. Yet in neither of these biographical introductions is there
the slightest suggestion that Herbert went into politics because
he was ambitious.

Perhaps Walton got the idea from Arthur Woodnoth, just as
he got his notions on Hooker's wife from the Cranmer relatives.
In Walton's account Herbert addresses a long speech to Woodnoth which is very like the speech that Hooker ostensibly delivers to George Cranmer, and it may be that in both cases
Walton was misled by a chance remark which he subsequently
elaborated. The point could hardly be checked with Woodnoth
since he had been dead for twenty years when the book was
published, and Walton had obviously never known him well
since he calls him John instead of Arthur in the first edition.

---

[1] There is no doubt whatever that Walton saw the final, printed copies of
his life of Herbert with the collection of letters at the end. The New York
Public Library has a copy of this first edition with corrections in Walton's
own hand.

For that matter, Woodnoth himself did not have an overmastering interest in the exact truth. He wrote an account of the Virginia Company, to justify the way his friends had handled its affairs, and the little tract is a biassed and inaccurate piece of work.

There is no outside evidence to support Walton's contention that George Herbert left God's service because he was tempted by ambition, and there is none within the poems themselves. *The Temple* is a highly personal work, written by a man with an abnormally sensitive conscience, and yet when Herbert speaks of his own past life there is no suggestion of blame. He is conscious of "missing my design." He is bitterly aware that his "power to serve" has been taken from him. He is tormented by a sense of uselessness and by the fact that the "thoughts and ends" of his younger days have come to nothing. But there is no suggestion anywhere that these "thoughts and ends" were for his personal advancement or that he had ever turned his back on his desire to serve God. Upon this subject Herbert must be considered a better witness than Walton. And since all the known facts of his outward life reinforce the impression given in the poems, it seems reasonable to conclude that Izaak Walton's interpretation is not the correct one.

Another difficulty, if a minor one, concerns the question of why George Herbert became a deacon. Walton says that Herbert retired to Kent after King James died in 1625 and "had many conflicts with himself, whether he should return to the painted pleasures of a court-life, or betake himself to a study of divinity." Herbert finally decides he will take up divinity and announces to a friend, "Though the iniquity of the late times have made clergymen meanly valued, and the sacred name of priest contemptible; yet I will labour to make it honorable." And so he becomes a deacon.

After this nothing happens until several years later when Herbert is offered the benefice at Bemerton and then, according to Walton, he goes through the same struggle all over again. Walton even uses some of the same wording to describe the second occasion, and again Herbert reaches the same conclusion. "I will be sure to live well, because the virtuous life of a clergy-

man is the most powerful eloquence to persuade all that see it
. . . to live like him. And this I will do, because I know we live
in an age that hath more need of good examples than precepts."
In other words, on both occasions and with no mental development or alteration in between, Herbert sees himself as setting a
good example to the clergy and delivers what almost amounts to
a recruiting lecture. This may well be the Herbert that Walton
designed as a model for the ministers of the Restoration, but it
is not the George Herbert of *The Temple.*

Yet it must be added that Walton's life of Herbert is a beautiful piece of work. All Walton's gentle, loving heart, all his literary skill and all his reverent admiration for "holy Mr. Herbert"
combine to produce a tender and luminous tribute that is very
close to a complete work of art. If there are errors of fact and of
interpretation, they are forgivable in the case of a biographer
who saved so much that would otherwise have been lost and
presented it so movingly. Walton loved George Herbert and
even considered him worthy to enter the select fellowship of
those who fished on the banks of the river Dove. For he "had a
spirit suitable to anglers" and insofar as it was innocent and holy
it was also a spirit most suited to Izaak Walton.

SELECTED BIBLIOGRAPHY

I WOULD LIKE TO MENTION MY SPECIAL GRATITUDE FOR TWO BOOKS
published by the Oxford Press, *The Works of George Herbert*
edited by F. E. Hutchinson and *The Poetical Works of Robert Herrick* edited by L. C. Martin.

WILLIAM ADDISON, *Worthy Dr. Fuller,* London: J. M. Dent and Sons,
Ltd., 1951.

The Anacreontea, translated by Judson France Davidson, London:
J. M. Dent and Sons, Ltd., 1915.

H. INCE ANDERTON, letter, *London Times Literary Supplement,* March
9, 1933.

ANONYMOUS, *The Life of George Herbert of Bemerton,* London:
Society for Promoting Christian Knowledge, 1893.

Archaeologia Cambrensis, series 3, Volume IV, London, 1858.

JOHN AUBREY, *Brief Lives,* edited by Andrew Clark, 2 volumes, Oxford: Clarendon Press, 1898.

JOHN AUBREY, *Wiltshire,* Devizes, 1862.

W. C. BACH, *A Tithing Table,* London, 1633.

FRANCIS BACON, *Works,* edited by James Spedding, Robert Leslie
Ellis and Douglas Denon Heath, 15 volumes, Boston, 1863-72.

THOMAS BAKER, *History of the College of St. John the Evangelist,
Cambridge,* 2 volumes, Cambridge: Cambridge University Press,
1869.

W. W. ROUSE BALL, *Cambridge Notes,* Cambridge, 1921.

W. W. ROUSE BALL AND J. A. VENN, editors, *Admissions to Trinity
College, Cambridge,* Volume I, London: Macmillan and Co.,
Ltd., 1916.

MARY BATESON, editor, *Records of the Borough of Leicester,* Volumes
III and IV, Cambridge: Cambridge University Press, 1905, 1923.

ALFRED BEAVER, *Memorials of Old Chelsea,* London, 1892.

JOAN BENNETT, *Four Metaphysical Poets,* Cambridge: Cambridge
University Press, 1934.

S. L. BETHELL, *The Cultural Revolution of the Seventeenth Century,*
London: Dennis Dobson, Ltd., 1951.

283

THOMAS BIRCH, *The Court and Times of Charles the First,* 2 volumes, London, 1848.

THOMAS BIRCH, *The Court and Times of James the First,* 2 volumes, London, 1849.

A Booke of Certaine Canons, London, 1571.

E. C. E. BOURNE, *The Anglicanism of William Laud,* London: Society for Promoting Christian Knowledge, 1947.

E. G. BOWEN, *Wales; A Study in Geography and History,* Cardiff, 1941.

IVOR BOWEN, "John Williams of Gloddaeth," *Transactions of the Honourable Society of Cymmrodorion,* London, 1927-8.

JOHN BRAND, *Observations on Popular Antiquities,* Newcastle upon Tyne, 1777.

JOHN S. BUMPUS, *A Dictionary of Ecclesiastical Terms,* London, 1910.

ARTHUR MEREDYTH BURKE, *Memorials of St. Margaret's Church, Westminster,* London: Eyre and Spottiswoode, Ltd., 1914.

GILBERT BURNET, *Bishop Burnet's History of His Own Time,* Volume I, London, 1724.

ISABELLA BURT, *Historical Notices of Chelsea, Kensington, Fulham and Hammersmith,* Kensington, 1871.

HENRY BURTON, *The Grand Impostor Unmasked . . . ,* London, 1645.

DOUGLAS BUSH, *English Literature in the Earlier Seventeenth Century, 1600-1660,* Oxford: Clarendon Press, 1946.

W. D. BUSHELL, *The Church of St. Mary the Great, the University Church at Cambridge,* Cambridge: Bowes and Bowes, 1948.

Calendar of State Papers, Domestic Series, of the Reign of Charles I, 23 volumes, London, 1858-97.

Calendar of Wynn (of Gwydir) Papers, 1515-1690, London: H. Milford, 1926.

WILLIAM CAMDEN, *Britain, Or a Chorographicall Description of the Most Flourishing Kingdomes, England, Scotland and Ireland,* London, 1610.

LILY B. CAMPBELL, "The Christian Muse," *Huntington Library Bulletin* 8, 1935.

MILDRED CAMPBELL, *The English Yeoman under Elizabeth and the Early Stuarts,* New Haven: Yale University Press, 1942.

GEORGE CAREW, *Letters from Sir George Carew to Sir Thomas Roe, 1615-1617,* edited by John MacLean, Royal Historical Society Publications 76, London, 1860.

S. C. CARPENTER, *The Church in England, 597-1688,* London: John Murray, 1954.

WILLIAM CHAFFERS, *Gilda Aurifabrorum,* London, 1897.

JOHN CHAMBERLAIN, *Letters,* edited by Norman Egbert McClure, 2 volumes, Philadelphia: American Philosophical Society, 1939.

JOHN FREDERICK CHANTER, *The Bishop's Palace, Exeter,* London: Society for Promoting Christian Knowledge, 1932.

CHARLES I, *The Letters, Speeches and Proclamations of King Charles I,* edited by Sir Charles Petrie, London: Cassell and Co., Ltd., 1935.

R. PEARSE CHOPE, editor, *Early Tours in Devon and Cornwall,* Exeter, 1918.

EDWARD, EARL OF CLARENDON, *The History of the Rebellion and Civil Wars in England,* 6 volumes, Oxford: Clarendon Press, 1888.

EDWARD, EARL OF CLARENDON, *The Life of Edward, Earl of Clarendon,* 3 volumes, Oxford: Clarendon Press, 1827.

HENRY W. CLARK, *History of English Nonconformity,* Volume I, London: Chapman and Hall, 1911.

ANNE CLIFFORD, *The Diary of the Lady Anne Clifford,* London: William Heinemann, Ltd., 1923.

WILLIAM COBBETT, *Cobbett's Parliamentary History of England,* Volume I, London, 1806.

Coleridge on the Seventeenth Century, edited by Roberta Florence Brinkley, Durham: Duke University Press, 1955.

Collection of Papers Relating to the Parish of Bemerton, Salisbury, 1893.

Collections Historical and Archaeological Relating to Montgomeryshire and Its Borders, London, Volume VI, 1873; Volume VII, 1874; Volume XIX, 1886; Volume XX, 1887; Volume XXI, 1887; Volume XXII, 1888.

WILLIAM COMBE, *A History of the University of Cambridge,* 2 volumes, London, 1815.

Constitutions and Canons Ecclesiastical, London, 1628.

CHARLES HENRY COOPER, *Annals of Cambridge,* Volume III, Cambridge, 1845.

CHARLES HENRY COOPER, *Memorials of Cambridge,* 3 volumes, Cambridge: Macmillan and Co., 1860-66.

CHARLES HENRY COOPER AND THOMPSON COOPER, *Athenae Cantabrigienses,* 3 volumes, Cambridge, 1858-1913.

WILLIAM COTTON, *Gleanings from the Municipal and Cathedral Records Relative to the History of the City of Exeter,* Exeter, 1877.

J. CHARLES COX, *The Parish Registers of England,* London: Methuen and Co., Ltd., 1910.

WESLEY FRANK CRAVEN, *Dissolution of the Virginia Company,* New York: Oxford University Press, 1932.

GODFREY DAVIES, *The Early Stuarts, 1603-1660,* Oxford: Clarendon Press, 1937.

GODFREY DAVIES, *The Restoration of Charles II,* San Marino: Huntington Library, 1955.

SIMON DEGGE, *The Parson's Counsellor,* London, 1820.

FLORIS DELATTRE, *Robert Herrick,* Paris, 1911.

SIMONDS D'EWES, *The Autobiography and Correspendence of Sir Simonds D'Ewes, Bart.,* edited by James Orchard Halliwell, 2 volumes, London, 1845.

Dictionary of National Biography, Oxford University Press, 1921-22.

P. H. DITCHFIELD, *Old English Sports, Pastimes and Customs,* London: Methuen and Co., 1891.

A. H. DODD, *Studies in Stuart Wales,* Cardiff: University of Wales Press, 1952.

JOHN DONNE, *The Divine Poems,* edited by Helen Gardner, Oxford: Clarendon Press, 1952.

JOHN DONNE, *The Poems of John Donne,* edited by Herbert J. C. Grierson, 2 volumes, London: Oxford University Press, 1953.

JOHN DONNE, *The Sermons of John Donne,* edited by George R. Potter and Evelyn M. Simpson, 6 volumes, Berkeley: University of California Press, 1953-57.

BRIAN W. DOWNS, *Cambridge, Past and Present,* London: Methuen and Co. Ltd., 1926.

GUILLAUME DE SALLUSTE DU BARTAS, *Du Bartas, His Devine Weekes and Workes,* translated by Joshua Sylvester, London, 1611.

O. JOCELYN DUNLOP, *English Apprenticeship and Child Labour,* London: T. Fisher Unwin, 1912.

JOHN EARLE, *Microcosmography,* London, 1811.

T. S. ELIOT, "George Herbert," *The Spectator,* March 12, 1932.

WILLA MCCLUNG EVANS, *Henry Lawes, Musician and Friend of Poets,* New York: Modern Language Association of America, 1941.

The Fairfax Correspondence, edited by George W. Johnson, 2 volumes, London, 1848.

THOMAS FAULKNER, *An Historical and Topographical Description of Chelsea and Its Environs,* 2 volumes, Chelsea, 1829.

EDMUND H. FELLOWES, *English Cathedral Music from Edward VI to Edward VII,* London: Methuen and Co., Ltd., 1941.

The Ferrar Papers, edited by B. Blackstone, Cambridge: Cambridge University Press, 1938.

The Forme and Manner of Making and Consecrating Bishops, Priests and Deacons, London, 1633.

J. E. FOSTER, editor, *The Churchwardens' Accounts of St. Mary the Great, Cambridge, from 1504 to 1635*, Cambridge Antiquarian Society Publications, octavo series no. 35, 1905.

ALLEN FRENCH, *Charles I and the Puritan Upheaval*, London: George Allen and Unwin, Ltd., 1955.

W. H. FRERE, *The English Church in the Reigns of Elizabeth and James I*, London: Macmillan and Co., Ltd., 1911.

W. H. FRERE AND C. E. DOUGLAS, editors, *Puritan Manifestoes*, London, 1907.

MORRIS FULLER, *The Life, Letters and Writings of John Davenant, D.D.*, London: Methuen and Co., 1897.

THOMAS FULLER, *The Church History of Britain*, 6 volumes, Oxford: Oxford University Press, 1845.

THOMAS FULLER, *The History of the University of Cambridge*, London, 1840.

THOMAS FULLER, *The History of the Worthies of England*, London, 1662.

SAMUEL RAWSON GARDINER, editor, *Debates in the House of Commons in 1625*, London: Royal Historical Society Publications, new series, Volume VI, 1873.

SAMUEL RAWSON GARDINER, *History of England, 1603-1642*, 10 volumes, London, 1863-84.

CHRISTINA HALLOWELL GARRETT, *The Marian Exiles*, Cambridge: Cambridge University Press, 1938.

HENRY GEE AND WILLIAM JOHN HARDY, editors, *Documents Illustrative of English Church History*, London, 1896.

The Gentleman's Magazine, London, 1796.

GODFREY GOODMAN, *The Court of King James the First*, 2 volumes, London, 1839.

EDMUND GOSSE, *The Life and Letters of John Donne*, 2 volumes, London: William Heinemann, 1899.

ROGER GRANVILLE, *The History of the Granville Family*, Exeter, 1895.

FULKE GREVILLE, *Life of Sir Philip Sidney*, edited by Nowell Smith, Oxford: Clarendon Press, 1907.

JOHN GUTCH, *Collectanea Curiosa*, 2 volumes, Oxford: Clarendon Press, 1781.

JOHN HACKET, *Scrinia Reserata, a Memorial Offer'd to the Great Deservings of John Williams*, London, 1693.

WILLIAM HALLER, *Liberty and Reformation in the Puritan Revolution*, New York: Columbia University Press, 1955.

WILLIAM HALLER, *The Rise of Puritanism*, New York: Columbia University Press, 1938.

ROBERT HALLEY, *Lancashire: Its Puritanism and Nonconformity*, 2 volumes, Manchester, 1869.

ALFRED HARBAGE, *Sir William Davenant*, Philadelphia: University of Pennsylvania Press, 1935.

HENRY A. HARBEN, *A Dictionary of London*, London, 1918.

FREDERICK J. HARRIES, *The Welsh Elizabethans*, Pontypridd, 1924.

HENRY HARTOPP, *Roll of the Mayors of the Borough and Lord Mayors of the City of Leicester*, Leicester, 1935.

ALBERT McHARG HAYES, "Counterpoint in Herbert," *Studies in Philology* 35, 1938.

EDWARD, LORD HERBERT OF CHERBURY, *The Autobiography of Edward, Lord Herbert of Cherbury*, edited by Sidney Lee, London, 1886.

EDWARD, LORD HERBERT OF CHERBURY, *De Veritate*, translated by Meyrick H. Carré, Bristol: University of Bristol, 1937.

EDWARD, LORD HERBERT OF CHERBURY, *The Expedition to the Isle of Rhé*, London, 1860.

EDWARD, LORD HERBERT OF CHERBURY, *The Poems, English and Latin, of Edward, Lord Herbert of Cherbury*, edited by G. C. Moore Smith, Oxford: Oxford University Press, 1923.

GEORGE HERBERT, *The Complete Works in Verse and Prose*, edited by Alexander B. Grosart, 3 volumes, 1874.

GEORGE HERBERT, *A Priest to the Temple*, with a preface by Barnabas Oley, London, 1671.

GEORGE HERBERT, *The Temple. Sacred Poems and Private Ejaculations*, Cambridge, 1633.

GEORGE HERBERT, *The Works of George Herbert*, edited by F. E. Hutchinson, Oxford: Clarendon Press, 1953.

HENRY HERBERT, *The Dramatic Records of Sir Henry Herbert, Master of the Revels, 1623-1673*, edited by Joseph Quincy Adams, New Haven: Yale University Press, 1917.

THOMAS HERBERT, *Memoirs of the Last Two Years of the Reign of King Charles I*, London, 1839.

WILLIAM HERBERT, *The History of the Twelve Great Livery Companies of London*, London, 1837.

ROBERT HERRICK, *The Complete Poems of Robert Herrick*, edited by Alexander B. Grosart, 3 volumes, London, 1876.

ROBERT HERRICK, *Hesperides: Or, the Works both Humane & Divine of Robert Herrick Esq.*, London, 1648.

ROBERT HERRICK, *The Poetical Works of Robert Herrick*, edited by L. C. Martin, Oxford: Clarendon Press, 1956.

PETER HEYLYN, *Cyprianus Anglicus*, London, 1668.

FLORENCE (M. GREIR EVANS) HIGHAM, *Lancelot Andrewes*, New York: Morehouse-Gorham Co., 1952.

FLORENCE (M. GREIR EVANS) HIGHAM, *The Principal Secretary of State*, Manchester: University of Manchester Press, 1923.

CHRISTOPHER HILL, *Economic Problems of the Church from Archbishop Whitgift to the Long Parliament*, Oxford: Clarendon Press, 1956.

JOHN H. HILL, *The History of Market Harborough*, Leicester, 1875.

RICHARD HOOKER, *Of the Laws of Ecclesiastical Polity*, 2 volumes, London: J. M. Dent and Sons, Ltd., 1907.

GERARD MANLEY HOPKINS, *The Letters of Gerard Manley Hopkins to Robert Bridges*, London: Oxford University Press, 1955.

HORACE, *Complete Works*, edited by Casper J. Kraemer, Jr., New York: Random House, 1936.

W. G. HOSKINS, "An Elizabethan Provincial Town: Leicester," in *Studies in Social History* edited by J. H. Plumb, London: Longmans, Green and Co., 1955.

W. G. HOSKINS AND H. P. R. FINBERG, *Devonshire Studies*, London: Jonathan Cape, 1952.

JAMES HOWELL, *Epistolae Ho-Elianae*, London, 1754.

HAROLD R. HUTCHESON, *Lord Herbert of Cherbury's "De Religione Laici,"* New Haven: Yale University Press, 1944.

F. E. HUTCHINSON, *Henry Vaughan, a Life and Interpretation*, Oxford: Clarendon Press, 1947.

LUCY HUTCHINSON, *Memoirs of the Life of Colonel Hutchinson*, London, 1846.

MATTHEW HUTTON, *The Correspondence of Dr. Matthew Hutton*, London, 1843.

WILLIAM HOLDEN HUTTON, *The English Church from the Accession of Charles I to the Death of Anne*, London: Macmillan and Co., Ltd., 1913.

A. G. HYDE, *George Herbert and His Times*, London, Methuen and Co., 1906.

HENRY ISAACSON, *The Life and Death of Lancelot Andrewes, D.D.*, London, 1829.

RICHARD IZACKE, *Remarkable Antiquities of the City of Exeter*, London, 1681.

JAMES I, *The Peace-Maker: or, Great Brittaines Blessing*, London, 1619.

JAMES I, *Serenissimi et Potentissimi Principis Iacobi . . . Opera*, London, 1619.

ALEXANDER JENKINS, *The History and Description of the City of Exeter*, Exeter, 1806.

IDRIS JONES, *Modern Welsh History from 1485 to the Present Day*, London: G. Bell and Sons, Ltd., 1934.

BEN JONSON, *Ben Jonson*, edited by C. H. Herford and Percy Simpson, 11 volumes, Oxford: Clarendon Press, 1925-52.

W. K. JORDAN, *The Development of Religious Toleration in England*, 4 volumes, London: George Allen and Unwin, 1932-40.

RALPH JOSSELIN, *The Diary of the Rev. Ralph Josselin, 1616-1683*, edited by E. Hockliffe, Royal Historical Society Publications, Camden third series, Volume XV, London, 1908.

MARY FREAR KEELER, *The Long Parliament, 1640-1641*, Philadelphia: American Philosophical Society, 1954.

A. F. KENDRICK, *The Cathedral Church of Lincoln*, London, 1898.

W. P. M. KENNEDY, *Elizabethan Episcopal Administration*, 3 volumes, London: A. R. Mowbray and Co., Ltd., 1924.

M. M. KNAPPEN, *Tudor Puritanism*, Chicago: University of Chicago Press, 1939.

L. C. KNIGHTS, *Explorations*, London: Chatto and Windus, 1946.

The Knyvett Letters, 1620-1644, edited by Bertram Schofield, Norfolk Record Society Publications, Volume XX, 1949.

WILLIAM LAUD, *The Archbishop of Canterbury's Speech: or His Funerall Sermon . . .* London, 1644.

WILLIAM LAUD, *Works*, 7 volumes, Oxford, 1847-60.

ARTHUR F. LEACH, *Educational Charters and Documents, 598-1909*, Cambridge: Cambridge University Press, 1911.

JOHN LE NEVE, *Fasti Ecclesiae Anglicanae*, 3 volumes, Oxford: Oxford University Press, 1854.

HAMON L'ESTRANGE, *The Reign of King Charles*, London, 1655.

SAMUEL LEWIS, *A Topographical Dictionary of Wales*, 2 volumes, London, 1842.

W. V. LLOYD, *The Sheriffs of Montgomeryshire*, London, 1876.

DONALD LUPTON, *London and the Country Carbonadoed*, Edinburgh: The Aungervyle Society, 1883.

DANIEL AND SAMUEL LYSONS, *Magna Britannia,* Volume VI, London, 1822.

JAMES MACKINNON, *Calvin and the Reformation,* London: Longmans, Green and Co., 1936.

F. N. MACNAMARA, *Memorials of the Danvers Family,* London, 1895.

FALCONER MADAN, *Oxford Books,* 3 volumes, Oxford: Clarendon Press, 1895-1931.

M. M. MAHOOD, *Poetry and Humanism,* London: Jonathan Cape, 1950.

HENRY ELLIOT MALDEN, *Trinity Hall,* London, 1902.

JOHN A. R. MARRIOTT, *The Crisis of English Liberty,* Oxford: Clarendon Press, 1930.

LOUIS L. MARTZ, *The Poetry of Meditation,* New Haven: Yale University Press, 1954.

DAVID MASSON, *The Life of John Milton,* 6 volumes, London: Macmillan and Co., 1859-80.

DAVID MATHEW, *The Age of Charles I,* London: Eyre and Spottiswoode, 1951.

DAVID MATHEW, *The Social Structure in Caroline England,* Oxford: Clarendon Press, 1948.

A. L. MAYCOCK, *Nicholas Ferrar of Little Gidding,* London: Society for Promoting Christian Knowledge, 1938.

KATHRYN ANDERSON McEUEN, *Classical Influence upon the Tribe of Ben,* Cedar Rapids: Torch Press, 1939.

JOHN T. McNEILL, *The History and Character of Calvinism,* New York: Oxford University Press, 1954.

JAMES A. S. McPEEK, *Catullus in Strange and Distant Britain,* Cambridge: Harvard University Press, 1939.

THOMAS M'CRIE, *Annals of English Presbytery,* London, 1872.

JAMES MELVILL, *Autobiography and Diary,* edited by Robert Pitcairn, Edinburgh, 1842.

EDMOND MILLER, *An Account of the University of Cambridge,* London, 1717.

PERRY MILLER, *The New England Mind; The Seventeenth Century,* New York: The Macmillan Co., 1939.

Miscellanea Genealogica et Heraldica, edited by Joseph Jackson Howard, second series, Volume I, London, 1886.

W. FRASER MITCHELL, *English Pulpit Oratory from Andrewes to Tillotson,* London: Society for Promoting Christian Knowledge, 1932.

WILLIAMS M. MITCHELL, *The Rise of the Revolutionary Party in the*

English House of Commons, 1603-1629, New York: Columbia University Press, 1957.

F. W. MOORMAN, *Robert Herrick*, London: Thomas Nelson and Sons, Ltd., 1924.

PAUL ELMER MORE AND FRANK LESLIE CROSS, *Anglicanism*, London: Society for Promoting Christian Knowledge, 1935.

SAMUEL ELIOT MORISON, *The Founding of Harvard College*, Cambridge: Harvard University Press, 1935.

JAMES BASS MULLINGER, *Cambridge Characteristics in the Seventeenth Century*, London, 1867.

JAMES BASS MULLINGER, *St. John's College*, London, 1901.

JAMES BASS MULLINGER, *The University of Cambridge*, 3 volumes, Cambridge: Cambridge University Press, 1873-1911.

S. MUSGROVE, *The Universe of Robert Herrick*, Auckland University College English series no. 4, Auckland, 1950.

EDWARD W. NAYLOR, *The Poets and Music*, London: J. M. Dent and Sons, Ltd., 1928.

J. E. NEALE, *Elizabeth I and Her Parliaments, 1559-1581*, London: Jonathan Cape, 1953.

J. E. NEALE, *Elizabeth I and Her Parliaments, 1584-1601*, London: Jonathan Cape, 1957.

J. E. NEALE, *The Elizabethan House of Commons*, London: Jonathan Cape, 1949.

JOHN NICHOLS, *The History and Antiquities of the County of Leicester*, Volumes I, II and III, London, 1798-1815.

JOHN NICHOLS, *The Progresses of King James the First*, 4 volumes, London, 1828.

WALLACE NOTESTEIN AND FRANCES HELEN RELF, editors, *Commons Debates for 1629*, Minneapolis: University of Minnesota Press, 1921.

DAVID NOVARR, *The Making of Walton's "Lives"*, Ithaca: Cornell University Press, 1958.

DAVID OGG, *Europe in the Seventeenth Century*, London: A. and C. Black, Ltd., 1925.

JOHN OGILBY, *The King's Coronation*, London, 1685.

JOHN OGLANDER, *A Royalist's Notebook*, London: Constable and Co., Ltd., 1936.

S. L. OLLARD AND GORDON CROSSE, *A Dictionary of English Church History*, London: A. R. Mowbray and Co., Ltd., 1919.

RICHARD PARKER, *The Presbyterian Movement in the Reign of Queen Elizabeth as Illustrated by the Minute Book of the Dedham*

Classis, 1582-1589, edited by Roland G. Usher, Royal Historical Society Publications, series 3, no. 8, London, 1905.

RICHARD PARR, *The Life of the Most Reverend Father in God, James Usher*, London, 1686.

HENRY PEACHAM, *The Compleat Gentleman*, London, 1634.

GEORGE PEACOCK, *Observations on the Statutes of the University of Cambridge*, London, 1841.

A. F. SCOTT PEARSON, *Thomas Cartwright and Elizabethan Puritanism, 1535-1603*, Cambridge: Cambridge University Press, 1925.

PETER PECKARD, *Memoirs of the Life of Mr. Nicholas Ferrar*, Cambridge, 1790.

CHARLES PENDRILL, *Old Parish Life in London*, London: Oxford University Press, 1937.

JOHN PENRY, *The Notebook of John Penry, 1593*, edited by Albert Peel, Royal Historical Society Publications, Camden third series, Volume LXVII, London, 1944.

ROBERT PHILLIMORE, *The Ecclesiastical Law of the Church of England*, 2 volumes, London, 1895.

EDWARD PHILLIPS, *Theatrum Poetarum*, London, 1675.

HENRY R. PLOMER, *A Dictionary of the Booksellers and Printers Who Were at Work in England, Scotland and Ireland from 1641 to 1667*, London, 1907.

RICHARD POLWHELE, *The History of Devonshire*, London, 1793.

JOHN PRINCE, *Danmonii Orientales Illustres: or, The Worthies of Devon*, London, 1810.

A Project Concerning the State, Order and Manner of Government of the University of Cambridge, Cambridge, 1769.

G. W. PROTHERO, *Select Statutes and Other Constitutional Documents Illustrative of the Reigns of Elizabeth and James I*, Oxford: Clarendon Press, 1913.

Quarterly Review, London, August, 1810.

THOMAS RANDOLPH, *The Poems and "Amyntas" of Thomas Randolph*, edited by John Jay Parry, New Haven: Yale University Press, 1917.

J. F. REES, *Studies in Welsh History*, Cardiff: University of Wales, 1947.

MAURICE F. REIDY, *Bishop Lancelot Andrewes*, Chicago: Loyola University Press, 1955.

TRISTRAM RISDON, *The Chorographical Description or Survey of the County of Devon*, London, 1811.

DORA H. ROBERTSON, *Sarum Close*, London: Jonathan Cape, 1938.

MALCOLM MACKENZIE ROSS, *Poetry & Dogma,* New Brunswick: Rutgers University Press, 1954.

JOHN RUSHWORTH, *Historical Collections,* 2 volumes, London, 1659-80.

JOHN SARGEAUNT, *Annals of Westminster School,* London: Methuen and Co., 1898.

ETHEL SEATON, *Literary Relations of England and Scandinavia in the Seventeenth Century,* Oxford: Clarendon Press, 1935.

JOHN SELDEN, *Table Talk,* edited by Sir Frederick Pollock, London, 1927.

WILLIAM SHAKESPEARE, *Poems Written by Wil. Shake-Speare, Gent.,* London, 1640.

WILLIAM A. SHAW, *A History of the English Church during the Civil Wars and under the Commonwealth, 1640-1660,* 2 volumes, London: Longmans, Green and Co., 1900.

EDGAR SHEPPARD, *Memorials of St. James's Palace,* 2 volumes, London, 1894.

PHILIP SIDNEY, *The Correspondence of Sir Philip Sidney and Hubert Languet,* edited by William Aspenwall Bradley, Boston: Merrymount Press, 1912.

C. J. SISSON, *The Judicious Marriage of Mr. Hooker and the Birth of "The Laws of Ecclesiastical Polity,"* Cambridge: Cambridge University Press, 1940.

FLORENCE E. SKILLINGTON, *The Plain Man's History of Leicester,* Leicester, 1950.

G. C. MOORE SMITH, "Thomas Randolph," *Proceedings of the British Academy,* Volume XIII, London, 1927.

JOHN THOMAS SMITH, *The Antiquities of Westminster,* London, 1837.

LOGAN PEARSALL SMITH, *The Life and Letters of Sir Henry Wotton,* 2 volumes, Oxford: Clarendon Press, 1907.

JAMES SPEDDING, *The Letters and the Life of Francis Bacon,* 7 volumes, London, 1861-74.

JOHN SPEED, *The Theatre of the Empire of Great Britain,* London, 1676.

THOMAS SPRAT, *The History of the Royal Society of London,* London, 1667.

DONALD A. STAUFFER, *English Biography before 1700,* Cambridge: Harvard University Press, 1930.

JOHN STOW, *The Survay of London,* with additions by Anthony Munday, London, 1618.

JOSEPH H. SUMMERS, *George Herbert; his Religion and Art,* Cambridge: Harvard University Press, 1954.

J. R. TANNER, editor, *Constitutional Documents of the Reign of James I*, Cambridge: Cambridge University Press, 1930.

J. R. TANNER, *English Constitutional Conflicts of the Seventeenth Century*, Cambridge: Cambridge University Press, 1928.

J. R. TANNER, editor, *The Historical Register of the University of Cambridge*, Cambridge: Cambridge University Press, 1917.

LAWRENCE E. TANNER, *Westminster School; a History*, London: Country Life, Ltd., 1934.

G. B. TATHAM, *Dr. John Walker and "The Sufferings of the Clergy,"* Cambridge: Cambridge University Press, 1911.

THOMAS TENISON, *Baconiana*, London, 1679.

JOHN THANE, *British Autography*, 3 volumes, London, 1793.

A. HAMILTON THOMPSON, *Cambridge and Its Colleges*, London: Methuen and Co., 1898.

A. HAMILTON THOMPSON, *The English Clergy and their Organization in the Later Middle Ages*, Oxford: Clarendon Press, 1947.

J. V. P. THOMPSON, *Supreme Governor, a Study of Elizabethan Ecclesiastical Policy and Circumstance*, London: Society for Promoting Christian Knowledge, 1940.

JOHN THROSBY, *The History and Antiquities of the Ancient Town of Leicester*, Leicester, 1791.

DOROTHEA TOWNSHEND, *Life and Letters of Mr. Endymion Porter*, London, 1897.

H. R. TREVOR-ROPER, *Archbishop Laud, 1573-1645*, London: Macmillan and Co., Ltd., 1940.

JOHN TUCKETT, *Devonshire Pedigrees Recorded in the Herald's Visitation of 1620*, London, 1859.

ROSEMOND TUVE, *A Reading of George Herbert*, London: Faber and Faber, 1952.

GEORGE UNWIN, *Industrial Organization in the Sixteenth and Seventeenth Centuries*, Oxford: Clarendon Press, 1904.

FREDERICK JOHN VARLEY, *Cambridge during the Civil War, 1642-1646*, Cambridge: W. Heffer and Sons, Ltd., 1935.

JOHN VENN AND J. A. VENN, compilers, *Alumni Cantabrigienses*, Part I, 4 volumes, Cambridge: Cambridge University Press, 1922.

JOHN VENN AND J. A. VENN, compilers, *The Book of Matriculations and Degrees . . . from 1544-1659*, Cambridge: Cambridge University Press, 1913.

FRANCES PARTHENOPE VERNEY, *Memoirs of the Verney Family*, 4 volumes, London, 1892-99.

LEOPOLD VON RANKE, *A History of England Principally in the Seventeenth Century*, 6 volumes, Oxford: Clarendon Press, 1875.

JOHN WALKER, *An Attempt towards Recovering an Account of the Numbers and Sufferings of the Clergy of the Church of England*, London, 1714.

ADAM WALL, *An Account of the Different Ceremonies Observed in the Senate House of the University of Cambridge*, Cambridge, 1798.

RUTH WALLERSTEIN, *Studies in Seventeenth-century Poetic*, Madison: University of Wisconsin Press, 1950.

IZAAK WALTON, *The Lives of Dr. John Donne, Sir Henry Wotton, Mr. Richard Hooker, Mr. George Herbert*, London, 1670.

IZAAK WALTON, *The Lives of Dr. John Donne, Sir Henry Wotton, Mr. Richard Hooker, Mr. George Herbert, and Dr. Robert Sanderson*, New York, 1903.

J. HEALD WARD, *Counsellor John Were of Silverton, and the Siege of Exeter*, Plymouth, 1910.

SEDLEY LYNCH WARE, *The Elizabethan Parish in its Ecclesiastical and Financial Aspects*, Baltimore: Johns Hopkins Press, 1908.

REBECCA WARNER, editor, *Epistolary Curiosities*, Bath, 1818.

AUSTIN WARREN, "George Herbert," *American Review*, no. 7, 1936.

PHILIP WARWICK, *Memoires of the Reigne of King Charles I*, London, 1701.

C. V. WEDGWOOD, *The King's Peace, 1637-1641*, New York: The Macmillan Co., 1955.

C. V. WEDGWOOD, *Oliver Cromwell*, London: Duckworth, 1939.

C. V. WEDGWOOD, *Velvet Studies*, London: Jonathan Cape, 1948.

THOMAS WESTCOTE, *A View of Devonshire*, Exeter, 1845.

H. F. WESTLAKE, *St. Margaret's, Westminster, the Church of the House of Commons*, London, 1914.

H. F. WESTLAKE, *Westminster; A Historical Sketch*, London: Society for Promoting Christian Knowledge, 1919.

BULSTRODE WHITELOCKE, *The History of England*, London, 1713.

BULSTRODE WHITELOCKE, *Memorials of the English Affairs*, London, 1732.

DAVID WILLIAMS, *A History of Modern Wales*, London: John Murray, 1950.

RICHARD WILLIAMS, *Montgomeryshire Worthies*, Newtown, 1894.

W. R. WILLIAMS, *The Parliamentary History of the Principality of Wales*, Brecknock, 1895.

GEORGE C. WILLIAMSON, *Lady Anne Clifford, Countess of Dorset, Pembroke and Montgomery*, Kendal, 1922.

ROBERT WILLIS, *The Architectural History of the University of Cambridge*, edited by John Willis Clark, 4 volumes, Cambridge: Cambridge University Press, 1886.

DAVID HARRIS WILLSON, *King James VI and I*, New York: Henry Holt and Co., 1956.

DAVID HARRIS WILLSON, *The Privy Councillors in the House of Commons, 1604-1629*, Minneapolis: University of Minnesota Press, 1940.

ARTHUR WILSON, *The History of Great Britain, Being the Life and Reign of King James the First*, London, 1653.

Wiltshire Archaeological and Natural History Magazine, Volume I, London, 1854.

WILLIAM WINSTANLEY, *Lives of the Most Famous English Poets*, London, 1687.

RALPH WINWOOD, *Memorials of Affairs of State in the Reigns of Queen Elizabeth and King James*, 3 volumes, London, 1725.

ANTHONY WOOD, *Athenae Oxonienses*, London, 1721.

ANTHONY WOOD, *The Life and Times of Anthony Wood*, collected by Andrew Clark, Volume I, Oxford: Clarendon Press, 1891.

ARTHUR WOODNOTH, *A Short Collection of the Most Remarkable Passages from the Originall to the Dissolution of the Virginia Company*, London, 1651.

HENRY WOTTON, *Reliquiae Wottonianae*, London, 1651.

WALTER YONGE, *Diary of Walter Yonge*, edited by George Roberts, Camden Society, 1848.

G. M. YOUNG, *Charles I and Cromwell*, London: Peter Davies, 1935.

INDEX

INDEX